WORLD HISTORY BY ERA

The Technological Revolution

VOLUME 10

Other titles in the
World History by Era series:

WORLD HISTORY BY ERA

The Technological Revolution

VOLUME 10

Scott Barbour, *Book Editor*

Daniel Leone, *President*
Bonnie Szumski, *Publisher*
Scott Barbour, *Managing Editor*

Greenhaven Press, Inc., San Diego, California

Every effort has been made to trace the owners of copyrighted material. The articles in this volume may have been edited for content, length, and/or reading level. The titles have been changed to enhance the editorial purpose.

Library of Congress Cataloging-in-Publication Data

The Technological revolution / Scott Barbour, book editor.
    p. cm. — (World history by era; vol. 10)
    Includes bibliographical references and index.
    ISBN 0-7377-0705-4 (pbk. : alk. paper) —
ISBN 0-7377-0706-2 (lib. : alk. paper)
    1. World politics—1989– 2. Technology—Social aspects.
3. National security. 4. Globalization. 5. Terrorism.
6. Computers—Social aspects. I. Barbour, Scott, 1963–
II. Series.

D860 .T363 2002
909.82'5—dc21   2001016158
                                                          CIP

Cover inset photo credits (from left):
Corel Professional Photos; Photodisc; Corel Professional
Photos; Corel Professional Photos; Planet Art; Digital Stock;
Photodisc
Main cover photo credit: © Bob Krist/Corbis
Terry Arthur/White House, 51
Department of Defense, 177
IBM, 71
Library of Congress, 58, 147, 247, 274
NASA, 87
UNHCR/22027/05.1992/A. Hollmann, 192

Copyright © 2002 by Greenhaven Press, Inc.
10911 Technology Place, San Diego, CA 92127

Printed in the USA

CONTENTS

Chapter 1: The Early 1980s: Political Crisis, Solidarity, and Technological Progress

December 1989. The government's dictatorial leader, Nicolae Ceausescu, was overthrown on December 22 and was swiftly executed, along with his wife Elena, on December 25.

Chapter 4: The Early 1990s: Competing Forces for Liberation and Aggression

ment of Web browser software, which led to the creation of the World Wide Web in 1993.

Chapter 5: Toward a New Millennium: The Late 1990s

FOREWORD

The late 1980s were a time of dramatic events worldwide. Tragedies such as the explosions of the space shuttle *Challenger* and the Chernobyl nuclear power plant shocked the world out of its complacent belief that humankind had mastered nature and firmly controlled its technological creations. In U.S. politics, scandal rocked the White House when several high-ranking officials in the Ronald Reagan administration were convicted of selling arms to Iran and aiding the Nicaraguan Contra rebels. In global politics, U.S. president Ronald Reagan and Soviet president Mikhail Gorbachev signed a landmark treaty banning intermediate-range nuclear forces, marking the beginning of an era of arms control. In several parts of the world—including Beijing, China, the West Bank and Gaza Strip, and several nations of Eastern Europe—people rose up to resist oppressive governments, with varying degrees of success. In American culture, crack cocaine and inner-city poverty contributed to the development of a new and controversial music genre: gangsta rap.

Many of these events were unrelated to one another except for the fact that they occurred at about the same time. Others were linked to global developments. Greenhaven Press's World History by Era series provides students with a unique tool for examining global history in a way that allows them to appreciate the seemingly random occurrences as well as the general trends of human progress. This series divides world history—from the time of ancient Greece and Rome to the end of the second millennium—into ten discrete periods. Each volume then presents a collection of both primary and secondary documents that describe the major events of the period in chronological order. This structure provides students with a snapshot of events occurring simultaneously in all parts of the world. The reader can then see the connections between events in far-flung corners of the world. For example, the Palestinian uprising (*Intifada*) of December 1987 was near in time—if not in character and location—to similar protests in Beijing, China; Berlin, Germany; Prague, Czechoslovakia; and Bucharest, Romania. While these events were different in many ways, they all involved ordinary citizens striving for self-autonomy and democracy against governments that were attempting to impose strict controls on their civil liberties. By making the connections between these events, students can see that they comprised a global movement for democracy and human rights that profoundly impacted social and political systems worldwide.

Each volume in this series offers features to enhance students' understanding of the era of world history under discussion. An introductory essay provides an overview of the period, supplying essential context for the readings that follow. An annotated table of contents highlights the main point of each selection. A more in-depth introduction precedes each document, placing it in its particular historical context and offering biographical information about the author. A thorough chronology and index allow students to quickly reference specific events and dates. Finally, a bibliography opens up additional avenues of research. These features help to make the World History by Era series an extremely valuable tool for students researching the rise and fall of civilizations, social and political revolutions, cultural movements, scientific and technological advancements, and other events that mark the unfolding of human history throughout the world.

INTRODUCTION

On December 31, 1999, people all over the world awaited the stroke of midnight with a mixture of excitement and dread. They were eagerly anticipating the dawn not only of a new year, but a new century and a new millennium as well. But beneath the festive mood lay a host of fears stemming from the possible effects of the "Y2K computer bug." Technology experts had long warned that as computers switched over to the year 2000, they would read only the last two numbers and interpret the date as 1900, causing them to crash. This breakdown in computer systems would result in the disruption of power, water, and financial systems. Airplanes would fall from the sky, ATMs would cease to distribute cash, nuclear weapons would automatically launch, and looters and terrorists would take advantage of the breakdown in order to wreak various forms of havoc.

Fortunately, midnight came and went with no such problems. In retrospect, some commentators credited human foresight for preventing the Y2K disasters by identifying the threat years in advance and investing millions of dollars, in both the private and public sectors, in correcting the glitch. More cynical critics suggested that the Y2K scare was simply and example of millennial hysteria. In either case, the incident reveals just how dependent humanity—especially in the developed nations—had become on computer technology by the end of the twentieth century. If the threat was real, major elements of the world's infrastructure had become reliant on the smooth functioning of computer systems. If the threat was an exaggerated scare, it was clear that regardless of the actual role of computers, the masses perceived their societies to be largely under the control of microchips and processors.

In the last two decades of the twentieth century, computers, which had previously been used mostly in science and industry, became ubiquitous in developed societies. In business, increasing numbers of processes and functions were taken over by computer technology. More significantly, The arrival of personal computers in the early and mid-1980s—which was arguably one of the most significant social developments of the twentieth century—brought computers out of the labs and into the lives of ordinary people. Computers, once the foray of experts, now became a common tool used in increasing numbers of homes, offices, and schools. With the advent of web browser software in the mid-1990s, more and more of these computers plugged into interconnected networks (the "Internet") and the World Wide Web, radically transforming the way people conducted business, accessed information, shopped, and engaged in personal communication. The development of computers could accurately be dubbed a "technological revolution."

Along with the revolution in computer technology, the last two decades of the twentieth century bought major transformations of governments worldwide as well as the relationships between nations. The most dramatic of these were the end of the cold war, the demise of communism in Eastern Europe, and the dissolution of the Soviet empire. In addition, the apartheid system of racial segregation in South Africa gave way to a democratic government headed by a black majority. And the map of Yugoslavia was redrawn following years of civil war in that nation. The era also saw its share of violent conflict. Besides war in the Balkans, armed struggle ensued to various degrees in Afghanistan, Israel, Northern Ireland, and elsewhere. Violence broke out in such faraway places as Tiananmen Square in Beijing, China, when the Chinese government quashed pro-democracy protesters in 1989, and the streets of Los Angeles, California, when residents rioted in response to a verdict in a racially charged trial in 1991. Perhaps the darkest event in the era occurred in Rwanda, Africa, where genocide took the lives of over a half-million people in 1994.

Besides political transformations and violence, the last two decades of the twentieth century saw significant social, cultural, and scientific changes. AIDS struck in the early 1980s, creating a major challenge for medical science and social policy. Crack cocaine arrived on the streets of America's cities, bringing with it a culture of guns and violence that would take a heavy toll on young people—especially African-American males—swelling the prisons and producing a new musical genre: gangsta rap. Scientists successfully cloned an adult mammal—a sheep named Dolly—for the fist time, raising major ethical concerns surrounding the prospect of cloning humans. Environmental concerns went global, with data on global warming and the hole in the ozone layer leading to international treaties designed to counter these cross-border problems.

Thus, the technological developments of the last two decades of the twentieth century did not occur in a vacuum. Rather, they took place against a backdrop of geopolitical flux, violence, and crises of various forms—some of which, such as the incidents in Rwanda and Yugoslavia, seemed to suggest that humanity, rather than progressing, had regressed to the level of stone age man. Perhaps this is the irony of the modern era: Humanity has evolved to the point that it has developed amazing machines that can perform extremely complex functions at rapid speeds, vastly improving the quality of life and increasing workers' productivity exponentially. Indeed, humanity has progressed to the point that it is capable of creating mammals and may even have the potential to replicate humans. Yet despite these advances, humans continue to revert to barbarism with alarming frequency.

THE REAGAN REVOLUTION

The 1980s began with a new president in the United States, when former Hollywood actor Ronald Reagan defeated the incumbent Jimmy Carter in November 1980. Carter's campaign had been harmed by his inability to secure the release of fifty-three American hostages being held by Islamic fundamentalists in Iran. In addition, he had exaggerated the seriousness of the energy crisis then affecting the nation and had presented a negative view of the country's future in his now-famous "national malaise" speech. As historian J.A.S. Grenville writes, "Ronald Reagan, by contrast, was upbeat and optimistic. He promised a new beginning, an America that would 'stand tall.'"[1] Reagan ran on a platform of increased defense and reduced government regulation of business and the environment. Once in office, the new president initiated these policies, taking a strong line against the Soviet Union, building up the nation's defenses, cutting taxes for the wealthy, rolling back environmental protections, and cutting spending on social programs.

In world affairs, Reagan adopted a confrontational posture toward the Soviet Union. Prior to the Reagan years, the defense policies of both the United States and the Soviet Union had been based on the concept of mutually assured destruction (MAD). Under this framework, both sides understood that a nuclear war initiated by either side would certainly result in the annihilation of both sides. This guarantee of mutual devastation served as a deterrent to both sides. Reagan believed that this policy would lead to an endless perpetuation of the arms race. In its stead, he sought to dramatically build up U.S. defenses in an effort to force the Soviets to negotiate. As explained by Richard V. Allen, former chief foreign policy adviser to Reagan, the president aimed to build up this country's strength by relying on its economic and technological advantages, and translating those elements into measurable national power— all in order to convince the other side that it was hopelessly expensive, even impossible to keep abreast. In other words, be believed that to disarm safely we first had to arm ourselves, deliberately and persuasively.[2]

One of the most controversial elements of Reagan's defense buildup was the Strategic Defense Initiative (SDI), a program to develop a system of space-based, computer-operated lasers and missiles designed to defend the nation from nuclear attack. Such a system threatened to render the Soviets' missiles useless and place the United States in a superior position. With SDI in place, Reagan reasoned, in the event of a nuclear attack, the destruction of the United States would no longer be assured. SDI was quickly dubbed "Star Wars" by critics who insisted it was an impossible scheme. The program never came fully to fruition, but talk of it may have served a role in persuading the Soviets to negotiate. According to historian Martin Gilbert, "More than any single American initiative, 'Star Wars' . . . spelt the end of the Soviet-American balance of power, and would tilt it significantly to the American side."[3]

THE GORBACHEV REVOLUTION

Progress on arms control would come slowly in the 1980s; no substantial agreements would be struck until the arrival of Mikhail Gorbachev as general secretary of the Communist Party of the Soviet Union in 1985. Soon after taking office, the new Soviet leader called a moratorium on the deployment of medium-range nuclear weapons in Europe. This action led the way to the resumption of the Strategic Arms Reduction Talks (START), which had broken off in 1983. Reagan and Gorbahev held their first summit meeting in October 1986 in Reykjavik, Iceland. They reached no agreements in Reykjavik, but in December 1987 they met again in Washington, where they signed a treaty banning intermediate-range nuclear forces (INF).

Progress in arms control was simply the tip of the iceberg of change under Gorbachev. Not long after he entered office, Gorbachev began to institute liberal reforms of Soviet economics, politics, and society. He frequently described these reforms as glasnost (openness) and perestroika (restructuring). Ironically, these reforms, which ultimately contributed to the collapse of the Soviet empire and the breakup of the Soviet Union itself, were conceived as strategies to preserve Soviet communism. As historian J.M. Roberts explains, Gorbachev

> sought to avoid the collapse of a communist system by opening it to his own vision of Leninism, a more pluralist system, involving the intelligentsia in the political nation. . . . His starting-point had been his recognition that without radical change the Soviet economy had not been and would not be able to provide the USSR with its former military might, sustain its commitments to allies abroad, improve (however slowly) living standards at home, and assure continuing self-generated technological innovation.[4]

However, rather than serving to preserve the communist system, liberalization—by loosening the grips of authoritarian control of the economic, political, and social spheres—accelerated the process of disintegration. By 1991, Roberts writes, "Mr. Gorbachev the reformer was, perhaps willy-nilly, proving to be a revolutionary."[5]

DEMOCRACY COMES TO EASTERN EUROPE

The seeds of revolution in Eastern Europe had been planted long before Gorbachev came to power. The first rumblings of change came from Poland. In 1979, a movement of Catholics, workers, and intellectuals opposed to the communist regime had been encouraged in their struggle by a visit from Pope John Paul II (known as the "Polish Pope") who had criticized communism for creating social divisiveness and banning independent trade organizations. In July, workers began to strike at various shipyards, most notably at Gdansk under the leadership of Lech Walesa. They formed a new union dubbed Solidarity. The strikers' demands expanded from economic issues to freedom of speech, the release of political prisoners, and the right to form independent trade unions.

On August 31, the Polish government agreed to many of the strikers' demands by signing the Gdansk Agreement. However, due in part to the disapproval of the Soviet Union, reforms came slowly. Eventually, amid increased pressure by Solidarity, Polish defense minister General Wojciech Jaruzelski imposed martial law on December 13, 1981. Tens of thousands of activists, intellectuals, and Solidarity leaders were arrested, strikes were quelled with force, and over two hundred protesters were killed. Martial law would remain in effect until July 1983.

Democracy would not come to Poland until 1989, the year communist regimes were also toppled in Czechoslovakia, Romania, and East Germany. Hungary and Bulgaria would follow suit, ousting their communist governments in 1990 and 1991, respectively. The collapse of the Soviet Union itself took place in 1991, bringing an end to over seventy years of socialism in Russia. The forces that led to these dramatic changes are disputed. Some historians give Reagan the majority of the credit for standing up to the Soviets. Others emphasize the popular national sentiments unleashed by Gorbachev's reforms. Still others point to bureaucratic inefficiency of the Soviet system or weaknesses inherent in the socialist form of government. It is likely that some combination of these and other factors caused the upheaval. Regardless of their cause, the events of 1989–1991 completely changed the nature of international relations. The bipolar world order that existed under the cold war gave way to a world with one superpower—the United States.

STRUGGLING FOR LIBERATION

Eastern Europe and the Soviet Union were not the only parts of the world witnessing liberation struggles in the late 1980s and early 1990s. One region of the world that did not jump on the democratic bandwagon in 1989 was China—despite the efforts of some citizens to bring about democratic reforms. In the spring of that year, students began to hold pro-democracy demonstrations in Tiananmen Square in the nation's capital, Beijing. On May 20, the government imposed martial law in Beijing, but the protesters refused to disperse. On the night of June 3–4, military troops entered the city and made their way to the square, killing all who obstructed them as well as bystanders. Estimates of the numbers killed range from the hundreds to over one thousand, but most fatalities appear to have occurred in the streets of Beijing, not in the square itself. In any event, the crackdown—which stood in sharp contrast to the relatively peaceful revolutions of Eastern Europe—was a major setback for pro-democracy activists in China and provoked extreme outrage from the international community.

Meanwhile, in another corner of the world—South Africa—the champions of freedom had slightly more success. In 1989, decades of legalized racial segregation (apartheid) began to come to an end under the policies of the new president, F.W. de Klerk. In 1990, de Klerk legalized the African National Congress, a black civil rights organization that had been banned since 1960. He also released its leader, Nelson Mandela, from prison. During his twenty-seven years of imprisonment, Mandela had served as a poignant symbol of the oppressiveness of apartheid. Once freed, he served as its most active critic. He and de Klerk began the difficult task of creating new governing structures granting blacks a share of power. In 1994, the nation's first multiracial elections were held, and Mandela was elected president.

NEW WORLD ORDER?

Many commentators hoped that the end of the cold war would usher in an era of peace and stability. The United States—the world's only remaining superpower—would lead by example and exercise its power (through the United Nations) in support of democracy and social justice across the globe. These were the ideals articulated by U.S. president George Bush, who succeeded Reagan in 1988.

This vision of international cooperation was most dramatically put to the test in 1990–1991 in the Middle East. Iraq, led by dictator Saddam Hussein, invaded and annexed its neighbor, the small, oil-rich country of Kuwait in August 1990. The international community responded with sanctions and diplomatic efforts in an attempt to force Hussein out of Kuwait—all of which proved fruitless. Finally, on January 17, 1991, a coalition of forces led by the United States launched a massive air war—Operation Desert Storm—against Iraq. Ground troops were added to the fray in the following weeks, eventually defeating Hussein and forcing his troops out of Kuwait.

Bush delivered his state of the union address for 1991 at the height of the air war. In it, he explained that the effort being undertaken in Iraq and Kuwait was necessary to preserve a "new world order" of stable international relations:

> What is at stake is more than one small country; it is a big idea: a new world order, where diverse nations are drawn together in common cause to achieve the universal aspirations of mankind—peace and security, freedom, and the rule of law. Such is a world worthy of our struggle and worthy of our children's future.[6]

Unfortunately, while Operation Desert Storm was a military success, and seemed to set the stage for post–cold war stability, it proved to be the exception rather than the rule. As Grenville explains:

> The near unanimity of the United Nations in ridding Kuwait, a member of the UN, of the Iraqi occupation forces had created the expectation that the UN would henceforth act to preserve peace and justice everywhere in the world and so live up to its most noble ideals. Such expectations could not be fulfilled.[7]

Instead, the 1990s would be a decade fraught with numerous regional wars that would elude the peacemaking efforts of the UN and the United States. Indeed, by the end of 2000, the number of nations experiencing civil unrest and other conflicts had nearly doubled since the height of the cold war, according to the National Defense Council Foundation.

Although the cold war had forced millions of people to live in repressive conditions and had threatened the globe with nuclear annihilation, it had imposed a measure of stability. As Grenville explains, from 1945 to the 1980s, the Soviet Union, China, the United States, and Western Europe had functioned as "four policemen" keeping the world relatively stable:

> The Soviet Union and China each kept her part of the world in order, at the point of a bayonet where necessary. The United States policed the Caribbean and Central America. Western Europe built up its defenses and the West safeguarded its vital interests in the Middle East. Without the Cold War, the policemen's roles diminished. A conflict in a country or region not vitally affecting the interests of the West or East was likely to be allowed to find its own bloody solution. Diplomatic good offices, sincere attempts at mediation within or outside the United Nations, and humanitarian aid might well be offered, but there would be a reluctance to intervene militarily. Possibly the economic carrot and stick, the granting or withholding of loans, aid and trade, would be the most common non-violent means by which the rich West would seek to influence the outcome of particular struggles.[8]

Thus, in various parts of the world throughout the 1990s—most notably in the Balkans and parts of Africa—the UN and the United States sought to bring about peace through means other than direct military involvement—with limited success.

THE WAR IN YUGOSLAVIA

Events in Yugoslavia most vividly illustrate the instability that ensued with the end of the cold war. The nation's six republics were populated by several ethnic groups—including Serbians, Croatians, and Muslims. These ethnic groups, who bore intense, longstanding hostilities toward one another, were not isolated in separate regions but were instead dispersed throughout the republics. Prior to 1980, the country's communist dictator, Marshal Tito, had succeeded in keeping the hostilities in check. His communist successors managed to sustain this stability until 1991. In June of that year, two of the republics, Croatia and Slovenia, declared independence. The Serbs opposed this move militarily, but following mediation by the European Community, they withdrew their forces ten days after the hostilities began. Slovenia then remained independent and experienced no more war. However, the Serbs renewed their hostilities against Croatia, winning one-third of Croatia after seven months of fighting. Despite these losses, the remainder of Croatia was declared independent in January 1992. Another republic, Macedonia, declared its independence in September 1991 in a relatively peaceful transition.

The worst fighting of the region was to begin in 1992, when Bosnia and Herzegovina (or simply Bosnia) declared its independence. The ethnic Serbs within Bosnia opposed this move and declared war on the Yugoslav government, which was composed of Serbs, Croats, and Muslims. The ensuing war would last until 1995, with the signing of the Dayton Agreement declaring Bosnia a sovereign nation composed of two states—one Bosnian and one Muslim and Croat. The war left 200,000 dead, created 2 million refugees, and left many cities and villages in ruins.

The international community's failure to stop this war exposed the failure of Bush's vision of a new world order to materialize. Without the heavy-handed communist control of citizens' daily lives, ethnic identities—and conflicts—were allowed to surface and find expression. With the demise of the Soviet Union, no superpower had a stake in maintaining the stability of the region. The West, with limited economic and political interests in the area, was willing to make only mostly symbolic and diplomatic gestures to end the conflict—gestures that failed repeatedly. The North Atlantic Treaty Organization (NATO), proved unwilling to intervene with significant force due to a lack of international support for such an effort. Although the Soviet Union was no longer in existence, its largest republic—Russia—was an ally of the Serbs. Any efforts to act against the Serbs threatened to antagonize this nation, which, while not a superpower, still wielded significant power.

In short, the war in Bosnia revealed that the post–cold war world would produce complex conflicts that would prove vexing to peacemakers. Indeed, the Bosnia scenario was repeated in various African and Asian countries throughout the 1990s, and in 1999, another Yugoslav republic—Kosovo—broke out in ethnic war. James Mayall, professor of international relations at the London School of Economics and Political Science, sums up the post–cold war international reality:

> The end of the cold war led to a brief period of triumphalism, particularly in the West. A vision opened up of a world at last made safe for democracy, the open

economy, and collective security. . . . Sadly, the optimism was short-lived. No sooner had it formed than the vision began to fade. It was obscured by the fact that, on the one hand, in a disintegrating world the costs of policing the new world order were likely to be beyond the resources of even the United States; and on the other, at the end of the century . . . nationalism retained its power to destroy as well as liberate.[9]

GENOCIDE IN RWANDA

The most violent of the world's ethnic conflicts in the 1990s occurred in the African nation of Rwanda. The two dominant ethnic groups in Rwanda, the Hutus and the Tutsis, had a long history of violent opposition and had competed for political control of the country for decades. In April 1994, the president of the country, Juvénal Habyarimana, a Hutu, was killed when his plane was shot down. It is not known who perpetrated this act, but immediately following the assassination, the nation's ethnic Hutus launched an attack on Tutsis and their moderate Hutu sympathizers. Within a few months they had succeeded in killing over 500,000.

Western observers originally perceived the violence as a spontaneous outbreak of hostilities. However, most experts now agree that the killings constituted genocide in the strictest sense of the term: "the deliberate and systematic destruction of a racial, political, or cultural group."[10] Members of the ruling party elite had planned and organized the killing in advance, and their goal was indeed to eliminate all Tutsis. To this end, they had established militias called *Interahamwe* ("those who attack together") and *Impuzamugambi* ("those who have the same goal"). In all, there were about 50,000 militia members, many armed simply with machetes. They simultaneously set up roadblocks throughout the country and set about their grizzly task, aided by ordinary citizens who were either forced to participate or swept up in the frenzy. They were urged on by messages from the government radio station, such as, "To kill thousands of people in a day means that you are very serious about what you are doing."[11]

The magnitude of the horror that descended on Rwanda in 1994 defies comprehension. Gérard Prunier, author of *The Rwanda Crisis: History of a Genocide*, estimates that more than 800,000 Tutsis were killed in a six-week period—a daily killing rate of "at least five times that of the Nazi death camps."[12] Journalist Scott Peterson writes that "the daily death rate *averaged* well more than 11,500 for two months, with surges as high as 45,000. During this peak, one murder was committed every 2 seconds of every minute, of every hour, for days."[13] Of course, untold numbers of others were injured, raped, and severely traumatized.

These numbers, as disturbing as they are, fail to fully communicate the extent of the horror. As with the Holocaust of World War II, it is important to remember the disturbing particulars of these events in order to understand the forces that produced them and to prevent their recurrence. The reader should be warned that the following passage contains extremely graphic descriptions of the genocide:

> The killings were not in any way clean or surgical. The use of machetes often resulted in a long and painful agony. . . . Sexual abuse of women was common and they were often brutally killed after being raped. If some children joining the *Interahamwe* became killers, others were victims, and babies were often smashed against rocks or thrown alive into pit latrines. Mutilations were common, with breasts and penises often being chopped off. In some cases, they became part of macabre rituals which would have puzzled a psychiatrist: "Brutality here does not end with murder. At massacre sites, corpses, many of them those of children, have been methodically dismembered and the body parts stacked neatly in separate piles" [the *Economist* reported].[14]

Clearly, the events in Rwanda—as well as Yugoslavia and elsewhere—illustrate that the post–cold war world of the 1990s bore little resemblance to George Bush's vision of a new world order.

INTO THE NEW MILLENNIUM

As the hoopla surrounding the arrival of the new millennium faded away, it became obvious that despite humanity's technological gains, many of the world's old problems persisted. While the computers continued to run smoothly, violent conflict and international tensions persisted in various regions of the world. Most notably, in September 2000, violence between Palestinians and Israeli soldiers broke out in the West Bank and Gaza strip. These Israeli-occupied zones had been the scene of much violence during a Palestinian uprising—*Intifada*—from 1987 to 1993. A relative level of peace had prevailed during the latter 1990s as the Palestinians had been gradually afforded a greater degree of autonomy. The calm was shattered on September 29, when Ariel Sharon, a right-wing former army general (who would subsequently be elected prime minister), visited a contested holy site— the Temple Mount—to assert Jewish claims there. Palestinians, who considered Sharon's action provocative, protested in violent confrontations with Israeli soldiers. In the months that followed, the violence escalated in an ongoing series of attacks and counterattacks until the conflict appeared more like a war than an uprising. By August 2001, more than 700 people had died in the renewed conflict.

The United States experienced its own share of conflict early in the new millennium. In November 2000, the presidential election between George W. Bush (the son of former president George Bush) and Al Gore (vice president under Bill Clinton) was left undecided after the state of Florida was declared too close to call. For several weeks the nation waited as a legal battle was fought over whether hand recounts should be allowed in several counties. On December 12, the U.S. Supreme Court declared the ballot recount unconstitutional, leaving Bush the winner.

In the early months of his presidency, Bush appeared to be taking a much more isolationist stance than his predecessor Bill Clinton. He pledged to pursue the development of a missile defense system despite the concerns of many European nations that opposed the plan. Europeans were also angered by Bush's decision to withdraw U.S. support of the Kyoto Protocol, an international treaty designed to address the problem of global warming by reducing greenhouse gas emissions. Various European leaders characterized this action as aggressive and arrogant. For example, Dominique Voynet, France's minister for the environment, called it "completely provocative and irresponsible."[15] However, Bush defended his move on the basis that the greenhouse-gas reductions required by the Kyoto Protocol would be too costly to U.S. industry: "We will not do anything that harms our economy, because first things first are the people who live in America."[16]

Bush also took a more isolationist posture toward Communist China early in his presidency following a tense international incident. In April 2001, a U.S. spy plane gathering intelligence in international airspace near the coast of China was involved in a mid-air collision with a Chinese fighter jet. The Chinese pilot was killed, and the damaged American plane was forced to make an emergency landing on a Chinese airfield. The twenty-four U.S. military personnel on board the plane were detained by the Chinese for eleven days while the two nations engaged in a game of high-pressure diplomacy reminiscent of cold-war relations with the USSR. Although the Americans were eventually released unharmed, Bush made it clear that while the Clinton administration had considered China a "strategic partner," the new White House viewed the communist nation a "strategic competitor."

Thus the new millennium started with international conflict and major shifts in U.S foreign policy.

AN ERA OF CONTRADICTIONS

The end of the twentieth century was an era of contradictions. The fall of oppressive regimes around the world produced both liberation and violent confrontation. The end of the largely non-violent cold war led to an escalation of smaller hot wars. While genocide—perhaps the most destructive activity imaginable—was taking place in Rwanda, scientists in other parts of the world were mapping the human genome and working on ways to create life through cloning. Thus the events chronicled in this anthology must be viewed against a complex backdrop of spellbinding technological progress, massive geopolitical change, ongoing ethnic and faith-based conflict, and dismaying levels of violence ranging from isolated acts of terrorism to ethnic conflicts, popular uprisings, border wars, and genocide. While the Y2K bug failed to shut down the computers on the eve of the new millennium, it is clear that many of humanity's oldest and most troubling problems remain to be resolved.

NOTES

1. J.A.S. Grenville, *A History of the World in the Twentieth Century, Volume Two: Conflict and Liberation, 1945–1996*. Cambridge, MA: Belknap Press of Harvard University Press, 1997, p. 816.

2. Quoted in James D. Torr, *The 1980s*. San Diego: Greenhaven, 2000, p. 84.

3. Martin Gilbert, *A History of the Twentieth Century, Volume Three, 1952–1999*. New York: W. Morrow, 1997, p. 597.

4. J.M. Roberts, *Twentieth Century: The History of the World, 1901–2000*. New York: Viking, p. 749.

5. Roberts, *Twentieth Century*, p. 751.

6. George Bush, Address Before a Joint Session of the Congress on the State of the Union, January 29, 1991. http://bushlibrary.tamu.edu//papers/1991/91012902.html.

7. Grenville, *A History of the World in the Twentieth Century*, p. 925.

8. Grenville, *A History of the World in the Twentieth Century*, p. 926.

9. James Mayall, "Nationalism," in *The Columbia History of the Twentieth Century*. Ed. Richard W. Bulliet. New York: Columbia University Press, p. 197.

10. *Webster's Ninth New Collegiate Dictionary*. Springfield, MA: Merriam-Webster, 1986, p. 511.

11. Quoted in Scott Peterson, *Me Against My Bother: At War in Somalia, Sudan, and Rwanda*. New York: Routledge, 2000, p. 254.

12. Gérard Prunier, *The Rwanda Crisis: History of a Genocide*. New York: Columbia University Press, 1995, p. 261.

13. Peterson, *Me Against My Bother*, p. 253.

14. Punier, *The Rwanda Crisis*, p. 255–56.

15. Quoted in Edmund L. Andrews, "Bush Angers Europe by Eroding Pact on Warming," *New York Times*, April 1, 2001, p. 3.

16. Quoted in Andrews, "Bush Angers Europe by Eroding Pact on Warming," p. 3.

The Early 1980s: Political Crisis, Solidarity, and Technological Progress

CHAPTER 1

THE 1980 MOSCOW OLYMPIC BOYCOTT

CHRISTOPHER R. HILL

Following the Soviet invasion of Afghanistan in December 1979, U.S. president Jimmy Carter called for a boycott of the 1980 Summer Olympic Games scheduled to be held in Moscow. In the following essay, Christopher R. Hill recounts the events of early 1980, as the Carter administration exerted extreme pressure on the United States Olympic Committee (USOC) to withdraw the U.S. team from the games. In the end, sixty-two nations—including West Germany and Japan—joined the boycott. The Soviet Union responded by declining to participate in the 1984 Summer Olympic Games held in Los Angeles. Hill, formerly a senior lecturer in politics at the University of York in the United Kingdom, is the author of *Olympic Politics*, from which this reading was excerpted.

L ate in December 1979 the Soviet Union invaded Afghanistan, nominally on the invitation of its government. In January President Jimmy Carter warned that the United States would boycott the Moscow Olympic Games, due to begin at the end of July, as a retaliation for the Soviet action. Although not well informed on Olympic procedures, he did understand that only the United States Olympic Committee could decide not to send a team to the Games, and in February he informed USOC that he expected it to withdraw the United States team. After extreme pressure had been put upon it by the government USOC duly agreed to withdraw by a substantial majority. It did so, not only because of the pressure, but also because of the traditional respect in which Americans hold Presidential policy in international affairs, and because many delegates to the meeting at which the decision was taken agreed with the government that it would be improper to take part in the Games.

The American boycott (a word which was never officially used) was almost certainly the direct cause of the Soviet counter-boycott of the Los Angeles Games in 1984 (when 'boycott' was avoided in favour of 'non-participation'), and threatened to split the Olympic movement. The choice of Seoul as host for the 1988 Games made a split even more likely, and it was largely thanks to the skill and determination of Juan Antonio Samaranch [President of the International Olympic Committee after 1980] that the Soviets took part in the 1988 Games. Since then it has become customary to say that the age of boycotts is past.

It may seem surprising that the International Olympic Committee should have awarded the Games to Moscow in the first place, since the choice must have been seen as likely to provoke the anti-communist West, even if no boycott could have been foreseen. The best clues to this puzzle may be found in the explanations offered by Lord Killanin, who was President of the IOC at the time. He asserts that the voting for Moscow was purely on sporting grounds, in recognition of its facilities and professional ability. If, he says, the vote had been taken on political grounds it might well have gone differently, since the IOC is basically a conservative body. (At the same time he admits that the vote was at the height of east-west detente and that some IOC members may have cast their votes with that in mind.) . . .

GENESIS OF THE U.S. BOYCOTT

There had been opposition to Moscow from the start, both outside and within the Soviet Union. David B. Kanin, a CIA man rather surprisingly writing in the *Journal of Sport and Social Issues*, believes that the Soviets timed the arrests of some of their dissidents well in advance of the Games, in order to allow any protest to die down before the West might have considered boycott as a policy option. Kanin, who must have had some inside knowledge, although he only used unclassified sources for his article, goes on that Carter ruled out a boycott in relation to the treatment of dissidents in 1978 but that after Afghanistan 'Sport, that most peripheral and most publicized form of international relations, provided the perfect answer'. He thinks Carter was reluctant to boycott, perhaps because the President wanted to be consistent with his earlier decision, or perhaps because he thought most Americans would prefer the United States team to compete.

The idea of a boycott may not have been Carter's own and

perhaps, as Kanin suggests, he would have preferred to send a team to the Games, had not polls and statements from public figures and such powerful bodies as the AFL-CIO (American Federation of Labour–Congress of Industrial Organizations) made it clear that boycott was a popular option—perhaps as an outlet for frustration over America's impotence in Iran. Be that as it may, the Soviet Union invaded Afghanistan on 27 December 1979, and in the first two weeks of January the boycott campaign began to roll. On 28 January Killanin was asked to see Lloyd Cutler, the President's Counsel, and Cutler called on him at his home in Dublin on 2 February.

There had been bad feeling between the IOC and Carter even before his boycott. On 20 October 1978 Tom Bradley, the Mayor of Los Angeles, had arranged that the ceremony of signing the contract between Los Angeles and the IOC for the 1984 Games should be held at the White House, expecting Carter to attend—but he did not, because his wife had been on television that morning, and he did not want to upstage her. Carter was only a few yards away and Killanin, used to being greeted by Presidents, was furious. It is, therefore, hardly surprising that his hackles rose when he found that Cutler had come to Dublin not to discuss the crisis, but to demand that the IOC should either postpone or cancel the Games. Killanin found Cutler ignorant about the Olympic movement and, once he had read the President's memoirs, passed the same verdict on Carter, whom he describes as 'scrambling for his political life'.

Denis Howell describes the campaign for the 1980 Olympics as 'the most epic political battle in which I have ever been engaged'. Like many other commentators, he shows that the Americans had no understanding of the Olympic movement. For example, Cyrus Vance, the Secretary of State, said the administration hoped there would be no American citizens in Moscow during the Games, a position he had to abandon when it was pointed out to him that, if all western countries followed suit, the control of all the federations could fall into non-western hands. Later in the American campaign Cutler came to London, where he met a small group including Howell and Roger Bannister, and seems to have come off worse. Among other *bon mots*, Howell told Cutler 'In this country Magna Carta rules, not Jimmy Carter'. . . .

THE BATTLE WITH USOC

Nor was life easy for the USOC, which alone could take the decision not to send a team to the Games. President Carter professed that his boycott was motivated partly by a concern for human rights, but his treatment of USOC suggests that he was not always interested in what went on in his own backyard.

USOC's President and Secretary-General, Robert J. Kane and Colonel Donald Miller, expressed shock, sadness and disappointment and feared that Carter's warning that a boycott of the Games was in his mind might reduce USOC's fund-raising capacity. USOC said, as Killanin had done, that it would not be physically possible to transfer the Games from Moscow and warned of possible repercussions on the Lake Placid [Winter 1980] and Los Angeles [Summer 1984] Games. It continued to reject boycott, relocation or the 'Free World Games' proposed by President Carter, but welcomed the opportunity to discuss the crisis with White House officials on 18 January 1980. After the meeting they were still brave enough to say that they would not necessarily comply with a decision by the US government to withdraw from the Games.

The government recognised that under Olympic rules the decision would ultimately be made by USOC, but that the athletes, working through their federations, would have some influence. It therefore put great pressure on them to decide in the right way. Some brave athletes resisted, like the oarswoman Anita DeFrantz, who simply went ahead with her training and later, when USOC had decided to withdraw, sought with eighteen other athletes to overthrow the decision, contending that the Committee was blocking the athletes' constitutional right to take part in the Games. She had presumably been waiting to announce the suit until the IOC had decided whether it could accept individual entries instead of teams chosen by federations and authorised by NOCs [national olympic committees], since a day earlier Killanin had said that individual entries would be impracticable.

PRESSURE FROM CONGRESS

As well as pressure from the administration, there was enormous pressure from both political parties and both Houses of Congress. The Republican National Committee approved a resolution urging USOC to boycott. The Senate Majority Leader, Robert C. Byrd, was in favour of moving the Games or boycotting if moving them were not possible. The House of Representatives' Foreign Affairs Committee overwhelmingly backed Carter, having spent a day hearing Kane, who again warned that Carter's boycott could produce counter-boycott of Los Angeles in 1984. The House itself approved by 386 to 12 a motion urging USOC to press for the Games' transfer or cancellation. The House of Representatives' pronouncement was followed closely by the Foreign Relations Committee of the Senate, which unanimously approved relocation, postponement or cancellation, while the full Senate went further and overwhelmingly approved the boycott, whether or not the Soviets withdrew from Afghanistan. Such opposition as there was came from a coalition of dyed-in-the-wool Republican Democrats to the left of Carter.

By mid-January Carter was saying that if there were no Soviet withdrawal within a month he wanted USOC to vote to transfer or cancel the Games; if that failed he would suggest USOC formally withdraw the American athletes. Senator Ted Kennedy, his main opponent for the Democratic nomination, reluctantly supported him. Killanin saw Carter's decision as a tragedy and reiterated that it would be legally and technically impossible to move the Games, but it is not surprising that Kane and Miller began to cave in and agreed to try to obtain other nations' agreement to moving them.

Killanin was thought to have chided USOC privately for having begun to give way to pressure from its government, in contravention of the Olympic ideal, which enjoins upon all the 'Olympic family' complete independence from political pressure. At the same time Carter sent a personal letter to more than a hundred heads of government asking support for a boycott, but gained no immediate new support, as most countries were anxious to defer a final decision for as long as possible, and many were not at all anxious to be seen to exert pressure on their NOCs. USOC's collapse gathered momentum when its Executive Board agreed to explore the possibility of a national sport festival to replace the Games. . . .

THE UNITED STATES VS. THE IOC

Meanwhile at USOC's headquarters in Colorado Springs its Executive Board unanimously agreed to ask the IOC to postpone, cancel or transfer the Games, which was exactly what the President had asked for. However, Julian K. Roosevelt, an American IOC member, remained loyal and attacked Carter's warning that he expected USOC to withdraw from the Games if the Soviet Union had made no significant move over Afghanistan by mid-February.

The next big encounter was at the IOC's Session, just before the winter Games at Lake Placid, which was opened by the Secretary of State, Cyrus Vance. He considerably irritated Killanin by allowing the world press to see his speech, under embargo, before Killanin saw it. When he did, he found it grossly political, and bound to offend the Soviets. So he warned them that they had better stay away from the ceremony, at which Vance's speech was received in complete silence. In response to Killanin's urgent summons, Kane also went to Lake Placid, where he duly urged the IOC's Executive Board to transfer the Games, although, according to Killanin, he did so with obvious lack of enthusiasm.

As Killanin emphasises, Vance's speech did have the good side-effect of drawing the IOC together; they were, after all, a conservative body of men (no women in those days), and it would have been surprising if none of them had been impressed by the American arguments. But their sense of propriety and dislike of being bullied were strong, and all seventy-three who were present at Lake Placid backed a document in Killanin's name, which stated that the Games must be held at Moscow as planned. . . .

THE BOYCOTTERS PREVAIL

The administration regretted the IOC's reaffirmation that the Games must be held at Moscow and stated that it now had no choice but to proceed with its plans. It therefore told USOC that it must reach a prompt decision. Kane and Miller said that they would accept any decision that Carter might make, but were against alternative Games being held. It was announced that USOC's final decision would be taken at the meeting of its House of Delegates at Colorado Springs on 11–13 April. Carter's deadline of 'mid-February' had become more precise over the preceding weeks, and he had fixed on 20 February as the date by which the Soviet Union must make a move which would persuade him that the Games could after all be held in Moscow. Once that date had passed without any response from the USSR he announced that his decision was firm and irreversible, and urged USOC not to send a team to the Games. Killanin points out that twelve days after the IOC's decision at its Lake Placid Session America suffered the humiliation of the bungled attempt to rescue hostages from Iran, and thinks that disaster may have stiffened Carter's resolve to prevent American athletes going to Moscow.

In April the administration began a drive to ensure that the House of Delegates' meeting would comply with its wishes. Vance, plus the chairman of the joint chiefs of staff, General David C. Jones, told USOC that the boycott was essential to national security. It was further reported that Carter was considering emergency economic powers to stop athletes going to Moscow and it was confirmed that there had been discussions with House Speaker Thomas P. O'Neill Jr and Senate Majority Leader Robert Byrd about stopping them with amendments to the Amateur Sports Act of 1978, which authorises USOC to field a team at Olympic events. USOC officials then had little choice but to say that the President's threats of legal actions seemed to have closed the door on American participation.

At the meeting at Colorado Springs a vast congregation of sportsmen and women and sports administrators was addressed by Vice-President Walter Mondale, after which the boycotters, by now including USOC's President, Robert Kane, won comfortably, by 1,604 to 797. Macfarlane, soon to become Britain's Minister for Sport, watched the meeting on television (as did Killanin) and wrote: 'It was almost embarrassing to watch the emotional nationalism that charged the meeting. It reminded me of an American political convention and there was no doubt about how a vote would go'. As the months went by at least one former athlete changed his mind towards favouring the boycott for a bizarre reason: this was Bruce Jenner, a former decathlon gold medal winner, who received letters from members of the patriotic public, threatening not to eat Wheaties, which he promoted. . . .

THE SOVIET REACTION

Once the prospect of a boycott became something to be reckoned with, the Soviet press began a counter-campaign. The Soviet campaign did not accept that the invasion of Afghanistan was the reason for the boycott. The 'real' reasons were that the USSR was a socialist country; that President Carter wished to undermine detente and that he needed to salvage his failing popularity. The campaign's main lines appeared in an article in *Sovietski Sport* on 20 January 1980:

> We understand clearly why all real friends of sports and Olympism decisively oppose the provocative manoeuvres of supporters of cold war in the United States, England and some other imperialist states, who are striving to utilise sport as an instrument of their policy and hinder the forthcoming meeting of world youth on the arenas of the Moscow Olympic Games. . . . The foreign policy of the USSR which is clear to the peoples of the world, corresponds with their basic interests . . . and serves as a reliable support of all forces struggling for peace and detente. Supporting the cause of preserving the unity of the Olympic movement, striving to prevent interference of politicians in sport and participating in Moscow's holiday of youth—despite threats, slanderous tricks and political pressure—this is the attitude of the sports world and the public of the countries participating in the Olympic movement toward the Olympiade in the first country of socialism.

Kanin thinks that by the middle of March Moscow had probably decided that the Americans would definitely not take part in the Games, because from then on their reaction to the boycott included extremely harsh attacks on Carter and hints that a boycott could harm overall East/West relations.

Baruch A. Hazan sees two stages in the campaign: up to 25 May the possible negative consequences were stressed; after that date had passed, and there was little prospect of further acceptances being received from NOCs, the line was that nothing serious had happened. There were vague threats of boycotting Los Angeles and the defeat of United States athletes by their own politicians was stressed. Afghanistan was seldom mentioned; when it was it was presented as Carter's excuse for something that he had long been planning. Some further Soviet arguments were that the boycott violated international law as well as the Helsinki agreement [on human rights] and the Charters of the United Nations and of UNESCO [United Nations Educational, Scientific, and Cultural Organization]. By denying athletes the right to compete it violated the fifth amendment to the American constitution, and it was rumoured that the CIA and FBI were to use the Games for subversive purposes. Thus the Soviet press fought back with a will, no doubt aided by the Soviet Union's long experience of using sport as a propaganda weapon.

As the Games approached, the Soviet authorities began to acknowledge that there would be fewer foreign visitors than had been expected (perhaps a blessing to the KGB) and lowered their guess from 300,000 or more to 70,000. As the final preparations for the Games began they closed Moscow to all Soviet citizens, except those who could prove that they lived and worked there.

THE GAMES AND AFTER

In the end 81 countries participated, compared with 88 at Montreal (1976), 122 at Munich (1972) and 113 at Mexico City (1968). The Games were attended by 5,326 competitors compared with 6,085 in 1972. The most important boycotters in terms of ability to win medals were the USA, West Germany and Japan. As Neil Macfarlane puts it: 'In some ways the Games were devalued but, had the boycott succeeded, there would have been a real danger that the Olympic movement would have been destroyed.'

For Killanin the Games were joyless. But he still believed that without the boycott, and with the presence of the three to four hundred thousand foreign visitors who had originally been expected, the Games might have played a part in breaking down the barriers between East and West, despite the difficulties of visitors meeting Soviet citizens. But so politicised had the Games become that the political journalists, according to Killanin, nearly outnumbered the sports writers, and many papers carried two accounts of the same events, though from two very different points of view.

After the Games were over, Samaranch told a press conference on 31 October 1980 that the Executive Board was happy with the Moscow Organising Committee's preliminary report on their Games. He asserted that the Moscow Games had won the Olympic movement new strength and respect and that the Executive Board had been keenly aware that it could save the Games from fiasco only by collaborating closely with the Moscow organising committee.

The Executive Board asked the sixty-six Olympic Committees which had stayed away to explain why they had done so. However, it seems that the enquiries were not very energetically pursued and that some quite feeble excuses were allowed to pass.

THE FAILED IRANIAN HOSTAGE RESCUE MISSION

GARY SICK

The year 1980 began with a crisis already in progress in Iran. In November 1979, militant Islamic students loyal to Iran's new leader, Muslim clergyman Ayatollah Ruhollah Khomeini, had stormed the U.S. embassy in Tehran and taken sixty-six Americans hostage. Thirteen of the hostages were quickly released, but the other fifty-three remained captive. In return for their release, the students demanded that the United States apologize for supporting Iran's former leader, Shah Muhammad Reza Pahlavi, who had been replaced by Khomeini in January 1979. They also demanded the return of large sums of money the shah had reportedly taken abroad.

Efforts to negotiate the hostages' release were unsuccessful, and in April 1980 the U.S. military attempted to extract the hostages by means of planes and helicopters. In the following essay, Gary Sick describes this operation, which was aborted prior to reaching Tehran due to mechanical failure and bad weather. In the wake of this failed rescue attempt, which resulted in the death of eight American servicemen, the United States resorted to economic sanctions and diplomacy in their efforts to secure the hostages' release. However, Sick concludes, the hostages were not released until the Iranian students considered them a liability rather than a bargaining chip. They were finally set free in January 1981 after 444 days in captivity.

Sick was a National Security Council staff member for Iran and the chief assistant to the national security adviser through-

Excerpted from "Military Options and Constraints," by Gary Sick, in *American Hostages in Iran: The Conduct of a Crisis*, edited by Warren Christopher et al. (New Haven, CT: Yale University Press). Copyright © 1985 by the Council on Foreign Relations. Reprinted by permission of Yale University Press.

out the Iranian hostage crisis. He is the author of *All Fall Down: America's Tragic Encounter with Iran.*

There was never any illusion on the part of anyone close to the planning of the rescue mission that it was anything but a high-risk venture. It was understood to be a highly complex and daring raid that would not only strain the limits of technology but would also press the endurance of men and machines to the outer margins. As Secretary of Defense Harold Brown commented in his press conference after the mission failed, there was no other country in the world that could even have attempted such an operation.

Ironically, the very improbability of attempting to extract more than fifty prisoners from a well-guarded site in the center of a major, hostile city halfway around the globe and more than 500 miles from the nearest available military facility was a factor in the plan's favor. One of the students in the embassy, when informed on Friday of the rescue attempt the previous evening, was reported to have replied: "Impossible!" In fact, the student captors had long before concluded that a rescue attempt was not feasible, and they had relaxed their security to such a degree that a raid was no longer the unattainable goal it had appeared in the earliest days when the student guards were suspicious of every shadow. . . .

THE PLAN

The rescue was designed to be conducted in a series of related steps, each of which would be reversible without escalation and with minimum casualties should something go wrong. The need to be able to terminate and withdraw at any point, together with the need for absolute secrecy, added to the complexity and difficulty of both planning and execution. The first stage of the plan involved the positioning of men, matériel, and support equipment at key locations in the Middle East and Indian Ocean. This movement had to be accomplished under the cover of other routinely scheduled activities to avoid signaling that an operation was being prepared. As a matter of security, the bulk of this matériel was held back until political authorization was granted to proceed with the operation. The practical effect of this decision was to extend the time lapse between the decision and the actual launching of the raid.

The insertion of the force into Iran was a grueling and technically difficult operation. Under cover of darkness, eight RH-53D helicopters and six C-130 aircraft were to depart from different locations, fly into Iran, and rendezvous at an airstrip some 500 miles inland. This airstrip, near the small town of Tabas, had been secretly prepared in advance and was known as "Desert I" in the plan. At Desert I, the helicopters were to be refueled and loaded with the men and equipment transported by the fixed-wing aircraft. Following the refueling and loading, the C-130s would leave Iran. The helicopters, still under cover of darkness, would proceed to a remote site in the mountains above Tehran, where they would be camouflaged and remain in hiding throughout the following day. This delay was required to insure that the assault on the embassy itself could be carried out under the cover of darkness. Because of the distances involved, it was impossible to insert the necessary forces, release the hostages, and depart in a single night.

For the nonspecialist, it is difficult to appreciate the demands this critical first phase of the operation placed on men, equipment, and technology. Simply flying 600 miles nonstop over sea and land in a helicopter is a remarkable feat. To do so at night, without lights, in complete radio silence, and at very low altitude is quite simply an heroic achievement. Many of those associated with planning the rescue mission believed—quite rightly as it turned out—that this was the most difficult segment of the entire operation.

Assuming the successful insertion of the team and its survival undetected during the following day, the actual rescue operation would be conducted under cover of darkness on the following night. The entry of the team into Tehran would be in local vehicles to attract minimum attention, with the helicopters making the briefest possible appearance to pick up the team and the hostages. The helicopters would then fly to an abandoned airfield near Tehran (called "Desert II" in the plan), where they would rendezvous with transport aircraft. The helicopters would be abandoned, and the personnel would be flown out of the country under heavy U.S. air cover.

SPECULATING ON LOSS OF LIFE

A great deal of attention has been focused on the actual assault on the embassy, where many believe there would have been an unacceptable loss of life among the hostages. The truth will never be known, but there is good reason to believe that these fears were exaggerated. The success of the entry into the embassy depended almost entirely on surprise. If the students guarding the embassy were alerted to the operation in advance, the risks to the lives of the hostages would have been very great, probably unacceptably so. If, however, the first twenty-four hours passed without detection of the team as *part of a rescue attempt*, the odds would have shifted substantially in favor of a successful extraction of the hostages with minimum loss of life.

It must be remembered that the student guards were in fact students, not trained military personnel. After nearly six months of guard duty, activities had settled into a comfortable and generally relaxed routine. How would these individuals react in the wee hours of a weekend night when confronted suddenly and without warning by seasoned combat troops?

No one could say with certainty that the students would not react by immediately beginning to shoot the prisoners they had been guarding for months, but human nature and past experience suggest otherwise. There was a curious parallel only a week after the rescue attempt, when a group of terrorists invaded the Iranian Embassy in downtown London and held its occupants hostage. On the sixth day of the siege, in broad daylight, with the terrorists on guard and alert, and with crowds and TV cameras filling the streets below, a small group of British commandos suddenly attacked and overcame the five terrorists with no loss of life to the hostages. Would a U.S. commando team have achieved the same success, striking without warning in the middle of the night in Tehran? We can only speculate.

MECHANICAL MALFUNCTIONS AND BAD WEATHER

The actual rescue mission failed long before it arrived at the embassy walls. Eight helicopters took off from the carrier USS *Nimitz* in the evening of April 24. Some two hours into the flight, while over Iranian territory, helicopter number 6 of the formation began receiving warning signals in the cockpit of a possible impending rotor blade failure. The pilot landed and, in accordance with normal operating procedures, abandoned his craft. The crew was picked up by one of the other helicopters and the flight continued.

The warning signal on the RH-53D helicopter is intended to provide advance warning of a crack in the rotor blade. However, it can be triggered by a number of nonthreatening circumstances. In the flight history of this aircraft, a total of forty-three warning light episodes had occurred. Subsequent investigation revealed that in none of those cases—or in any other case in the 38,000 hours of total flight experience with the RH-53D—had a rotor crack actually been present. Even if a crack is present, it does not prevent the craft from flying for a considerable period of time. Peacetime safety regulations prescribe that an RH-53D not fly more than five hours after appearance of a warning light. At the time this helicopter was abandoned, the craft was approximately three hours from Desert I.

Shortly after this event, the helicopter flight unexpectedly encountered a cloud of suspended dust, making visual observation extremely difficult. Since the helicopters were observing strict communications silence and were unable to maintain contact with each other visually, they became separated. The flight broke out of the dust cloud, only to encounter another shortly thereafter that was more dense than the first. Because of the dense, swirling dust, the helicopters were forced to rely almost entirely on the inertial navigation equipment and instruments specially designed for this operation. Approximately four hours into the flight, helicopter number 5 began to experience malfunction of essential flight instruments. The pilot reversed course, flew back for more than two hours through the dust cloud, and returned safely to the carrier. The crew of helicopter number 5 was unaware that, at the moment when this decision was taken, they were only twenty-five minutes from the end of the dust cloud and that the weather conditions at Desert I itself, less than one hour away, were clear.

At approximately the same moment when helicopter 5 reversed course, number 2 was beginning to experience hydraulic problems. Number 2 continued on to the rendezvous site and arrived safely. However, inspection after arrival revealed that a hydraulic leak had occurred, leading to contamination of the hydraulic system and the failure of a pump. Repair of this malfunction required not only replacement of the pump but a thorough flushing of the entire hydraulic system, a process that could not be accomplished at the desert site. The helicopter would have to be abandoned.

ABORTING THE MISSION

At this stage, the mission commander at Desert I was faced with a critical situation. Because of the dust storms, the helicopters had arrived as much as eighty-five minutes late. Dawn was fast approaching, and he had only five workable helicopters. It had been determined in advance that a minimum of six helicopters was required in order to proceed with the second stage and to assure the availability of sufficient lift to conduct the actual mission the following night. As a consequence, the mission commander at the site determined that the operation should be aborted. This decision was relayed to the White House, where President Carter approved, and the force prepared to withdraw. During the refueling operation preparatory to withdrawal, one helicopter collided with the C-130 refueling aircraft, which immediately burst into flames. Eight crew members died, and five others were wounded. The remaining helicopters were abandoned, and the force withdrew on board the C-130s.

At 1:00 A.M. on the morning of April 25, the White House issued an announcement that a rescue mission had been attempted, and President Carter later went on national television to take personal responsibility for the failure. The purpose of the announcement and its timing were intended to insure that Iran would not mistake the events at Desert I for an invasion attempt and retaliate against the hostages. From all accounts, Iran became aware of the raid only when officially informed of it by President Carter. . . .

If one wished to identify a single factor that was ultimately the cause of the failure, it would have to be the clouds of suspended dust, which had not been foreseen and which interfered disastrously with the timing and execution of the raid almost from the start. The flight path of the helicopters was, by necessity, across virtually uninhabited desert, where regular weather observations were sporadic or nonexistent. Satellite observations were used extensively but were incapable of identifying low-level dust clouds. Historical information about the phenomenon was available and was even incorporated into the weather annex to the operational plan; however, its importance was not adequately appreciated, and crews were not briefed. Ironically, two international meteorological stations that would normally have been providing a continuous stream of data about the region had broken down and were no longer operational, as Iranian technical services had collapsed after the fall of the Shah [Muhammad Reza Pahlavi]. If the seriousness of the dust problem had been understood in advance, there were relatively simple remedies available even on short notice to overcome the problem.

A great deal of attention has been paid to the question of providing a larger number of helicopters. Indeed it would have been possible from an operational perspective to employ up to twelve helicopters without unduly straining existing support capacity. The decision to proceed with only eight was based on exercise experience with the RH-53D over desert terrain and was consistent with the lean military profile adopted for the operation as a whole in order to preserve security and minimize the risks of detection.

Was it a fatal error? Accounts of the raid seldom point out that, of the eight helicopters sent on the mission, only one suffered an irreparable mechanical failure. Two others encountered significant problems, but their withdrawal from the operation was due to *pilot discretion* rather than mechanical necessity. Again, one may ask what would have happened if the two pilots had chosen to press on, rather than abandon ship in one case and reverse course in the other. There is no way to know. . . .

The larger policy issue of whether a rescue mission should have been undertaken at all, in view of the inherent risks, is a question that admits no easy answer. The negative consequences were tangible and of great moment. Eight brave men lost their lives. The hostages themselves were dispersed to remote sites, in some cases with considerable discomfort and danger. America's allies, who had been led to believe that their imposition of more stringent sanctions would forestall any unilateral U.S. military action, believed with some justification that their trust had been abused. America's military reputation was dealt a devastating blow. And the President of the United States was politically wounded, perhaps fatally.

Some severe critics of the operation have maintained that it may have been fortunate that the operation failed at the beginning. Even a successful operation, it is argued, would have entailed unacceptably high costs to the United States for three essential reasons: (1) There was a very high risk of an armed confrontation within Tehran itself, which could have resulted in very high loss of life among the rescue team, the hostages themselves, or the Iranian population; (2) The Islamic world might have reacted by sparking a conflagration with the West generally and the United States in particular; and (3) Even if all the hostages had been removed successfully, Iran might have retaliated by imprisoning a new set of American hostages, specifically the many American journalists who were present in the country. These are essentially the arguments that Secretary of State Cyrus Vance advanced in opposition to the mission before it was launched and that subsequently led him to resign when his counsel was rejected by President Carter. For obvious reasons, there was substantial support for this position among journalists, particularly those in Tehran, who were furious to realize not only that they had been taken by surprise by the rescue attempt but that they might have been its victims.

Those who supported the rescue attempt did not share this assessment. They believed that, if the rescue team could be delivered without warning to the embassy, it would succeed in carrying out its task with a minimum of bloodshed. They did not believe that Iran had much support even within the Islamic world for its actions and felt that most Islamic states would be secretly pleased to see the crisis terminated. If the operation could be conducted with little loss of *civilian* lives in Tehran, there seemed to be a reasonable prospect that most Islamic states would stop short of making it a major international incident.

There was indeed a significant risk that other hostages would be taken, possibly including journalists. In the weeks prior to the mission, the administration made it illegal to conduct even the most routine financial transactions with anyone in Iran. Paying a hotel bill in Tehran became a criminal offense under U.S. law. Repeated warnings were issued that individuals traveling to Iran did so at their own risk and that the U.S. government could offer no protection or support. However, journalists, because of first amendment protection of freedom of the press, were exempted from the travel ban (although they were supposed to report their travel to the Treasury Department), and they were accustomed to traveling in areas where there was significant risk. It is uncertain whether the Iranian students would have launched a massive search for other Americans to replace the hostages at the embassy, and it is not clear that the government would have acquiesced in such an effort had it been attempted. The only thing one can say with certainty is that the very nature of the crisis would have been changed if the original hostages had been spirited out of Iran in April 1980.

A SILVER LINING

The views of both the critics of the rescue mission and those who supported it have tended to harden in subsequent years. It is an argument that is not likely to be settled authoritatively, since the operation failed before these hypotheses could be tested. However, even the failure was not without its silver lining. It must be reiterated that the actual policy choice made by President Carter was not between a rescue mission and no action at all. On the contrary, given the relatively weak response of our allies to the U.S. call for sanctions, even after some fairly severe arm-twisting, a decision to impose a partial or total economic blockade by military force would have been virtually impossible to resist in the face of Tehran's persistent flouting of its responsibilities under international law. The rescue attempt, though unsuccessful, lanced the boil, removing the pressures that had been building with deadly inevitability toward a wider military confrontation.

Though unintentional, the failure of the rescue attempt created a quieter policy environment that permitted Washington to de-emphasize the crisis and allowed time for the peculiar rhythms of Iranian internal politics to play themselves out. By the end of August, an Islamic government consistent with Ayatollah Khomeini's theocratic vision had been installed. Very shortly thereafter, the Iranian leadership concluded that the continued retention of the hostages was a net liability, and they took the initiative to seek a solution. The fact that those four critical months passed without resort to violence must be attributed to the tragic experience of the rescue attempt.

THE REAGAN REVOLUTION

ROWLAND EVANS AND ROBERT NOVAK

In 1980, Republican candidate Ronald Reagan defeated incumbent Jimmy Carter to become the fortieth president of the United States. Many commentators and historians, including well-known columnists Rowland Evans and Robert Novak, argued that Reagan's election represented a political revolution on a scale that has never been surpassed. Reagan's agenda included major reforms of foreign and domestic policies, including tax cuts, a reduction in the scope of the federal government, decreased environmental protections, stepped-up military spending, and a posture of confrontation with the Soviet Union. In the following selection, excerpted from their book *The Reagan Revolution*, Evans and Novak explain that Reagan's victory was in large part the result of the public's dissatisfaction with the blunders of his predecessor, including Carter's failure to resolve the Iran hostage crisis and manage the economy. Reagan would be elected to a second term in 1984 and would be replaced by another Republican, George Bush, in 1988. This Republican era would end, however, with the election of Democrat Bill Clinton in 1992.

REAGAN'S MANDATE

After pollsters and politicians had graded the outcome too close to call, it was an electoral landslide on November 4, 1980—489 electoral votes for Reagan to 49 for Carter. The popular vote was less clear: 43,195,000 (50.9 percent) for Reagan; 34,911,000 (41.1 percent) for Carter; 5,581,000 (6.6

From *The Reagan Revolution* by Rowland Evans and Robert Novak. Copyright © 1981 by Rowland Evans Jr. and Robert Novak. Used by permission of Dutton, a division of Penguin Putnam Inc.

percent) for independent candidate John Anderson. Accepting the conventional wisdom that Anderson's votes would have otherwise gone to Carter, it was a squeaker on the order of 1948, 1960, 1968 and 1976, with the winner barely getting half the vote. But many polls indicated less than half of Anderson's vote would have ended up with Carter under any circumstances, indicating a Reagan mandate that, if not the landslides of 1964 and 1972, was close to those of 1952 and 1956.

However, the question of Reagan's mandate depended less on raw numbers than on the motive of the great rush of voters to Reagan the last weekend of the campaign. That they were expressing dissatisfaction with the current state of affairs in the nation and Jimmy Carter's responsibility for it could not be denied. But whether the voters were also consciously accepting Reagan's alternative was less clear.

One distant vote for the latter alternative came from an unlikely source. On December 7, 1980, on a snowy, windswept plain on the outskirts of Gdansk, Lech Walesa, hero of Poland's free labor movement, talked about world politics and quietly turned to the recent American election. "It was intuition, perhaps," he said, "but one year ago I envisioned what would happen. Reagan was the only good candidate in your presidential campaign, and I knew he would win."

But why would this devout Catholic layman, a political liberal and economic socialist who had extracted unprecedented concessions from Poland's Communist regime, be moved to support the likes of Ronald Reagan? Walesa spoke cautiously, aware that he led a movement accused by his government of consorting with Western "imperialists." "Someday the West will wake up," he said, "and you may find it too late, as [Soviet novelist Alexander] Solzhenitsyn has written. Reagan will do it better. He will settle things in a more efficient way. He will make the U.S. strong and make it stand up."

There, from within the restive European empire of the Soviet Union, came the answering echo to Reagan's warning that national weakness would inevitably lead to national humiliation and even defeat at the hands of ruthless adversaries who knew the meaning of power. In his Inaugural Address, Reagan put the capstone on what he had been proclaiming so long, using a word—the noun *will*—not used in such context by any recent president. In addition to military power, Reagan said, "we must realize that no arsenal or no weapon in the arsenals of the world is so formidable as the *will* and moral courage of free men and women" (emphasis added). The word *will* had become the metaphor for the worries and fears of citizens who

saw the systematic decay of America's once impregnable position in the world; it was heard in the think tanks and study
groups of conservatives, moderates and ex-liberals, and it was
voiced quietly by military leaders. It was what Walesa was talking about. First *will*, then a rebirth of power.

On May 10, 1980, the small homes with their neatly tended
lawns in Warren, Michigan, were full of surprises for the in-
quiring political reporter. Although the sample of opinion
would not be completed until sixty-four households had been
visited and the questionnaires prepared by pollster Pat Caddell
had been filled in, a shocking fact was apparent from the start:
Reagan was cutting beyond the 50 percent mark into a vote that
normally went Democratic by a 3-to-1 margin.

The revolution of the sixties and seventies was over; counterculture had withered; the three-piece suit was back, and getting a college education and a good job was in. The talk in the
cluttered living rooms dominated by the constantly playing
television sets was of Soviet troops in Cuba and Afghanistan
and Cubans in Africa. It was about American hostages imprisoned in Tehran in what their countrymen believed was an unprecedented humiliation visited on their country.

On one question after another, the voters of Warren, Michi-
gan, expressed rising contempt for their president, preferring
Reagan over Carter to rebuild U.S. strength, to deal with the
Russians, to handle inflation, taxes and the economy, to restore
America's image.

That image was especially tarnished on February 14, 1979,
fifteen months before the voters of Warren told a reporter of
their contempt for Carter's handling of affronts and insults to
their country. The bleak events on that Valentine's Day started
with the first invasion of the American Embassy in Tehran.

Within hours of the Iranian takeover of the American Embassy on Taleghani Avenue in Tehran, Telex machines in the
State Department's operations center announced the kidnap-
ping of Adolph (Spike) Dubs, the U.S. ambassador in Kabul,
Afghanistan. Dubs stayed alive four hours more. The Soviet-
dominated government of Afghanistan rejected the appeal of
Secretary of State Cyrus Vance and stormed the room in the Hotel Kabul where Dubs had been taken by the terrorists. He was
killed in the "rescue" attempt supervised by Soviet advisers. Almost simultaneously, the marine guards at the embassy in
Tehran were ordered to surrender, a decision dictated both by
the circumstance that faced the one hundred American Embassy officials caught in the seizure and by the presence of
seven thousand other Americans throughout Iran. It proclaimed

President Reagan's considerable charisma and amiable personality were major political assets that contributed to his popularity and successful dealings with world leaders as well as the American public.

the decline of American power from its postwar peak, when the CIA in 1953 had helped oust a leftist demagogue from power in Iran and restored a pro-American government.

It upset voters beginning for the first time to concentrate on the 1980 presidential election and to take the measure of Carter and Reagan. In Warren, Michigan, voters were asked: Which candidate, Carter or Reagan, would be stronger in handling defense? Reagan won, by 4 to 3.

The anti-Carter resentment was widened by more dramatic disasters closer to the election: the second takeover of the Tehran embassy in November 1979, resulting in the hostage crisis; the Soviet invasion of Afghanistan in December; Carter's acquiescence in the existence of a Soviet combat brigade in Cuba, after momentary bluster following its discovery (belated or not) in December 1978; the grudging acknowledgment by Carter that the Russians really had been testing a whole new generation of dreaded long- and intermediate-range nuclear missiles that soon could threaten U.S. and European safety with a knockout blow. The hobgoblins that Ronald Reagan had been conjuring up all those years were suddenly reality, and Reagan was there not just as a polemicist to say "I told you so," but as the presumptive Republican presidential nominee.

Foreign troubles were bad enough for the incumbent president, but they did not pack the political punch of the domestic variety. Not since the Great Depression had American wage-earners been so confused and distracted by economic events neither they nor their government fully understood or could come to grips with. Here, too, Ronald Reagan had been sounding the alarm for sixteen years.

In Warren, Michigan, that day in May, voters picked Reagan by 2 to 1 over Carter on ability "to handle the economy" and by 3 to 1 on tax policy. Among these auto-worker Democrats, Reagan had become digestible in a community where ten years earlier his kind of Republican was as popular as a Hoover soup kitchen. One pro-Reagan Chrysler production-line worker, asked to define what Reagan stood for, showed by his answer how deeply etched was the Reagan imprimatur: "If you don't know what Reagan stands for, you shouldn't be taking this poll." What Reagan stood for in Warren was lowered taxes, lessened government, reduced welfare, higher defense spending. The perception that cut deepest was less definable and more inflammatory: "We just can't go along this way any longer, mister, things gotta change in this country."

The task of making things change in the America of the 1980s was profound, and not just because of Jimmy Carter. Reagan was a chosen instrument of change in policies made by administrations of both parties—for foreign policy dating back a dozen years and for domestic policy all the way back to the beginning of the New Deal a half century ago.

The sixteen years of Republican rule since Franklin Roosevelt (Eisenhower, 1953–1961, and Nixon-Ford, 1969–1977) had never intended to effect revolutionary change and certainly had not done so. General Eisenhower was the establishment's choice over Senator Robert A. Taft as the Republican less likely to roil the waters. While Nixon was no establishment favorite, neither was he interested in radical change; he took the word of his Democratic adviser Daniel Patrick Moynihan that he should reassure the nation and fortify social stability by continuing most of the policies of the preceding Johnson Administration.

The unmistakable decline of U.S. power in the world began in the Nixon Administration. Unable in the latter days of the Vietnam War to sell adequate defense programs to Congress, Nixon retreated to his policy of détente with the Soviet Union, replete with treaties that critics insisted were unequal in favor of the Kremlin. What followed in the Carter Administration was not a new direction but acceleration of the old.

Like Eisenhower, Nixon disdained a massive assault to trim down the federal government. By 1971, he decided to cure the problem of too much government with more government by imposing wage and price controls. Simultaneously, he severed all remaining links between gold and the dollar (for the first time since 1876), ensuring that (contrary to the expectations of his advisers) gold would rise and the dollar would fall. Chronic inflation was at hand.

As government spending and government regulation expanded, Uncle Sam's share of the citizen's dollar rose—the steeply graduated income tax system ensuring ever greater revenues as inflation climbed. Belatedly awakening to the threat of inflation, Carter would not take Nixon's disastrous route of wage-price controls but neither would he come to grips with the soaring federal budget. Fighting all tax rate reduction plans, he proposed annual revenue increases of more than $100 billion in each of his last two years in office, thereby perpetuating the "stagflation" of Nixon and Ford—a stagnant economy amid rising inflation. Indeed, Carter had even less success than Nixon and Ford in slowing the engines of inflation.

Carter's pledge of a balanced budget by the end of his first term became a multibillion-dollar embarrassment: nearly $60 billion of deficit, the third largest in all history, in fiscal 1981 (the year ending September 30, 1981). Voters had lost any fiscal respect they might have had for Carter. While chafing under ever-rising tax rates, they were most visibly angry at the extraordinary speed with which entitlements had grown from almost nothing to multibillions: food stamps, one of those Great Society ideas backed both by farmers (glutted with overproduction) and the poor (wanting federal food subsidies), started modestly at a few millions of dollars. Carter's last budget put the cost to taxpayers at nearly $13 billion. Among the grateful recipients: well-heeled students.

Social Security, the granddad and foundation of social welfare programs—supposedly self-financed by contributions from both wage-earners and employers—had exploded to the point where it was consuming 30 percent of the entire federal budget. Social Security liability was far beyond the wildest dreams of the New Dealers who established the system's tax at 1 percent for both employee and employer on a maximum wage base of $3,000 in 1935. The steady increase in the tax burden to almost seven times that rate, on a maximum wage base of $29,700, contributed to the tax revolt of the seventies.

The growth of entitlements—legal obligations of the federal government to pay cash for one purpose or another directly to citizens—kept narrowing the slice of budget pie that was cuttable. Carter, wiser in January 1981 than he had been four years earlier, spoke in uncharacteristic words when he sent his final budget to Congress January 15, 1981. Noting that entitlements, interest on the national debt and other "mandatory contracts" now consumed 75 percent of the total budget, he appealed for restraint in words reminiscent of the language Reagan had been using for almost two decades: "We can no longer, as individuals or groups, make special pleas for exceptions to budget discipline. Too often we have taken the attitude that there must be alternative sources for reduction in programs that benefit our particular group. That attitude is in part responsible for the rapid budget growth we . . . can no longer afford."

That accurately represented what Reagan had been promoting for so long: the concept that for every problem an answer lay in the Treasury in Washington, D.C., did not work any longer.

The voters on November 4, 1980, declared that they felt the impact of an overpowering weight of big government with growing malice. Reagan was the identified enemy of big government. Coupled with the public perception of him far in front of Carter on the question of neutralizing Soviet pressure around the world, the result of the 1980 election should not have been in doubt.

DEATH OF A BEATLE

ALLAN J. MAYER, SUSAN AGREST, AND JACOB YOUNG

One of the most tragic events of the early 1980s was the assassination of former Beatle John Lennon by a mentally deranged fan named Mark David Chapman. In the following article, journalist Allan J. Mayer writes that Lennon's murder was a shocking event akin to the assassinations of John F. Kennedy, Robert Kennedy, and Martin Luther King Jr. in the 1960s. To many, Lennon symbolized the ideals of the 1960s counterculture, Mayer points out, and his passing marked the end of that era.

Although Chapman's motives were unclear, Mayer explains, it is clear that the twenty-five-year-old shooter planned the attack for weeks and waited outside Lennon's apartment building for three days for an opportunity to strike. He immediately confessed to the shooting and remains in prison for the crime.

C ome together, he had once asked them in a song, and now they came, tens of thousands of them, to share their grief and shock at the news. John Lennon, once the cheeky wit and sardonic soul of the Beatles, whose music had touched a generation and enchanted the world, had been slain on his doorstep by a confused, suicidal young man who had apparently idolized him. Along New York's Central Park West and West 72nd Street, in front of the building where Lennon had lived and died, they stood for hours in tearful vigil, looking to each other and his music for comfort. The scene was repeated in Dallas's Lee Park, at San Francisco's Marina Green, on the Boston Common and in countless other gathering places around the country and the world. Young and old, black and white, they lit candles and softly sang his songs. "All you need is love," they chanted in the rain. "Love is all you need."

From "Death of a Beatle," by Allan J. Mayer, Susan Agrest, and Jacob Young. *Newsweek*, December 22, 1980;

As the unofficial leader of the Beatles, Lennon had exerted a numinous influence on the popular culture of the 1960s and 1970s. But in recent years he had been something of a recluse, a refugee from the maelstrom of pop superstardom who had abandoned the recording studio and public life in an effort to devote himself to raising his son Sean, now 5 (page 45). He emerged from his self-imposed retreat just five months ago, on the eve of his 40th birthday, a man finally at peace with himself, the creative juices once again flowing. He and his wife, Yoko Ono, released their first album in eight years and were putting the finishing touches on a second. He was, as he titled his most popular new song, "Starting Over." "[I'm only] 40," he said cheerfully. "God willing, there are another 40 years of productivity to go." But as he and Yoko returned home from a late-night session at a recording studio early last week, a 25-year-old doppelganger named Mark David Chapman popped out of the darkness and shot Lennon.

Distraught: The killing stunned the nation—and much of the world—as nothing had since the political assassinations of the 1960s. "At first I didn't believe he was really dead," said Chris Backus, one of a thousand mourners who assembled the next day at the ABC entertainment complex in Los Angeles to pay tribute to Lennon. "When I realized it was true, then—bang!—part of my childhood was gone forever." As the news spread, radio stations throughout North America and Europe threw away their play lists and began broadcasting nothing but music by Lennon and the Beatles. Even Radio Moscow devoted 90 minutes to his songs. "The phones started ringing right after the news and they didn't stop all day," reported discjockey Traver Hulse of KATT-FM in Oklahoma City. "It was like losing a President." Distraught fans also descended on record stores, snapping up virtually every Lennon album available. "It was like they had just been robbed of something," said manager Gary Crawford of Strawberries, a downtown Boston record store. "They wanted to replace that something right away."

The question asked over and over again was why—why had Chapman, a moody, unemployed amateur guitar player who lived and worked in the South before moving to Hawaii three years ago, killed a man he was said to have admired for fifteen years? There were no simple answers. Police said Chapman told them of hearing "voices," of having "a good side and a bad side," of being annoyed at the way Lennon scrawled his autograph when Chapman first approached him six hours before the shooting. Friends talked of Chapman's obsessive identification with Lennon—how he used to play Beatles songs constantly on his guitar, how he taped the name "John Lennon" over his own on the ID badge he wore as a maintenance man at a Honolulu condominium, how he emulated Lennon by marrying a Japanese woman several years his senior. And psychologists noted that before taking Lennon's life, Chapman had twice tried to take his own. "He had already tried to kill himself and he was unsuccessful, so he decided to kill Lennon," speculated a forensic psychiatrist in Hawaii. "The homicide was simply a suicide turned backward."

Normal Dude: Chapman had apparently been planning to shoot Lennon for weeks. Late in October he quit his job as a maintenance man and applied to the Honolulu police for a pistol permit. Since he had no criminal record, the permit was granted—and on Oct. 27, he went to J&S Sales, Ltd., in Honolulu and paid $169 for a five-shot Charter Arms .38 special. "Just a normal dude," said J&S manager Tom Grahovac. At about the same time, Chapman called local art dealer Pat Carlson, who had sold him a number of expensive lithographs. He wanted to sell one, he told her, because he needed to raise some money. He also called the employment counselor who had found him the condominium job. "He said to me that he had something really big he was planning to do," she recalled.

A week or so later, Chapman left Honolulu for Atlanta, Ga., where he had grown up and gone to school. He told acquaintances that he was in town to see his father, but he never did. Instead, he dropped in on an old girlfriend and visited his highschool chorus teacher, Madison Short. Though the girlfriend's parents said he seemed depressed, Short recalled him insisting that "he was happy, content with his lot in life." Chapman said nothing about going to New York or seeking out John Lennon. After a few days he returned home to Honolulu, but on Dec. 5 he was off again. His wife, Gloria, had no idea of his plans. "She knew he was going somewhere," Gloria's lawyer, Brook Hart, said, "but she didn't know precisely where."

Boast: He arrived in New York on Saturday, Dec. 6, and checked into a $16.50-a-night room at a YMCA just nine blocks from the Dakota, the elegant, century-old apartment building where Lennon and his family lived. That afternoon, taxi driver Mark Snyder picked up Chapman in his cab. According to Snyder, Chapman boasted that he was Lennon's sound engineer, that he was in the midst of a recording session with him and that he had just learned that Lennon and his long-estranged songwriting partner Paul McCartney were going to make an album together.

The same day, Chapman was seen for the first time loitering near an entrance to the Dakota. No one took much notice; the building is home to a number of celebrities—among them, conductor Leonard Bernstein, actress Lauren Bacall and comedienne

The Beatles wave to thousands of screaming teenagers after their arrival at Kennedy Airport in 1964.

Gilda Radner—and sidewalk gawkers are a common sight. Chapman reappeared outside the Dakota on Sunday as well. He also changed hotels on Sunday, moving from the Y to a more comfortable $82-a-day room at the Sheraton Centre farther downtown.

On Monday evening Chapman's and Lennon's paths finally crossed. Once again Chapman had spent the afternoon on the sidewalk outside the Dakota—this time in the company of Paul Goresh, a Beatles fan and amateur photographer from North Arlington, N.J. Goresh, who was also hoping to catch a glimpse of Lennon, said Chapman struck up a conversation as they waited. "He said he spent the last three days trying to see Lennon and get an autograph," Goresh recalled. At about 5 P.M., Lennon and his wife finally emerged from the building on their way to The Record Plant Studios on West 44th Street. Chapman approached Lennon timidly, holding out a copy of John and Yoko's latest album, "Double Fantasy." Lennon took it and scrawled his signature ("John Lennon 1980") across the cover, while Goresh snapped a picture. Chapman was delighted. "John Lennon signed my album," he exulted to Goresh after the Lennons had left. "Nobody in Hawaii is going to believe me."

The two men remained outside the Dakota for another two hours. When Goresh finally decided to go home, Chapman tried to change his mind. Lennon, he said, "should be home soon and you can get your album signed." Goresh replied that he could get Lennon's autograph another day. "I'd wait," Chapman advised somberly. "You never know if you'll see him again."

The Lennons worked at The Record Plant until 10:30 P.M., mixing the sound for a new single, tentatively titled "Walking on Thin Ice." "We had planned to go out to eat after leaving the recording studio," Yoko said later, "but we decided to go straight home instead." Their rented limousine delivered them to the Dakota's 72nd Street entrance at about 10:50 P.M. The limousine could have driven into the entranceway, but it stopped at the curb. Yoko got out first, with John trailing a few steps behind. As he passed under the ornate archway leading to the Dakota's interior courtyard, he heard a voice call out from behind, "Mr. Lennon." He turned to see Chapman crouched 5 feet away gripping his .38 special with both hands. Before Lennon had a chance to react, Chapman opened fire, pumping four bullets into his back and left shoulder. "I'm shot!" Lennon gasped. Leaving a trail of blood behind him, he staggered six steps into the doorman's office, where he collapsed.

Calm: While Yoko cradled her husband's head in her arms, Chapman dropped his gun, and the doorman kicked it away. "Do you know what you just did?" the doorman asked Chapman dazedly. "I just shot John Lennon," came the calm reply.

Summoned by the doorman, police were on the scene within minutes. Chapman waited for them, thumbing through a copy of J.D. Salinger's classic novel of adolescent rebellion, "The Catcher in the Rye." While two officers frisked and handcuffed him, two others attended to Lennon. "I turned him over," said Patrolman Anthony Palma. "Red is all I saw." Palma turned to a rookie cop, who was on the verge of being sick. "The guy is dying," he said. "Let's get him out of here."

Lennon, semiconscious and bleeding profusely, was placed in the back seat of Officer James Moran's patrol car. "Do you know who you are?" Moran asked him. Lennon couldn't speak. "He moaned and nodded his head as if to say yes," Moran said. While Moran raced Lennon to Roosevelt Hospital fifteen blocks away, Palma followed in his car with Yoko. "Tell me it isn't true, tell me he's all right," she implored him over and over again.

Though doctors pronounced Lennon dead on arrival at Roosevelt, a team of seven surgeons labored desperately to revive him. But his wounds were too severe. There were three holes in his chest, two in his back and two in his left shoulder. "It wasn't possible to resuscitate him by any means," said Dr. Stephen Lynn, the hospital's director of emergency services. "He'd lost 3 to 4 quarts of blood from the gun wounds, about 80 per cent of his blood volume." After working on Lennon for about half an hour, the surgeons gave up, and Lynn went to break the news to Yoko. "Where is my husband?" she asked him frantically. "I want to be with my husband. He would want me to be with him.

Where is he?" Lynn took a deep breath. "We have very bad news," he told her. "Unfortunately, in spite of massive efforts, your husband is dead. There was no suffering at the end." Yoko refused to comprehend the message. "Are you saying he is sleeping?" she sobbed.

Accompanied by David Geffen, whose Geffen Records was producing the Lennons' new album, Yoko returned home around midnight. She made three phone calls, to "the three people that John would have wanted to know"—his 17-year-old son by his first marriage, Julian; his aunt, Mimi Smith, who had raised him, and his onetime collaborator, Paul McCartney.

Shrine: As word of the shooting spread throughout the city, a spontaneous vigil began to form outside the Dakota. By 1 A.M., a crowd of nearly a thousand had gathered. They sang Lennon songs, lit candles and turned the building's gate into an impromptu shrine, covering it with flowers and pictures of John and Yoko. Within minutes, news of Lennon's death had been flashed round the world, sparking a public outpouring not seen since John Kennedy was assassinated in 1963. President Carter spoke of the irony that Lennon "died by violence, though he had long campaigned for peace"; President-elect Reagan pronounced it "a great tragedy."

In London, a portrait of the Beatles draped with a floral tribute was placed at the entrance to the Tate Gallery. "We usually do this when a British artist whose work is represented in the Tate dies," a spokesman said. "But we thought John Lennon was a special case." In Lennon's hometown of Liverpool, the lord mayor announced plans to hold a memorial service for him at the city's giant cathedral, and local teen-agers placed wreaths at the parking lot that was once the site of the Cavern club, where the Beatles had gotten their start. In New York, hundreds of thousands of mourners planned to gather for a Sunday afternoon memorial in Central Park, not far from the Dakota.

Of the three other former Beatles, only Ringo Starr came to New York to be with Yoko. George Harrison canceled a recording session and reportedly went into seclusion. And McCartney, who called his ex-partner "a great man who will be sadly missed," said he would mourn Lennon in private.

Yoko also stayed out of sight. Two days after the shooting, she released a poignant statement describing how she told Sean of his father's death. "Now Daddy is part of God," she reported Sean as saying. "I guess when you die you become much more bigger because you're part of everything." Yoko also announced there would be no funeral; after Lennon's body was cremated privately, she invited mourners to participate—"from wherever you are at the time"—in a ten-minute silent vigil on Sunday afternoon. "John loved and prayed for the human race," she said. "Please pray the same for him."

Chapman, meanwhile, was charged with second-degree murder (since New York has abandoned the death penalty, first-degree murder is no longer used as a charge) and ordered to undergo 30 days of extensive psychiatric testing. He was first sent, under heavy guard, to a cell at the city's famous Bellevue Hospital, where he was placed on a 24-hour "suicide watch." But as fears of a Jack Ruby-style revenge killing grew, officials decided to transfer him to the more remote jail on Riker's Island.

Chapman's second courtappointed attorney, Jonathan Marks, who was assigned the case after the accused murderer's first lawyer quit, said his client probably would plead not guilty by reason of insanity. "Obviously, Mark Chapman's mental state is a critical issue in this case," Marks told reporters. "In order to convict, the [prosecution] must show criminal intent."

Though Lennon appealed to people of all ages, races and classes, it was the baby-boom generation, now in its 20s and 30s, that was hardest hit by his murder. "We grew up together," said Julie Cohen, a 27-year-old teacher who was among the 2,000 mourners who gathered at San Francisco's Marina Green last week to honor him. "I felt there must be some way it could not be true, that it must be a mistake." Secretary Christy Lyou, 32, who showed up along with 2,500 others in Dallas's Lee Park for a similar memorial, said: "It's the last nail in the coffin of the '60s."

However keen the sense of loss, those closest to Lennon rejected the notion that his death marked the passing of an era. "We had planned so much together," Yoko said the day her husband was cremated. "We had talked about living until we were 80. We even drew up lists of all the things we could do for all those years. Then, it was all over. But that doesn't mean the message should be over. The music will live on." And with it, so will John Lennon.

THE EMERGENCE OF
THE AIDS EPIDEMIC

DOUGLAS A. FELDMAN AND JULIA WANG MILLER

In the early 1980s, gay men in Los Angeles and New York City began to die of unusual forms of cancer and pneumonia. These were
the first casualties of a new disease—acquired immune deficiency
syndrome, or AIDS. In the following selection, Douglas A. Feldman and Julia Wang Miller recount the early days of the AIDS
epidemic as doctors struggled to discover how the disease was
transmitted. Feldman and Miller write that over 1,000 Americans
had died of AIDS by mid-1985. By 1995, the number of deaths
would reach 319,849 worldwide.

Feldman is the president of D.A. Feldman & Associates, a
health research organization, and the editor of *Global AIDS Policy*
and *Culture and AIDS*. Miller is a sociologist and co-editor (with
Feldman) of *The AIDS Crisis: A Documentary History*, from which
the following essay was excerpted.

A merican physicians with predominately gay male patients began to notice that something unusual was happening in 1979. Some of their patients were showing up
with a form of cancer called Kaposi's sarcoma (KS), which pro-
duces purplish or brownish blotches on the body. Before then, in
the United States, KS usually was seen only in elderly men, and
was a fairly chronic condition. Now it was occurring in younger
gay and bisexual men, spreading rapidly through their bodies
and often killing them. Other patients were coming down with
a previously rare form of pneumonia called *Pneumocystis carinii*
pneumonia (PCP for short), which is often fatal and is known to

occur only in people with weakened immune systems. Some patients had both KS and PCP.

In June 1981, the first report in the medical literature appeared in the *Morbidity and Mortality Weekly Report (MMWR)*, the main publication for the Centers for Disease Control and Prevention (CDC). It simply stated that five gay men in Los Angeles had developed PCP for no known reason and two of them had died. A month later, *MMWR* reported that ten more cases of PCP had occurred in California and that there were also twenty-six cases of KS in gay men. Seven weeks later, *MMWR* reported an additional seventy persons with KS and/or PCP throughout the United States, mostly in New York City and California. The disease was spreading rapidly. By the end of 1981, 150 adults (mostly, but not entirely, gay men) and nine children in the United States were dead of this new mysterious illness.

At first, it was unclear what was spreading it. Could it be spread through the air? Or a handshake? No one knew for sure. Hospitals were beginning to use extreme precautions to protect health care workers from becoming infected by this mystery disease, including masks and gloves when touching or even standing near a patient. And no one knew quite what to call the new disease. Some called it gay-related immune deficiency (or GRID), others termed it KSOI (for Kaposi's sarcoma and opportunistic infections), and others coined the term "gay plague." By September 1982, the term "acquired immunodeficiency syndrome" (AIDS) had become popular and widely accepted.

PROVOKING FEAR

There was growing concern within the gay communities of large American cities; the first community-based organization to fight AIDS was established in New York City in 1982 and named the Gay Men's Health Crisis (GMHC). Similar organizations were set up soon after in San Francisco, Los Angeles, and Miami. There was considerable fear among gay men at that time about this new disease; one study shows that gay men in New York City were already changing their sexual behavior, reducing by half their number of sex partners.

Subsequent articles in *MMWR* made it increasingly clear that AIDS was affecting not only gay men but also persons with hemophilia, injecting drug users, and Haitian-Americans. Though it was assumed by many people that AIDS was sexually transmitted, the evidence was not certain until July 1982, when the *MMWR* reported a cluster of AIDS cases among gay men who had sex together in Orange County, California. As the additional evidence grew that AIDS could not be transmitted through the

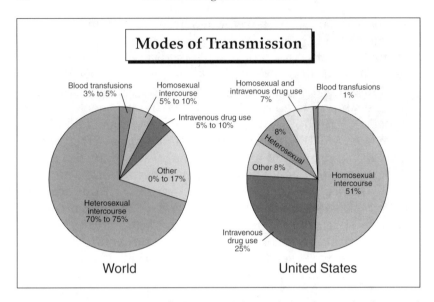

Modes of Transmission

World

United States

air by a sneeze or a cough, like a cold or tuberculosis, the fear and extreme precautions used by health care workers treating persons with AIDS gradually subsided. By the end of 1982, over five hundred men, women, and children had died of AIDS in the United States.

By 1983, the first report in the medical literature indicated that AIDS was found in wealthy Africans seeking medical treatment in Europe. It was quickly learned that AIDS had been spreading rapidly through parts of central Africa. Reports of AIDS were coming in from Zaire, Rwanda, Uganda, and Zambia. Increasingly, AIDS was being seen as an international epidemic.

In 1983, Dr. Luc Montagnier of the Pasteur Institute in France discovered the virus that causes AIDS, which he called LAV. He sent his findings to Dr. Robert Gallo of the National Institutes of Health in Maryland to have him examine them. Although what exactly transpired still remains debatable, Dr. Gallo maintains that he independently discovered the AIDS virus, which he named HTLV-III, in 1984. By 1986, the AIDS virus had been renamed "human immunodeficiency virus," or HIV. In April 1984, a month after Dr. Gallo announced that he "discovered" the AIDS virus, Secretary of Health and Human Services Margaret Heckler held a press conference where she predicted that a cure for AIDS would be found in a few months. Unfortunately, her prediction proved untrue; no cure has been found.

A commercial test to detect antibodies (proteins produced by the body that react specifically with a foreign substance in the body) to HIV first became available in early 1985, and people were encouraged to be tested for HIV. It was then learned that thousands of blood transfusion recipients and persons with he-mophilia had become infected with HIV through infected blood or blood products. Mass screening of all donated blood for HIV began. By the middle of 1985, however, nearly one thousand Americans were dead from AIDS.

AIDS INTO THE 1990S

The definition of what is considered AIDS changed in 1987 and again in 1993, becoming more accurate as we learned more about the opportunistic diseases that affect persons with HIV. The num-ber of reported AIDS cases grew with each change in definition. By the end of 1997, there were an estimated 30.6 million persons with HIV in the world, mostly in Africa, and at least one million persons with HIV in the United States. By December 1995, a to-tal of 513,486 people had been reported to the CDC as AIDS pa-tients, of whom 319,849 (including 3,921 children) had died. Of those adults and teenagers with AIDS, 51 percent were men who had sex with men, 25 percent were men and women who in-jected recreational drugs, 7 percent were men who had sex with men and injected recreational drugs, 4 percent were men and women who had heterosexual sex with an injecting drug user, 4 percent were men and women who had heterosexual sex with someone other than an injecting drug user (or the behavior of their partner was unknown), 1 percent were men and women who received a blood transfusion, 1 percent were men and women with hemophilia, and 7 percent were men and women whose risk was not reported or identified.

By the middle of the 1990s, HIV had become truly pandemic, spreading throughout the globe. In spite of the new treatments available in the developed nations, it was clear that the best hope to slow the spread of the disease was still through educa-tion and behavioral change.

THE BIRTH OF THE PERSONAL COMPUTER

MARTIN CAMPBELL-KELLY AND WILLIAM ASPRAY

In the following article, Martin Campbell-Kelly and William Aspray describe the development of the IBM personal computer (or IBM PC), which hit the market in August 1981, initiating the era of the personal computer for use in homes and offices. The authors explain that the IBM PC was enormously successful, leading many other companies to produce "IBM clones"—computers with many of the same hardware components and software used by IBM. At the same time that IBM was developing its PC, Apple was at work on its "Macintosh" PC, which would reach the market in early 1984. These two computers—the IBM PC (along with its clones) and the Macintosh—would dominate the personal computer market throughout the late twentieth century.

Campbell-Kelly is a reader in computer science at the University of Warwick in the United Kingdom. Aspray is the executive director of the Computing Research Association in Washington, D.C., a nonprofit organization that seeks to strengthen research and advanced education in computer science and related fields. Campbell-Kelly and Aspray are co-authors of *Computer: A History of the Information Machine*.

There has, of course, been no shortage of published accounts of the development of the personal computer. Scores of books and hundreds of articles, written mostly by journalists, have appeared in response to a demand from the general public for an understanding of the personal computer. Much of this reportage is bad history, though some of it is good reading.

From *Computer: A History of the Information Machine*, by Martin Campbell-Kelly and William Aspray. Copyright © 1996 by Martin Campbell-Kelly and William Aspray. Reprinted by permission of Basic Books, a member of Perseus Books, L.L.C.

Perhaps its most serious distortion is to focus on a handful of individuals, portrayed as visionaries who clearly saw the future and made it happen: Apple Computer's Steve Jobs and Microsoft's Bill Gates figure prominently in this genre. By contrast, IBM and the established computer firms are usually portrayed as dinosaurs: slow-moving, dim-witted, deservedly extinct. When it comes to be written, the history of the personal computer will be much more complex than this. It will be seen to be the result of a rich interplay of cultural forces and commercial interests. . . .

IBM ENTERS THE PC BUSINESS

IBM was not, in fact, the giant that slept soundly during the personal-computer revolution. IBM had a sophisticated market research organization that attempted to predict market trends. The company was well aware of microprocessors and personal computers. Indeed, in 1975 it had developed a desktop computer for the scientific market (the model 5100), but it did not sell well. By 1980 IBM was selling a dedicated word processor based on microprocessor technology. But its sales came a poor second to its traditional electric typewriters, of which IBM was still selling a million a year.

Once the personal computer became clearly defined as a business machine in 1980, IBM reacted with surprising speed. The proposal that IBM should enter the personal-computer business came from William C. Lowe, a senior manager who headed the company's "entry-level systems" in Boca Raton, Florida. In July 1980 Lowe made a presentation to IBM's senior management in Armonk, New York, with a radical plan: Not only should IBM enter the personal-computer market but it should also abandon its traditional development processes in order to match the dynamism of the booming personal-computer industry.

For nearly a century IBM had operated a bureaucratic development process by which it typically took three years for a new product to reach the market. Part of the delay was due to IBM's century-old vertical integration practice, by which it maximized profits by manufacturing in-house all the components used in its products: semiconductors, switches, plastic cases, and so on. Lowe argued that IBM should instead adopt the practice of the rest of the industry by outsourcing all the components it did not already have in production, including software. Lowe proposed yet another break with tradition—that IBM should not use its direct sales force to sell the personal computer but should instead use regular retail channels.

Surprisingly, in light of its stuffy image, IBM's top management agreed to all that Lowe recommended, and within two weeks of his presentation he was authorized to go ahead and build a prototype, which had to be ready for the market within twelve months. The development of the personal computer would be known internally as Project Chess.

IBM's relatively late entry into the personal computer market gave it some significant advantages. First, it could make use of the second generation of microprocessors (which processed sixteen bits of data at a time instead of eight); this would make the IBM personal computer significantly faster than any other machine on the market. IBM chose to use the Intel 8088 chip, thereby guaranteeing Intel's future prosperity.

Although IBM was the world's largest software developer, paradoxically it did not have the skills to develop software for personal computers. Its bureaucratic software development procedures were slow and methodical, and geared to large software artifacts; the company lacked the critical skills needed to develop the "quick-and-dirty" software needed for personal computers.

ENTER BILL GATES

IBM initially approached Gary Kildall of Digital Research—the developer of the CP/M operating system—for operating software for the new computer, and herein lies one of the more poignant stories in the history of the personal computer. For reasons now muddied, Kildall blew the opportunity. One version of the story has it that he refused to sign IBM's nondisclosure agreement, while another version has him doing some recreational flying while the dark-suited IBMers cooled their heels below. In any event, the opportunity passed Digital Research by and moved on to Microsoft. Over the next decade, buoyed by the revenues from its operating system for the IBM personal computer, Microsoft became the quintessential business success story of the late twentieth century, and Gates became a billionaire at the age of thirty-one. Hence, for all of Gates's self-confidence and remarkable business acumen, he owes almost everything to being in the right place at the right time.

The IBM entourage arrived at Bill Gates and Paul Allen's Microsoft headquarters in July 1980. It was then a tiny (thirty-two–person) company located in rented offices in downtown Seattle. It is said that Gates and Allen were so keen to win the IBM contract that they actually wore business suits and ties. Although Gates may have appeared a somewhat nerdish twenty-nine-year-old who looked fifteen, he came from an impeccable background, was palpably serious, and showed a positive eagerness to accommodate the IBM culture. For IBM, he represented as low a risk as any of the personal-computer software firms, almost all of which were noted for their studied contempt for Big Blue. It is said that when John Opel, IBM's president, heard about the Microsoft deal, he said, "Is he Mary Gates's son?" He was. Opel and Gates's mother both served on the board of the United Way.

At the time that Microsoft made its agreement with IBM for an operating system, it did not have an actual product, nor did it have the resources to develop one in IBM's time scale. However, Gates obtained a suitable piece of software from a local software firm, Seattle Computer Products, for $30,000 cash. Eventually, the operating system, known as MS-DOS, would be bundled with almost every IBM personal computer and compatible machine, earning Microsoft a royalty of between $10 and $50 on every copy sold.

THE ACORN

By the fall of 1980 the prototype personal computer, known internally as the Acorn, was complete; IBM's top management gave final authorization to go into production. Up to this point the Acorn had been only a development project like any other—now serious money was involved. Lowe, his mission essentially accomplished, moved up into the higher echelons of IBM, leaving his second-in-command, Don Estridge, in overall charge. Estridge was an unassuming forty-two-year-old. Although, as the corporate spokesman for the IBM personal computer, he later became as well-known as any IBMer apart from the company's president, he never attracted as much media attention as the Young Turks such as Gates and Jobs.

The development team under Estridge was now increased to more than a hundred, and factory arrangements were made for IBM to assemble computers using largely outsourced components. Contracts for the bulk supply of subsystems were finalized with Intel for the 8088 microprocessor, with Tandon for floppy disk drives, with Zenith for power supplies, and with the Japanese company Epson for printers. Contracts were also firmed up for software. Besides Microsoft for its operating system and BASIC, arrangements were made to develop a version of the VisiCalc spreadsheet, a word processor, and a suite of business programs. A games program, Adventure, was also included with the machine, suggesting that even at this late date it was not absolutely clear whether the personal computer was a domestic machine, a business machine, or both.

Not everyone in IBM was happy to see the personal computer—whether for home or business—in the company's product line. One insider was reported as saying:

Why on earth would you care about the personal computer? It has nothing at all to do with office automation. It isn't a product for big companies that use "real" computers. Besides, nothing much may come of this and all it can do is cause embarrassment to IBM, because, in my opinion, we don't belong in the personal computer business to begin with.

MARKETING THE NEW MACHINE

Overriding these pockets of resistance inside the company, IBM began to actively consider marketing. The economics of the personal computer determined that it could not be sold by IBM's direct sales force because the profit margins would be too slender. The company negotiated with the Chicago-based Sears Company to sell the machine at its Business Centers and contracted with ComputerLand to retail the machine in its stores. For its traditional business customers, IBM would also sell the machines in its regular sales offices, alongside office products such as electric typewriters and word processors.

Early in 1981, only six months after the inception of Project Chess, IBM appointed the West Coast–based Chiat Day advertising agency to develop an advertising campaign. Market research suggested that the personal computer still lay in the gray area between regular business equipment and a home machine. The advertising campaign was therefore ambiguously aimed at both the business and home user. The machine was astutely named the IBM Personal Computer, suggesting that the IBM machine and the personal computer were synonymous. For the business user, the fact that the machine bore the IBM logo was sufficient to legitimate it inside the corporation. For the home user, however, market research revealed that although the personal computer was perceived as a good thing, it was also seen as intimidating—and IBM itself was seen as "cold and aloof." The Chiat Day campaign attempted to allay these fears by featuring in its advertisements a Charlie Chaplin lookalike and alluding to Chaplin's famous movie *Modern Times*. Set in a futuristic automated factory, *Modern Times* showed the "little man" caught up in a world of hostile technology, confronting it, and eventually overcoming it. The Charlie Chaplin figure reduced the intimidation factor and gave IBM "a human face."

THE BIRTH OF THE IBM PC

During the summer of 1981 the first machines began to come off the IBM assembly plant in Boca Raton, and by early August initial shipments totaling 1,700 machines had been delivered to

In 1981 IBM revolutionized the business world and family life with its invention of the personal computer.

Sears Business Centers and ComputerLand stores ready for the launch. A fully equipped IBM Personal Computer, with 64 Kbytes of memory and a floppy disk, cost $2,880.

The IBM Personal Computer was given its press launch in New York on 12 August. There was intense media interest, which generated many headlines in the computer and business press. In the next few weeks the IBM Personal Computer became a runaway success that exceeded almost everyone's expectations, inside and outside the company. While many business users had hesitated over whether to buy an Apple or a Commodore or a Tandy machine, the presence of the IBM logo convinced them that the technology was for real: IBM had legitimated the personal computer. There was such a demand for the machine that production could not keep pace, and retailers could do no more than placate their customers by placing their names on a waiting list. Within days of the launch, IBM decided to quadruple production.

During 1982–83 the IBM Personal Computer became an industry standard. Most of the popular software packages were converted to run on the machine, and the existence of this software reinforced its popularity. This encouraged other manufacturers to produce "clone" machines, which ran the same software. This was very easy to do because the Intel 8088 microprocessor used by IBM and almost all the other subsystems was readily available on the open market. Among the most successful of the clone manufacturers was Houston-based Compaq, which produced its first machine in 1982. In its first full year of business, it achieved sales of $110 million. Adroitly swimming with the tide, several of the leading manufacturers such as Tandy, Commodore, Victor, and Zenith switched into making IBM-compatible products. Alongside the clone manufacturers, a huge subindustry developed to manufacture peripherals, memory boards, and add-ons. The software industry published thousands of programs for the IBM-compatible personal computer—or the IBM PC, as the machine soon became known. In 1983 it was estimated that there were a dozen monthly magazines and a score of weekly newspapers for users of the machine. Most famously, in January 1983, the editors of *Time* magazine nominated as their Man of the Year not a person but a machine: the PC.

Almost all the companies that resisted the switch to the IBM standard soon went out of existence or were belatedly forced into conforming. The only important exception was Apple Computer, whose founder, Steve Jobs, had seen another way to compete with the IBM standard: not by making cheaper hardware but by making better software.

MARTIAL LAW IN POLAND

NEAL ASCHERSON

During the 1980s, the countries of Eastern Europe underwent a political transformation, as communist regimes gave way to democratic forms of government. Poland was one of the first Eastern European countries to experience a pro-democracy movement. In response to food price increases in August 1980, workers at the Gdansk shipyard went on strike, led by an unemployed electrician named Lech Walesa. The strike spread to other shipyards throughout Poland and evolved from a wage protest to a major confrontation with Poland's communist leadership. It also produced a new trade union—Solidarity—led by Walesa. After intense negotiations, a settlement, known as the Gdansk Agreement, was brokered in August 1980. The agreement promised sweeping reforms of Polish employment and social policies, granting workers the right to set up their own trade unions and to strike, increasing freedom of the press, raising the minimum wage, reforming welfare and pension plans, improving health services, and ending all Saturday and Sunday work for miners, among other changes.

The promises of the Gdansk Agreement failed to materialize, as Neal Ascherson writes in the following essay. Throughout 1981, tensions between Solidarity and the Polish government escalated. Finally, on December 12, 1981, General Wojciech Jaruzelski, the leader of the Communist Party, imposed martial law, seizing Solidarity buildings, arresting the union's leaders, cutting all telephone communications, and imposing curfew. Between fifty and one hundred persons were killed during the eighteen months of martial law. Ascherson contends that while martial law succeeded in limiting the actions of Solidarity in the short term, the union survived as an underground movement.

Although martial law was lifted in July 1983, advocates for democracy made little progress in Poland until the end of the decade, when liberal reforms swept Eastern Europe. Solidarity was re-legalized in 1989 and claimed major victories in that year's political elections.

Ascherson is a journalist and the author of several books, including *The Polish August* and *Struggles for Poland*.

O n 13 December 1981, a young Pole living in a tower block near the centre of Warsaw overslept. 'When I woke up, I tried to ring the office, but the phone was dead. I thought: some sort of power cut. I looked out of the window and saw military trucks standing everywhere in the snow. I thought: some sort of manoeuvres. Then I turned on the radio and there was no news, no chat shows, nothing but Chopin, Chopin and more Chopin. And suddenly I knew what had happened.'

A few hours later, the police came to search the flat. The young Pole's wife managed to eat the latest Solidarity bulletin, and threw the others out of the kitchen window. General Wojciech Jaruzelski, now not only minister of defence but prime minister and first secretary of the party as well, had declared a 'state of war' and imposed martial law.

The brief Solidarity period lasted for just under a year after the 16 December 1980 ceremony of 'national unity' at Gdańsk [an elaborate event to commemorate the violent suppression of protesters in 1970]. That hopeful mood evaporated only a few weeks into the New Year. Mutual mistrust wrecked all efforts to reach a durable compromise between Solidarity and the régime, while in late 1981 the economy had almost completely broken down. By the autumn, both sides had almost abandoned hope of reaching agreement. Solidarity prepared openly for political action. General Wojciech Jaruzelski laid secret plans to solve the crisis by force.

The truce had ended in January 1981, as the government announced that it could not fulfil its promise in the Gdańsk Agreement to end all Saturday work. Strikes broke out in several cities and towns, ending with a compromise at the end of the month which allowed the Poles three free Saturdays out of four. At the same time, a long sit-in strike at Rzeszów in south-east Poland marked the start of a campaign for a 'Rural Solidarity' of private farmers, which won the open support of the Catholic Church.

On 19 March, security police burst into the prefecture at Bydgoszcz and beat up a group of Solidarity members who were negotiating there. Whether this was an act of local stupidity or a deliberate provocation engineered by hard-line party leaders in Warsaw is still not clear. But it led to the most violent upsurge of protest since August 1980. Solidarity took the Bydgoszcz incident as a direct challenge to its existence. A countdown to a general strike began as union members and supporters prepared the factories for siege.

Soviet troops began to move, and there were fresh warnings from the West. General Jaruzelski had become prime minister on 9 February, and had appointed Mieczysław Rakowski, the editor of *Polityka* [a weekly Communist Party publication] who was generally seen as a party 'liberal', as deputy prime minister in charge of negotiation with Solidarity. Pope John Paul II and President Ronald Reagan appealed for restraint and compromise. Then, only a day before the strike was to begin, Rakowski and Lech Wałesa managed to make a shaky deal.

The police action at Bydgoszcz would be investigated. More importantly, Rural Solidarity would be allowed to exist. This was an enormous concession, and a perilous one. The Soviet Union might tolerate independent unions for the working class, but in the Soviet view private peasants were a reactionary and anti-socialist element in society. In the event, Rural Solidarity spread rapidly throughout the countryside. . . . .

'RENEWAL' OF THE GOVERNMENT

Most of June was taken up with party preparations for an emergency congress. This time, the membership made sure that the process of electing delegates and committees was genuinely free and democratic. There was a great slaughter of the old guard. When the congress met in July, seven out of every eight members of the old central committee were thrown out, including seven out of the eleven members of the politburo and forty out of forty-nine district party secretaries.

This looked like a true 'renewal'. But the new central committee and politburo turned out, unexpectedly, to be even more passive and disorganised than the last one. There was an ironic reason for this. The ultra-democratic voting system made it easy to block an opponent but difficult to elect a friend. As a result, most of the best-known party veterans and the most prominent reformers managed to knock each other out of the lists. Those who were elected tended to be nonentities, who proved easy for the surviving party 'apparatchiks' to manipulate.

The new party leadership and the government remained paralysed. Jaruzelski's appointment as head of the government had raised some hopes of a fresh, military vigour at the top. But nothing coherent was done to halt the steady slither of the economy into disaster. As a result, Solidarity finally began to lose patience with its own original idea of a sort of 'dualism' in Poland: the régime governing and applying the Gdańsk reforms, while Solidarity restricted itself to the business of a trade union. If the government refused to act, then—so, increasingly, the argument went—Solidarity had a responsibility to take action and save the nation by its own initiatives.

SOLIDARITY CONGRESS

Solidarity held its own first congress at Gdańsk in September and October. Some 900 delegates from all over Poland assembled in the bleakly modern Olivia sports hall, which became a living theatre of the nation as speeches, pageantry, desperate arguments, ceremonies to welcome veterans of Polish history, messages from foreign guests, recitations of poetry or epic prose, debates and elaborate ballot after ballot filled the days. Outside the Olivia, small crowds listened to the speeches relayed from the hall, or shopped in the flea-market of Solidarity badges and leaflets. Inside, the delegates struggled to agree on a permanent structure for Solidarity, and on a platform over which the nation could be led to safety. . . .

At the congress, Solidarity set out on a new track. It would not wait for the authorities to act, but would act itself. It called for free elections to the Sejm [Polish parliament]. It agreed to make a start on the economic reforms at factory level, without delaying any longer for the government. 'We are the only guarantor for society, and that is why the union considers it to be its basic duty to take all short-term and long-term steps to save Poland from ruin, poverty, despondency and self-destruction.' And the congress, on an impulse, issued an appeal to the workers of the Soviet Union and eastern Europe, calling on them to follow Solidarity's example of free trade unions.

TASS, the Soviet news agency, retorted that this 'villainous appeal' had been drafted by 'a whole conglomerate of counter-revolutionaries, including agents of imperialist secret services'. The régime was terrified. It condemned the appeal to workers in other socialist countries as 'an insane act', and accused the congress of 'breathing hatred' and of 'declaring war on the government of its country'. A week later, the despairing Stanisław Kania was induced to step down and was replaced as party leader by General Jaruzelski.

ON A COLLISION COURSE

Poland was on a collision course. It was probably now that Jaruzelski, with all power in his hands, began the detailed plans to impose martial law. On all sides, there were calls for a new authority in Poland, a powerful and almost dictatorial coalition including Communists, Catholics, Solidarity leaders and the heads of the armed forces in a 'government of national salvation'. Even in Solidarity, there were some who argued that the best solution might be an army takeover. There was a blind faith, based on Polish wishful thinking rather than on Polish experience of history, that the army was a non-political, patriotic force which would put the national interest above all ideologies.

By now, the economy was approaching final breakdown. The factories were stopping for lack of spare parts, raw materials and fuel. The currency was losing all value, and urgent transactions were being done with dollars or by barter. People slept on the pavements to keep their place in the food queues. . . .

By the late autumn of 1981, General Jaruzelski was operating on two levels. In public, he issued a series of calls for a new 'national accord' and a 'unity front' to include Solidarity and representatives of the Church. In secret, he drove ahead with the planning of martial law. Solidarity, admitting that it was beginning to lose control of its followers, responded to his public appeal, and on 4 November Wałesa, Jaruzelski and Archbishop Glemp met in Warsaw for two hours of talks.

For a few days, there was hope that a real 'national accord' was near. But strikes continued to break out, and the régime accused Solidarity of launching a campaign to evict party cells from their offices in factories throughout Poland.

PROVOKING SOLIDARITY

Suddenly the government began a series of sharp actions against Solidarity, apparently aiming to provoke the union into acts or words which would justify the imposition of martial law. Riot police stormed the Fire Brigade Academy in Warsaw, where a strike was in progress, on 25 November. Solidarity retorted by threatening a general strike and by again demanding free elections to the Sejm. At a meeting of the union executive in Radom, Wałesa was reported to have said that confrontation was now inevitable, while others—according to the official media—called for the overthrow of the government and the formation of a workers' militia.

The 'national committee' of Solidarity met at Gdańsk on 11 December. A confused two-day debate began, some calling for a truce with the authorities, others suggesting a referendum to seek a vote of no confidence in the government. It was decided to call a day of national protest on 17 December.

In the last hours of 12 December, Jaruzelski struck. A 'state of war' was proclaimed. All Solidarity buildings were seized, most of the leadership was rounded up at Gdańsk by riot police, and there were mass arrests throughout Poland, as tanks and armoured vehicles poured out into the streets. All telephone and cable links with the outside world were cut, the entire civilian telephone network was disconnected, and a curfew was imposed.

In the morning, Jaruzelski told the nation that he had installed a 'military council of national salvation'. Solidarity 'extremists' had been interned, but so, too, had a group of Poland's pre-1980 leaders, including Edward Gierek. Jaruzelski insisted that he had acted to prevent a 'national catastrophe' and that the course of reform and renewal would go on.

In the short term, the coup was completely successful. Solidarity was taken utterly by surprise, and there was no coherent resistance or general strike. But Poland did not escape bloodshed. In many places, workers defended factories and mines against the ZOMO [mobile units of citizens' militia] riot police. Tanks were used to storm the Lenin shipyard at Gdańsk, and at the Wujek colliery near Katowice seven miners were killed. Miners in several other collieries began underground occupation strikes, which lasted until 28 December. The total death roll, in these first weeks and in conflicts through the next twelve months, was probably between fifty and a hundred. Over 10,000 people were confined in internment camps or prisons, including Lech Wałesa himself.

A Long-Term Failure

Seen in longer terms, however, martial law was a failure. It was another example of a Polish half-measure. It was carried out with a brutality which appalled and alienated the nation, and yet it was not brutal enough to terrorise the Poles into passivity. Within a short time, Solidarity set up a clandestine provisional committee led by Zbigniew Bujak, who had escaped arrest in December 1981 and was able to elude the police for no less than four-and-a-half years.

Jaruzelski's real self-justification, which was difficult to state openly, was that by crushing Solidarity he had prevented a power struggle which would have led to civil war and Soviet intervention. He almost certainly believed this. In the years that followed, he was to be accused of being 'a Russian in Polish uniform'. A stiff, reserved figure behind his black spectacles, Jaruzelski—who had been a forced labourer in the Soviet Union after his family were deported from eastern Poland in 1940—bitterly resented this, and continued to insist that he had acted as a patriot to ensure the survival of his country.

Not much came from his promises to carry on the 'renewal'.

Worst of all, the military government wasted its chance to force through a sweeping reform of the over-centralised economy while the nation still lay under the anaesthetic of martial law. Some prices were increased, and a little progress was made towards introducing the laws of supply and demand into economic management. But when the Poles came round from the anaesthetic, they proved uncooperative. The creative intellectuals and a large part of the technical intelligentsia refused to help; the working class was mutinous; old vested interests in heavy industry revived and were able to slow the reforms down into insignificance.

The West was outraged by martial law and the crushing of Solidarity, and declared a wide range of economic and political sanctions against Poland. Although these were at first welcomed by many Poles as a token that they had not been forgotten, the sanctions made Poland's dire economic condition even worse. For the next few years, a lifeline of food, clothing, and medical supplies brought in by Western voluntary organisations and mostly distributed by the Catholic Church helped to hold in check the worst of the malnourishment and epidemics. But Poland felt degraded and humiliated. The author visited Polish hospitals in this period; sights like critically ill children sleeping in corridors because of gross overcrowding in the wards, or surgeons washing over and over again masks, needles and catheters made for one-time use, or old razor-blades being used to take skin grafts while microtomes stood by unusable for lack of spares—these were the normal conditions of medical care.

Helped by strict rationing and steep price rises, the economy eventually stabilised at a low level. A gradual start was made on rescheduling Poland's enormous foreign debt.

Martial law finally ended in July 1983, . . . although it was replaced by a battery of almost equally severe emergency laws. A general amnesty for political and other prisoners followed, which opened the way for a resumption of political contact with the West. . . .

Martial law and its aftermath did not really destroy the pluralism of Polish society. The Solidarity atmosphere persisted; although the press was tightly censored, people continued to say what they thought without inhibition, and little was done to silence them.

RONALD REAGAN ANNOUNCES "STAR WARS"

RONALD REAGAN

From the 1950s to the 1980s, the United States and the Soviet Union had been engaged in a nuclear arms race based on the concept of deterrence—the belief that neither side would strike first when faced with the reality that the other side would launch a destructive counterattack. In a March 1983 speech, excerpted here, U.S. president Ronald Reagan proposed altering U.S. nuclear policy to include defensive capabilities. Although he provided few specifics, Reagan's speech marked the launch of his Strategic Defense Initiative (SDI), a program to develop a system of computer-controlled, space-based lasers and weapons to detect and destroy incoming nuclear missiles.

This proposal—which came to be known as "Star Wars"—proved to be extremely controversial due in part to its high cost, doubts about its potential effectiveness, and fears that it might be used offensively. Although the system was never completed, $30 billion was spent on the project. In 2001, U.S. President George W. Bush proposed a similar system of missile defenses.

M y predecessors in the Oval Office have appeared before you on other occasions to describe the threat posed by Soviet power and have proposed steps to address that threat. But since the advent of nuclear weapons, those steps have been directed toward deterrence of aggression

Ronald Reagan, speech on defense and national security, March 23, 1983.

through the promise of retaliation—the notion that no rational nation would launch an attack that would inevitably result in unacceptable losses to themselves. This approach to stability through offensive threat has worked. We and our allies have succeeded in preventing nuclear war for three decades. In recent months, however, my advisors, including in particular the Joint Chiefs of Staff, have underscored the bleakness of the future before us.

Over the course of these discussions, I have become more and more deeply convinced that the human spirit must be capable of rising above dealing with other nations and human beings by threatening their existence. Feeling this way, I believe we must thoroughly examine every opportunity for reducing tensions and for introducing greater stability into the strategic calculus on both sides. One of the most important contributions we can make is, of course, to lower the level of all arms, and particularly nuclear arms. We are engaged right now in several negotiations with the Soviet Union to bring about a mutual reduction of weapons. I will report to you a week from tomorrow my thoughts on that score. But let me just say I am totally committed to this course.

If the Soviet Union will join us in our effort to achieve major arms reduction we will have succeeded in stabilizing the nuclear balance. Nevertheless it will still be necessary to rely on the specter of retaliation—on mutual threat, and that is a sad commentary on the human condition.

Would it not be better to save lives than to avenge them? Are we not capable of demonstrating our peaceful intentions by applying all our abilities and our ingenuity to achieving a truly lasting stability? I think we are—indeed, we must!

A Vision of Hope

After careful consultation with my advisors, including the Joint Chiefs of Staff, I believe there is a way. Let me share with you a vision of the future which offers hope. It is that we embark on a program to counter the awesome Soviet missile threat with measures that are defensive. Let us turn to the very strengths in technology that spawned our great industrial base and that have given us the quality of life we enjoy today.

Up until now we have increasingly based our strategy of deterrence upon the threat of retaliation. But what if free people could live secure in the knowledge that their security did not rest upon the threat of instant U.S. retaliation to deter a Soviet attack; that we could intercept and destroy strategic ballistic missiles before they reached our own soil or that of our allies?

I know this is a formidable technical task, one that may not be accomplished before the end of this century. Yet, current technology has attained a level of sophistication where it is reasonable for us to begin this effort. It will take years, probably decades, of effort on many fronts. There will be failures and setbacks just as there will be successes and breakthroughs. And as we proceed we must remain constant in preserving the nuclear deterrent and maintaining a solid capability for flexible response. But is it not worth every investment necessary to free the world from the threat of nuclear war? We know it is!

In the meantime, we will continue to pursue real reductions in nuclear arms, negotiating from a position of strength that can be ensured only by modernizing our strategic forces. At the same time, we must take steps to reduce the risk of a conventional military conflict escalating to nuclear war by improving our non-nuclear capabilities. America does possess—*now*—the technologies to attain very significant improvements in the effectiveness of our conventional, non-nuclear forces. Proceeding boldly with these new technologies, we can significantly reduce any incentive that the Soviet Union may have to threaten attack against the United States or its allies.

As we pursue our goal of defensive technologies, we recognize that our allies rely upon our strategic offensive power to deter attacks against them. Their vital interests and ours are inextricably linked—their safety and ours are one. And no change in technology can or will alter that reality. We must and shall continue to honor our commitments.

I clearly recognize that defensive systems have limitations and raise certain problems and ambiguities. If paired with offensive systems, they can be viewed as fostering an aggressive policy and no one wants that.

RENDERING NUCLEAR WEAPONS OBSOLETE

But with these considerations firmly in mind, I call upon the scientific community who gave us nuclear weapons to turn their great talents to the cause of mankind and world peace; to give us the means of rendering these nuclear weapons impotent and obsolete.

Tonight, consistent with our obligations under the A.B.M. [Antiballistic Missile] Treaty and recognizing the need for close consultation with our allies, I am taking an important first step. I am directing a comprehensive and intensive effort to define a long-term research and development program to begin to achieve our ultimate goal of eliminating the threat posed by strategic nuclear missiles. This could pave the way for arms control measures to eliminate the weapons themselves. We seek neither military superiority nor political advantage. Our only purpose—one all people share—is to search for ways to reduce the danger of nuclear war.

My fellow Americans, tonight we are launching an effort which holds the promise of changing the course of human history. There will be risks, and results take time. But with your support, I believe we can do it.

The Late 1980s: Disaster, Scandal, and Conflict

CHAPTER 2

TRAGEDY IN SPACE: THE *CHALLENGER* EXPLOSION

CLAUDIA GLENN DOWLING

On January 28, 1986, the space shuttle *Challenger* exploded during launch, killing all seven crew members on board. This tragedy, which was shown live on television and replayed repeatedly on news reports, was shocking in part because Americans had become relatively nonchalant about the safety of space travel. In the following selection, published on the tenth anniversary of the explosion, Claudia Glenn Dowling recalls the tragedy and describes its impact on the families of the crew. Dowling is a senior writer at *Life* magazine.

T hree, two, one . . ." Roger. Go with throttle up," shuttle commander Dick Scobee radioed on a freezing January morning in 1986. His daughter Kathie, 25, huddled with her mother, brother and infant son on a roof at Cape Canaveral, along with the assembled families of the six other *Challenger* astronauts about to blast into space. She felt the rumble of liftoff and hugged her baby closer in the cold. "Wow, look how pretty," she said 74 seconds later. "Is that normal?" someone else in the crowd asked. "They're gone," said Jane, wife of pilot Michael Smith. "What do you mean, Mom?" asked her son. "They're lost," she replied. All over the country, the millions watching that awful bloom spread across their television screens realized that something had gone wrong before they heard the voice of Mission Control: "Obviously . . . a major malfunction." Blam.

From "The Mission Continues," by Claudia Dowling, *Life*, February 1996. Reprinted with permission from Time Inc.

The bolt out of the blue shattered the U.S. space program. The 25th shuttle flight was scheduled to kick off the busiest year ever for the National Aeronautics and Space Administration, a year in which Halley's comet would be observed, the Hubble telescope lofted and no fewer than 15 shuttle missions flown. Moreover, space travel for every man was to be popularized by Christa McAuliffe, a gung-ho schoolteacher from Concord, N.H., selected from 11,000 applicants to be the first average American in space. Her motto was "reach for the stars." During four months of training at Johnson Space Center in Houston, Christa kidded that her greatest fear of flying was of waste compartment malfunction. Calling himself a "space husband," lawyer Steve McAuliffe cared for their two children, who seemed to take space exploration for granted. Christa, more aware of the risks, told *Life*'s David Friend, "If anything happened, my husband would have to deal with that as the time came."

On January 28, 1986, as schoolchildren everywhere gazed skyward, what Christa had promised would be "the ultimate field trip" ended in disaster. The families were hustled off the roof, down elevators, into buses. Still bewildered, Kathie clung to baby Justin and eyed the NASA staff. "The looks on their faces told me that something was really, absolutely, terribly wrong," she recalls. The families waited for news in the crew's quarters. Steve McAuliffe, with Scott, nine, and Caroline, six, sat in Christa's dorm room, her sneakers still on the floor. "This is not how it's supposed to be," he said.

THE AFTERMATH

Mission Control turned rapidly to spin control. Rather than delivering the State of the Union address that evening as scheduled, President Ronald Reagan made a brief speech. "We'll continue our quest in space," he promised traumatized Americans, for whom the word shuttle had once sounded so routine. "There will be more shuttle flights and more shuttle crews and, yes, more volunteers, more civilians, more teachers in space." But there would be no shuttle flights for almost three years. There would be no teacher in space. And for those left on the ground, for the families of the seven adventurers who died, there would be years of bitterness, of grief and pain and anger before, finally, lives could heal. On the tenth anniversary of the explosion, the *Challenger* commander's son, Rich Scobee, now an Air Force pilot, will fly his F-16 over the Super Bowl in Tempe, Ariz., leading a formation of jets in a memorial tribute.

In 1986, NASA planes flew the McAuliffes home to New Hampshire, the Scobees and three other families who lived near

Millions of Americans watched in horror as the space shuttle **Challenger** *exploded just seconds after take-off. All seven passengers, including teacher Christa McAuliffe, were killed in the blast.*

Johnson Space Center back to Houston. Each family was assigned an astronaut to help out—to run interference with the reporters camped on their lawns, respond to roomfuls of mail, arrange insurance payments. In the midst of their own mourning, the parents' first concern was for the children. Cheryl, the wife of astronaut Ronald McNair and a technical writer for NASA, explained to her toddlers that "we wouldn't be able to see Daddy anymore, physically, but that we would be able to feel him, spiritually." In addition to their grief, the children had practical worries. Hawaiian-born astronaut Ellison Onizuka's daughters asked: "Are we going to have enough money to eat? Am I like a child from a divorced family? Will we still live in this house?" Recalls mother Lorna, "There were so many things to be done, so many wounds to salve."

In those early months, the Houston women often gathered in the Scobees' living room. "As the commander's wife, I felt such responsibility," recalls June. "I needed help myself, and I was trying to carry the weight of the world." With new information, the wounds reopened. At the outset of a search for shuttle debris that would take seven months, 31 ships, 52 aircraft and 6,000 workers, Christa McAuliffe's lesson plans for space were found floating in the Atlantic Ocean. The crew compartment was found 40 days later. When the bodies were brought up, it became clear that some of the astronauts had been alive during the three-to-four-minute fall to the sea.

THE PRICE OF COMPLACENCY

Shortly after the last funerals were held, a commission chaired by former Secretary of State William Rogers revealed the conclusions of its investigation: The explosion of the $1.2 billion spacecraft was due to a faulty O-ring seal on the solid rocket fuel booster, a $900 synthetic rubber band that engineers had warned was vulnerable at temperatures below 51deg. The *Challenger* launch, canceled three times, had finally taken place in 36deg weather. The Rogers Commission found both the company that made the O-rings, Morton Thiokol, and NASA itself guilty of allowing an avoidable accident to occur. The survivors' first response was anger. "It shouldn't have happened," says Christa's mother, Grace Corrigan. "They were told not to launch, and they decided, 'Twenty-four other shuttle flights went off O.K.' They were complacent."

The government scrambled to settle with the survivors. In December 1986 the families of Christa McAuliffe, Ellison Onizuka, Bruce Jarvis and Dick Scobee accepted some $7.7 million from the U.S. and Morton Thiokol. The unrevealed sums designated for each family were based on the age and number of dependents of the deceased. The families of Ronald McNair and unmarried astronaut Judith Resnick sued Morton Thiokol and settled independently more than a year later, reportedly for multiple millions. The last suit to be resolved was that of Jane Smith, who, on the second anniversary of the *Challenger* accident, filed a $1.5 billion suit against Morton Thiokol. "No one in big business should be allowed to make a faulty product and profit from it," she said. Her suit was settled for an undisclosed sum in 1988, just before the shuttle resumed flying. Like several of the other widows—Cheryl McNair works for a foundation for teenage mothers, and Marcia Jarvis clears hiking trails near her Mammoth Mountain, Calif., home—Jane has a favorite charity, the Virginia Beach Society for the Prevention of Cruelty to Animals. Her dogs, she says, helped her through mourning. Despite her marriage five years ago to a Naval Academy pal of her first husband's and a move to Virginia, she still misses Mike Smith every day: "I waited, and he never came back."

MOVING ON

At the time of the accident, television host Larry King asked June Scobee, "Do you think you will ever remarry?" She responded,

"Dick Scobee loved me enough to last a lifetime." But two and a half years afterward, she felt "alone." Her son, Rich, was in the Air Force, as his father would have wished. Her daughter, Kathie, had her own problems with an unraveling marriage. And suddenly, June found, "I couldn't function." She checked into a hospital, then saw a psychologist. "I knew that I had to let Dick Scobee go," she says. In 1989 she married Lt. Gen. Don Rodgers, whose wife had died, and moved to Tennessee. For her part, after agonizing about a decision contrary to her Christian upbringing, daughter Kathie got a divorce: "Daddy was so young when he died—I just thought, life is too short."

There were delayed reactions in the other families, too. Lorna Onizuka, who hasn't remarried, noticed the changed dynamics without a man in the house: "He was an equilibrium for us. With no El to come in and say, 'Ladies,' it was like a den of she-lions." When she overheard her younger girl "talking" to her father on the telephone, she built a house without so many memories. In the attic is a cedar closet storing her husband's fishing tackle and flight bag. On the household's Buddhist altar, she makes offerings of flowers, favorite foods and, on El's birthday, a can of Coors Light—"He used to enjoy a beer now and then." The older daughter, now out of college, works for NASA like her mother, who deals with the Japanese space agency. "Ten years down the road, there are still moments that my daughters break down and cry," Lorna says. "Moments, usually, of accomplishment. When one wins a soccer tournament, when she's invited to be a debutante and doesn't have a father to escort her, when she graduates and we're missing one person." But the anger has long passed. "I could spend the rest of my life being angry at something I couldn't change," says Lorna. "My husband believed that this mission was worth his life."

The families wanted a living memorial. "We didn't want to dwell on how the crew died, but what they had lived for," says Chuck Resnik, brother of astronaut Judy. June Scobee quit her job as an education professor at the University of Houston to found the Challenger Center, an organization promoting space science for kids. Members of each of the seven astronauts' families sit on the board. Among the initial supporters: Morton Thiokol and Rockwell International, which built the orbiter.

"O.K., astronauts, let's go." A team of fifth-graders at a Challenger Center in Framingham, Mass., one of 30 around the U.S., receives its orders: Launch a probe to Halley's comet. "We don't dwell on the sad part," says teacher Mary Liscombe. "We say, 'The mission continues.'" Grace Corrigan, who lives nearby, often visits the center, which she supports with proceeds of her

1993 book, *A Journal for Christa*. "That's Christa's mom," the kids whisper. Christa's own kids, kept out of the public eye, are big now. Scott is in college, downloading musical riffs from the Internet. Caroline is 16 and a horsewoman. Their father, now a federal judge, took up flying and, in 1993, married a reading teacher. He too supports the centers. The faculty nationwide includes some of the 114 Teacher in Space finalists—not least, Christa's backup, Idaho teacher Barbara Morgan. NASA chief Daniel Goldin has appointed a committee to decide whether to end the Teacher in Space program. But for now, Barbara, 44, still has a flight physical every year. "What happened was horrible, and you can't ever erase that," she says. "But our job as teachers is to help kids reach their potential. *Challenger* reminds us that we should never quit reaching for the stars."

One frequent visitor to the Challenger Center in Houston is Dick Scobee's grandson, the infant in Kathie's arms when she watched that fatal flowering in the sky. "I like the shuttle simulator best," says Justin. "It would be fun in space. You can float because it's zero g. I would like to become an astronaut."

A NUCLEAR NIGHTMARE: THE CHERNOBYL DISASTER

NIGEL HAWKES, GEOFFREY LEAN, DAVID LEIGH, ROBIN MCKIE, PETER PRINGLE, AND ANDREW WILSON

One of the worst disasters of the 1980s took place on April 26, 1986, at the Chernobyl nuclear power plant in Ukraine, which was then part of the Soviet Union. During an experiment, Unit 4, one of the plant's reactors, exploded, causing fires and releasing dangerous amounts of radioactive gas. In the following essay, Nigel Hawkes and his colleagues explain that the accident primarily resulted from a series of mistakes committed by technicians, including shutting off the reactor's safety systems. Thirty-one workers died as a direct result of injuries or radiation poisoning, including many who bravely remained to fight fires that threatened other reactors, thus preventing a much wider tragedy. In the aftermath of the explosion, over 100,000 people were evacuated from the area around the plant due to the health risk posed by radiation, and official estimates of cancer deaths resulting from radiation poisoning ranged from 2,800 to 49,000. Hawkes is a journalist and co-author of *Chernobyl: The End of the Nuclear Dream*, from which the following selection was excerpted.

N ear the meeting of the rivers Uzh and Pripyat, there stands an uninspiring, simple one-storey building. This is Chernobyl weather station, one of a chain that crosses the Ukraine and which provides forecasts for Russian farmers. There, Soviet scientists work in the secluded calm of a remote, relatively unimportant meteorology centre. Eight times a day, the

Excerpted from *Chernobyl: The End of the Nuclear Dream,* by Nigel Hawkes, Geoffrey Lean, David Leigh, Robin McKie, Peter Pringle, and Andrew Wilson (New York: Vintage Books). Copyright © 1986 by The Observer Ltd. Reprinted with permission.

six station workers carry out a ritual of checking wind flow and direction, of analysing soil moisture and of observing cloud movements—standard procedures that are familiar routine for meteorologists throughout the world.

'SOMETHING HAD GONE BADLY WRONG'

But in the early hours of Saturday 26 April, that calm routine was abruptly disrupted. At the time, station chief Zinaida Kordyk was carrying out morning measurements. Carefully, she took down the different readings, as she had done on countless previous occasions, until she stopped at one piece of equipment—the station's Geiger counter. To her horror, the counter was giving a reading that showed there was a sudden and severe increase in radiation levels outside her station.

An experienced meteorologist, Kordyk knew that rapid rise could only mean one thing. 'There was only one explanation—something had gone badly wrong at the Chernobyl atom plant,' she recalls.

Kordyk's assessment was to prove to be horribly accurate. Her discovery also has historical significance. She was the first person outside the stricken atom plant to discover that its deadly outpourings had already begun their journey across Europe. The readings on the weather station's dials were, however, a pale shadow of the dark cloud that was about to cover Europe.

Indeed by late Saturday morning, much of reactor No. 4 and its surrounding buildings were fiercely ablaze. Vast plumes of highly radioactive debris were being hurled high into the atmosphere.

No accident has ever rivalled its severity. But what on earth triggered such a calamity?

Many western newspapers later speculated wildly about explanations and causes. Few of their theories have subsequently survived close scrutiny. Indeed, Soviet authorities took weeks merely to establish the basic sequence of events that occurred that morning.

Details of that sequence were first given by Soviet leader, Mikhail Gorbachev, on 14 May. 'During planned decommissioning of the No. 4 generating set, the power of the reactor suddenly increased,' he stated. 'The considerable discharge of steam and subsequent reaction led to the formation of hydrogen, its explosion, the destruction of the reactor and the radioactive emission connected with it.'

AN APPALLING CATALOGUE OF ERRORS

Such a stark description gave little away. Gorbachev was probably still unaware of the appalling catalogue of operators' errors at the plant. In fact, there had been 'deliberate, systematic and numerous violations of procedure', a long and frank Soviet report informed the International Atomic Energy Authority conference on the accident. This was backed by an even franker speech by the leader of the Soviet delegation, Academician Valery Legasov; and the combined picture they painted was one of devastating complacency and irresponsibility.

At the time, the reactor was due to be shut down for annual maintenance. Its operators decided to use the opportunity to test how long the power station's steam turbines could generate electricity after its steam supply had been shut off. [Academician Valerii A.] Legasov [who presented the findings of a commission investigating the accident] revealed that there 'had been a lot of discussion concerning the justification of the test.' Nevertheless, they had decided to go ahead. The operators wanted to be sure that—in the event of an accidental cut-off of the steam—the turbines could continue to generate power which was needed to keep the reactor's safety systems working. The power station did have emergency diesel generators, but these took time to start up, and in the interval the freewheeling turbines would have to carry the load. Two previous experiments at Chernobyl reactors, in 1982 and 1984, had shown the turbines could not supply the necessary electricity before the diesel generators cut in. So new equipment, designed to solve the problem, was installed and a test was arranged.

But the technicians who drew up the plans did not discuss them with the physicists or other nuclear safety staff at the plant, though they did send experiment plans to the designers of the power station. However, the designers did not get round to looking at them, and never issued any authorisation for the experiment. Yet the tests proceeded.

'DANGEROUS VIOLATIONS'

And from the beginning, the operators seemed hell-bent on self-destruction. Their first serious error was to switch off the emergency core cooling system. This was unnecessary and meant that the reactor would be without one of its most vital safety systems. It was the first of six 'dangerous violations' of the Chernobyl operating rules. It did not cause the accident, but it made its consequences more severe.

The official report also revealed that 'the operators involved were not adequately prepared for the tests, and were not aware of the possible dangers.' This failure was to have grim consequences. When things began to go wrong, operators overrode one fail-safe system after another—any one of which could have prevented the accident occurring.

At 1 A.M. on Friday, 25 April—almost exactly 24 hours before the accident was to occur—operators began the task of gradually reducing the power of reactor No. 4. They were aiming to bring it down from 3,200 MW [megawatts] (thermal) to between 700 and 1,000 MW, the level set for the experiment. By lunchtime, it had reached 1,600 MW, and at 2 P.M. they switched off the emergency cooling system.

But then the operators received an urgent call from the local grid controller at Kiev. He needed the reactor's electricity for several more hours, and told the operators to stop running down the power. They obeyed, but failed to turn the emergency cooling back on again. So the reactor went on running without this crucial safety system—a clear violation of the rules.

At 11.10 P.M. the grid controller said he no longer needed the electricity, and the operators returned to reducing the reactor's power. Then at 28 minutes past midnight, on 26 April, the operators made another simple, fateful error. They forgot to set a regulator properly. 'This is the kind of operator error that we all experience in our plants, and it is difficult to eliminate,' said Dr Pierre Tanguy, chairman of the commission that examined the accident sequence at the conference [of the International Atomic Energy Agency, Vienna, August 1986]. 'But without it, there would have been no accident.' It was the second crucial violation of safety procedures.

ATTEMPTING TO RESTORE POWER

As a result of the incorrect regulator setting, the reactor's power slumped dramatically. Instead of stabilising at 700–1,000 MW, it crashed to 30 MW—far too low for the test. At this point the operators should have simply abandoned the experiment and closed the reactor down. But they decided to try to rescue it. Their motive was straightforward. If the experiment had been abandoned, it could not have been repeated for another year when the reactor would have been next shut down for maintenance. The senior authorities who had ordered the test would have been furious and would have found out the regulator error. So the operators decided, literally, to pull out the stops to try to restore the reactor's power.

But they faced a major problem—a phenomenon called 'xenon poisoning'. Xenon-135, a gas, is one of the fission products produced during reactor operation. It absorbs neutrons, the lifeblood of nuclear fission. During full-power operation, there are enough neutrons to overcome this absorption. But at very low power, xenon build-up is a dominating factor.

This led to the operators' third dangerous violation. They

started pulling out control rods [rods made of boron that absorb neutrons, thus controlling the nuclear reaction]. The plant's operating rules state there should never be less than 30 control rods at one time, though a minimum of 15 is occasionally permitted. In their desperation, however, the operators removed rods until there were only six to eight left in the core.

By 1 A.M. the power had climbed to 200 MW, which was still far too low for the experiment. Yet the operators decided to press ahead with the test —and made their fourth violation. At 1.03 and 1.07 they switched on two extra pumps to join the six that were already circulating cooling water through the core. This was a measure laid down in the test programme. Under normal conditions, it would have added to the safety of the reactor, but at this low power it crucially altered the balance of steam and water in the circuit and made the reactor, in Legasov's words, 'extremely unstable'.

Water and steam levels began changing unpredictably from second to second, and the operators could not control them. And then they made their fifth major mistake. At about 1.20 A.M., in response to steam pressures that were sagging and to the water level that was dropping below the emergency mark, they blocked the automatic shut-down system that would normally have closed down the reactor.

At 1.23 A.M. they started the experiment. Four seconds later they performed the sixth, and final, violation. They switched off the last safety system which would have come into operation automatically when the turbines shut down. Their motives are unclear, but whatever they were, the operators had now closed the last mechanism that might have prevented disaster.

The reactor was now running free, isolated from the outside world, its control rods out, and its safety systems disconnected. As Legasov told the Vienna conference: 'The reactor was free to do as it wished'.

It took the shift manager just 30 seconds to realise something was seriously wrong. He shouted at an operator to press button AZ–5. This should have driven all the control and scram rods into the core. The rods fell, but did not go fully home, probably because the fuel or the rods were already distorted by heat. 'Banging noises' were heard, and the rods were disconnected to allow them to fall into the core by their own weight. But it was too late.

EXPLOSION

In the last second of the reactor's life its power surged from 7 per cent to several hundred times its normal level. A small part of the reactor's core went 'prompt critical'. The effect was the equivalent of half a ton of TNT exploding in the core. In fact, it was very like the detonation of an atomic bomb—something that the nuclear industry had always insisted could never happen in a reactor. (The main difference is that in a bomb the reaction goes much faster, taking only a few billionths of a second.) Disaster struck so fast that the fuel did not have time to melt—it simply shattered into fragments.

Four seconds later a second explosion occurred. The Vienna conference could not agree on its cause, however. Some experts thought it must have been a repetition of the first one. The Soviet scientists disagreed, insisting it was caused by steam. Whatever the causes, the explosions blasted the 1,000-tonne lid clean off the reactor, and brought the giant 200-tonne refuelling crane crashing down on the core, destroying more cooling circuits. Within seconds, the zirconium cladding of the fuel rods began to react with the steam to form hydrogen. This was to cause, as the official Russian report describes it, 'a fireworks display of glowing particles and fragments escaping from the units'. It set off 30 separate fires in the building. The huge blocks of graphite in the reactor core also caught fire.

The entire deadly sequence was summed up with admirable brevity in the Russian report, which said: 'The continuing reduction of water flow through the fuel channels as the power rose led to intensive steam formation and then to nucleate boiling, over-heating of the fuel, destruction of the fuel, a rapid surge of coolant boiling with particles of destroyed fuel entering the coolant, a rapid and abrupt increase of pressure in the fuel channels, destruction of the fuel channels, and finally an explosion which destroyed the reactor and part of the building and released radioactive fission products into the environment.' . . .

By now the entire Chernobyl complex was facing complete destruction. 'Fire had broken out in over 30 places as a result of the explosions in the reactor, which had ejected fragments of its core, heated to high temperatures, onto the roofs above several areas housing the reactor section, the de-aeration stages and the machine hall. Because of damage to some oil pipes, electric cable short circuits and the intense heat radiation from the reactor, focuses of fire formed in the machine hall over turbogenerator number 7, in the reactor hall and in the adjoining, partially destroyed buildings,' the official report stated.

The fate of Chernobyl reactor No. 4 was now sealed. Its double containment was breached and the top of its core had been smashed open. Broken pressure tubes were no longer providing coolant to the top of the core, which continued to overheat, triggering further reactions between the steam that now poured over the reactor's zirconium and its red-hot blocks of graphite. The graphite itself caught fire and began pouring out plumes of highly radioactive fission products—such as lanthanum-140, ruthenium-103, caesium-137, iodine-131, tellurium-132, strontium-89, strontium-90, and yttrium-91—which Soviet scientists later found contaminating the surrounding countryside. The cloud escaped through a gaping hole in the reactor hall roof and into the night. In addition, fire began to spread to reactor No. 3 and threatened to spark an even greater calamity. Only human bravery and self-sacrifice prevented that from happening.

FIGHTING THE FIRES

A minute after the fatal surge had begun to wreak its dreadful damage, the first warnings were sounded. The duty crew of the No. 2 military fire-fighting unit heard a roar. A second later their quarters echoed to the howl of sirens. The crew struggled into their protective gear and raced towards their vehicles. By the time they reached the plant, the blaze had already taken a grip. 'In the reactor hall, flames were raging on various floors, at five points at least, including the roof and the adjoining turbine hall,' recalled Leonid Telyatnikov, the Chernobyl fire chief, from his hospital bed in Moscow.

As soon as Telyatnikov had arrived at the burning reactor building, racing from his home 6 km away, he saw that the 28 firefighters already there were losing against the fire. The flames were threatening to spread through the cable channels to other parts of the reactor complex, including nearby reactor No. 3.

Telyatnikov split his men into groups and several times led one group by climbing to the highest part of the station roof where the turbine section towers 69 metres above the ground. This section was the most seriously ablaze.

Here the Soviet firemen showed the extraordinary heroism that was to become the hallmark of their battle to contain the Chernobyl reactor fire. All knew radiation must be leaking from the damaged reactor core for dosimetric emergency teams had already warned of the danger. None flinched from his task. 'The fire had to be fought whatever happened,' said Telyatnikov. At this point, he and his men were struggling to combat a blaze in desperate conditions. Fumes and smoke were pouring from the blazing hall below while the bitumen on the turbine hall roof melted rapidly in the intense heat. Soon the men found their boots were becoming heavier by the minute. Their feet were caught in the molten mass and turned 'leaden' as the resin stuck.

Under these conditions, the firemen fought the blaze for three hours, until they halted the spread of the flames and prevented fire damaging Chernobyl's three other operational reactors. The actions of these men undoubtedly saved a far greater disaster from occurring, as the other technicians struggled to shut down the whole power station, and put the three adjoining reactors on emergency stand-by cooling. They could not be abandoned, however fierce were the waves of radioactivity and fire that surrounded them. Those on duty that night would later pay dearly for their heroism.

Telyatnikov had already summoned support from Kiev Region fire headquarters, which ordered all units to the reactor. Among the fire leaders who first arrived was Lieutenant Ivan Saureye. It was immediately clear to Saureye that many of the firemen on the roof were by this time in a very bad state, having fought the fire in smoke and intense radiation for several hours. Saureye and his men brought the fire team down to the ground on ladders and had them taken away in ambulances before taking their places on the roof. For twenty minutes they continued to spray the roof of No. 3 reactor hall with water to prevent it from igniting from the heat of the blaze in No. 4, before being forced to come down themselves.

Saureye and Telyatnikov were later taken to the same hospital ward. A Soviet journalist interviewing the two men was told by the hospital staff: 'We do not abandon hope that they will recover,' although by that time six of their colleagues were already dead from the effects of the radiation that poured over them that night.

VICTIMS OF RECKLESSNESS

The first victim of Chernobyl was Valeriy Hodiemchuk. Described simply as a power station operator, Hodiemchuk was pinned beneath collapsing masonry at his work station as the explosion went off. Nearby his fellow worker and friend, Vladimir Sashionok, who was described as the auto-system setter, was also caught in the blast. Staggering from the wrecked block with 80 per cent burns, Sashionok fell into the arms of horrified workmates and gasped only two words, 'Valeriy. Inside', before losing consciousness. Sashionok died in the ambulance. He never had a funeral. The ambulance crew, fearing radioactive contamination, buried him on the spot, in the cemetery of the first village that they came to.

Such small tragedies put the devastating events at Chernobyl in a particularly chilling perspective. But how could the accident have been allowed to happen in the first place? Scientists now know what caused it. Why could they not have foreseen disaster?

The answer is, as Legasov put it in Vienna, that the extraordinary series of deliberate operator violations was, quite simply, 'impossible to foresee'. He described their behaviour as the 'pilot of a plane deciding to test it while flying very high, by opening the doors and switching off the safety systems'. And he added with some justice: 'I do not think any designer of the plane could foresee that'.

Human error—or, rather, astonishing human recklessness—was therefore the overwhelming cause of the Chernobyl disaster.

SCANDAL IN THE WHITE HOUSE: THE IRAN/CONTRA AFFAIR

LAWRENCE E. WALSH

In October and November of 1986, two illegal covert operations conducted by the Reagan administration came to light. Between 1984 and 1986, the government had sold military arms to Iran in an attempt to win Iran's assistance in obtaining the release of American hostages in Lebanon. At the same time, the administration had illegally aided the rightist Contra rebels fighting the left-wing regime in Nicaragua. These two operations, both of which violated U.S. policies, were linked by the fact that profits from the Iranian arms sales were diverted to the Contras. After these activities were exposed, lengthy congressional and legal investigations implicated numerous high-level Reagan administration officials in the crimes and attempts to cover them up.

The following selection is excerpted from the final report of the independent counsel appointed to the case. The report's author, Lawrence E. Walsh, concludes that while there is no evidence that Reagan himself committed any crimes, the president was aware of the arms sale to Iran and endorsed the continued support of the Contras despite a congressional ban on such aid. Walsh was the independent counsel in the Iran/Contra investigation from 1986 to 1993. He has also served as a prosecutor, a federal district judge, and a deputy attorney general of the United States.

Excerpted from the Executive Summary of the *Final Report of the Independent Counsel for Iran/Contra Matters,* by Lawrence E. Walsh, Washington, D.C., 1993.

I n October and November 1986, two secret U.S. Government operations were publicly exposed, potentially implicating Reagan Administration officials in illegal activities. These operations were the provision of assistance to the military activities of the Nicaraguan contra rebels during an October 1984 to October 1986 prohibition on such aid, and the sale of U.S. arms to Iran in contravention of stated U.S. policy and in possible violation of arms-export controls. In late November 1986, Reagan Administration officials announced that some of the proceeds from the sale of U.S. arms to Iran had been diverted to the contras.

As a result of the exposure of these operations, Attorney General Edwin Meese III sought the appointment of an independent counsel to investigate and, if necessary, prosecute possible crimes arising from them.

The Special Division of the United States Court of Appeals for the District of Columbia Circuit appointed Lawrence E. Walsh as Independent Counsel on December 19, 1986, and charged him with investigating:

(1) the direct or indirect sale, shipment, or transfer since in or about 1984 down to the present, of military arms, materiel, or funds to the government of Iran, officials of that government, persons, organizations or entities connected with or purporting to represent that government, or persons located in Iran;

(2) the direct or indirect sale, shipment, or transfer of military arms, materiel or funds to any government, entity, or person acting, or purporting to act as an intermediary in any transaction referred to above;

(3) the financing or funding of any direct or indirect sale, shipment or transfer referred to above;

(4) the diversion of proceeds from any transaction described above to or for any person, organization, foreign government, or any faction or body of insurgents in any foreign country, including, but not limited to Nicaragua;

(5) the provision or coordination of support for persons or entities engaged as military insurgents in armed conflict with the government of Nicaragua since 1984.

This is the final report of that investigation.

OVERALL CONCLUSIONS

The investigations and prosecutions have shown that high-ranking Administration officials violated laws and executive orders in the Iran/contra matter. Independent Counsel concluded that:

—the sales of arms to Iran contravened United States Government policy and may have violated the Arms Export Control Act;

—the provision and coordination of support to the contras violated the Boland Amendment ban on aid to military activities in Nicaragua;

—the policies behind both the Iran and contra operations were fully reviewed and developed at the highest levels of the Reagan Administration;

—although there was little evidence of National Security Council level knowledge of most of the actual contra-support operations, there was no evidence that any NSC member dissented from the underlying policy—keeping the contras alive despite congressional limitations on contra support;

—the Iran operations were carried out with the knowledge of, among others, President Ronald Reagan, Vice President George Bush, Secretary of State George P. Shultz, Secretary of Defense Caspar W. Weinberger, Director of Central Intelligence William J. Casey, and national security advisers Robert C. McFarlane and John M. Poindexter; of these officials, only Weinberger and Shultz dissented from the policy decision, and Weinberger eventually acquiesced by ordering the Department of Defense to provide the necessary arms; and

—large volumes of highly relevant, contemporaneously created documents were systematically and willfully withheld from investigators by several Reagan Administration officials.

—following the revelation of these operations in October and November 1986, Reagan Administration officials deliberately deceived the Congress and the public about the level and extent of official knowledge of and support for these operations.

In addition, Independent Counsel concluded that the off-the-books nature of the Iran and contra operations gave line-level personnel the opportunity to commit money crimes.

PROSECUTIONS

In the course of Independent Counsel's investigation, 14 persons were charged with criminal violations. There were two broad classes of crimes charged: Operational crimes, which largely concerned the illegal use of funds generated in the course of the operations, and "cover-up" crimes, which largely concerned false statements and obstructions after the revelation of the operations. Independent Counsel did not charge violations of the Arms Export Control Act or Boland Amendment. Although apparent violations of these statutes provided the impetus for the cover-up, they are not criminal statutes and do not contain any enforcement provisions.

All of the individuals charged were convicted, except for one CIA official whose case was dismissed on national security grounds and two officials who received unprecedented pre-trial pardons by President Bush following his electoral defeat in 1992. Two of the convictions were reversed on appeal on constitutional grounds that in no way cast doubt on the factual guilt of the men convicted. The individuals charged and the disposition of their cases are:

(1) Robert C. McFarlane: pleaded guilty to four counts of withholding information from Congress;

(2) Oliver L. North: convicted of altering and destroying documents, accepting an illegal gratuity, and aiding and abetting in the obstruction of Congress; conviction reversed on appeal;

(3) John M. Poindexter: convicted of conspiracy, false statements, destruction and removal of records, and obstruction of Congress; conviction reversed on appeal;

(4) Richard V. Secord: pleaded guilty to making false statements to Congress;

(5) Albert Hakim: pleaded guilty to supplementing the salary of North;

(6) Thomas G. Clines: convicted of four counts of tax-related offenses for failing to report income from the operations;

(7) Carl R. Channell: pleaded guilty to conspiracy to defraud the United States;

(8) Richard R. Miller: pleaded guilty to conspiracy to defraud the United States;

(9) Clair E. George: convicted of false statements and perjury before Congress;

(10) Duane R. Clarridge: indicted on seven counts of perjury and false statements; pardoned before trial by President Bush;

(11) Alan D. Fiers, Jr.: pleaded guilty to withholding information from Congress;

(12) Joseph F. Fernandez: indicted on four counts of obstruction and false statements; case dismissed when Attorney General Richard L. Thornburgh refused to declassify information needed for his defense;

(13) Elliott Abrams: pleaded guilty to withholding information from Congress;

(14) Caspar W. Weinberger: charged with four counts of false statements and perjury; pardoned before trial by President Bush.

At the time President Bush pardoned Weinberger and Clarridge, he also pardoned George, Fiers, Abrams, and McFarlane.

THE BASIC FACTS OF IRAN/CONTRA

The Iran/contra affair concerned two secret Reagan Administration policies whose operations were coordinated by National Security Council staff. The Iran operation involved efforts in 1985 and 1986 to obtain the release of Americans held hostage in the Middle East through the sale of U.S. weapons to Iran, despite an embargo on such sales. The contra operations from 1984 through most of 1986 involved the secret governmental support of contra military and paramilitary activities in Nicaragua, despite congressional prohibition of this support.

The Iran and contra operations were merged when funds generated from the sale of weapons to Iran were diverted to support the contra effort in Nicaragua. Although this "diversion" may be the most dramatic aspect of Iran/contra, it is important to emphasize that both the Iran and contra operations, separately, violated United States policy and law. The ignorance of the "diversion" asserted by President Reagan and his Cabinet officers on the National Security Council in no way absolves them of responsibility for the underlying Iran and contra operations.

The secrecy concerning the Iran and contra activities was finally pierced by events that took place thousands of miles apart in the fall of 1986. The first occurred on October 5, 1986, when Nicaraguan government soldiers shot down an American cargo plane that was carrying military supplies to contra forces; the one surviving crew member, American Eugene Hasenfus, was taken into captivity and stated that he was employed by the CIA. A month after the Hasenfus shootdown, President Reagan's secret sale of U.S. arms to Iran was reported by a Lebanese publication on November 3. The joining of these two operations was made public on November 25, 1986, when Attorney General Meese announced that Justice Department officials had discovered that some of the proceeds from the Iran arms sales had been diverted to the contras.

When these operations ended, the exposure of the Iran/contra affair generated a new round of illegality. Beginning with the testimony of Elliott Abrams and others in October 1986 and continuing through the public testimony of Caspar W. Weinberger on the last day of the congressional hearings in the summer of 1987, senior Reagan Administration officials engaged in a concerted effort to deceive Congress and the public about their knowledge of and support for the operations.

Independent Counsel has concluded that the President's most senior advisers and the Cabinet members on the National Security Council participated in the strategy to make National Security staff members McFarlane, Poindexter and North the scapegoats whose sacrifice would protect the Reagan Administration in its final two years. In an important sense, this strategy succeeded. Independent Counsel discovered much of the best evidence of the cover-up in the final year of active investigation, too late for most prosecutions. . . .

THE OPERATIONAL CONSPIRACY

The operational conspiracy was the basis for Count One of the 23-count indictment returned by the Grand Jury March 16, 1988, against Poindexter, North, Secord, and Hakim. It charged the four with conspiracy to defraud the United States by deceitfully:

(1) supporting military operations in Nicaragua in defiance of congressional controls;

(2) using the Iran arms sales to raise funds to be spent at the direction of North, rather than the U.S. Government; and

(3) endangering the Administration's hostage-release effort by overcharging Iran for the arms to generate unauthorized profits to fund the contras and for other purposes.

The charge was upheld as a matter of law by U.S. District Judge Gerhard A. Gesell even though the Justice Department, in a move that Judge Gesell called "unprecedented," filed an amicus brief supporting North's contention that the charge should be dismissed. Although Count One was ultimately dismissed because the Reagan Administration refused to declassify information necessary to North's defense, Judge Gesell's decision established that high Government officials who engage in conspiracy to subvert civil laws and the Constitution have engaged in criminal acts. Trial on Count One would have disclosed the Government-wide activities that supported North's Iran and contra operations.

Within the NSC, McFarlane pleaded guilty in March 1988 to four counts of withholding information from Congress in connection with his denials that North was providing the contras with military advice and assistance. McFarlane, in his plea agreement, promised to cooperate with Independent Counsel by providing truthful testimony in subsequent trials.

Judge Gesell ordered severance of the trials of the four charged in the conspiracy indictment because of the immunized testimony given by Poindexter, North and Hakim to Congress. North was tried and convicted by a jury in May 1989 of altering and destroying documents, accepting an illegal gratuity and aiding and abetting in the obstruction of Congress. His conviction was reversed on appeal in July 1990 and charges against North were subsequently dismissed in September 1991 on the ground that trial witnesses were tainted by North's nationally televised, immunized testimony before Congress. Poindexter in April 1990 was convicted by a jury on five felony counts of conspiracy, false statements, destruction and removal of records and obstruction of Congress. The Court of Appeals reversed his conviction in November 1991 on the immunized testimony issue. . . .

THE FLOW OF FUNDS

The off-the-books conduct of the two highly secret operations circumvented normal Administration accountability and congressional oversight associated with covert ventures and presented fertile ground for financial wrongdoing. There were several funding sources for the contras' weapons purchases from the covert-action Enterprise formed by North, Secord and Hakim:

(1) donations from foreign countries,

(2) contributions from wealthy Americans sympathetic to President Reagan's contra support policies; and

(3) the diversion of proceeds from the sale of arms to Iran.

Ultimately, all of these funds fell under the control of North, and through him, Secord and Hakim.

North used political fundraisers Carl R. Channell and Richard R. Miller to raise millions of dollars from wealthy Americans, illegally using a tax-exempt organization to do so. These funds, along with the private contributions, were run through a network of corporations and Swiss bank accounts put at North's disposal by Secord and Hakim, through which transactions were concealed and laundered. In late 1985 through 1986 the Enterprise became centrally involved in the arms sales to Iran. As a result of both the Iran and contra operations, more than $47 million flowed through Enterprise accounts.

Professional fundraisers Channell and Miller pleaded guilty in the spring of 1987 to conspiracy to defraud the Government by illegal use of a tax-exempt foundation to raise contributions for the purchase of lethal supplies for the contras. They named North as an unindicted co-conspirator.

Secord pleaded guilty in November 1989 to a felony, admitting that he falsely denied to Congress that North had personally benefited from the Enterprise. Hakim pleaded guilty to the misdemeanor count of supplementing the salary of North. Lake Resources Inc., the company controlled by Hakim to launder the Enterprise's money flow, pleaded guilty to the corporate felony of theft of Government property in diverting the proceeds from the arms sales to the contras and for other unauthorized purposes. Thomas G. Clines was convicted in September 1990 of four tax-related felonies for failing to report all of his income from the Enterprise.

AGENCY SUPPORT OF THE OPERATIONS

Following the convictions of those who were most central to the Iran/contra operations, Independent Counsel's investigation focused on the supporting roles played by Government officials in other agencies and the supervisory roles of the NSC principals. The investigation showed that Administration officials who claimed initially that they had little knowledge about the Iran arms sales or the illegal contra-resupply operation North directed were much better informed than they professed to be. The Office of Independent Counsel obtained evidence that Secretaries Weinberger and Shultz and White House Chief of Staff Donald T. Regan, among others, held back information that would have helped Congress obtain a much clearer view of the scope of the Iran/contra matter. Contemporaneous notes of Regan and Weinberger, and those dictated by Shultz, were withheld until they were obtained by Independent Counsel in 1991 and 1992.

THE WHITE HOUSE AND OFFICE OF THE VICE PRESIDENT

The investigation found no credible evidence that President Reagan violated any criminal statute. The OIC could not prove that Reagan authorized or was aware of the diversion or that he had knowledge of the extent of North's control of the contra-resupply network. Nevertheless, he set the stage for the illegal activities of others by encouraging and, in general terms, ordering support of the contras during the October 1984 to October 1986 period when funds for the contras were cut off by the Boland Amendment, and in authorizing the sale of arms to Iran, in contravention of the U.S. embargo on such sales. The President's disregard for civil laws enacted to limit presidential actions abroad—specifically the Boland Amendment, the Arms Export Control Act and congressional-notification requirements in covert-action laws—created a climate in which some of the Government officers assigned to implement his policies felt emboldened to circumvent such laws.

President Reagan's directive to McFarlane to keep the contras alive "body and soul" during the Boland cut-off period was viewed by North, who was charged by McFarlane to carry out the directive, as an invitation to break the law. Similarly, President Reagan's decision in 1985 to authorize the sale of arms to Iran from Israeli stocks, despite warnings by Weinberger and Shultz that such transfers might violate the law, opened the way for Poindexter's subsequent decision to authorize the diversion. Poindexter told Congress that while he made the decision on his own and did not tell the President, he believed the President would have approved. North testified that he believed the President authorized it.

Independent Counsel's investigation did not develop evidence that proved that Vice President Bush violated any criminal statute. Contrary to his public pronouncements, however, he was fully aware of the Iran arms sales. Bush was regularly briefed, along with the President, on the Iran arms sales, and he participated in discussions to obtain third-country support for the contras. The OIC obtained no evidence that Bush was aware of the diversion. The OIC learned in December 1992 that Bush had failed to produce a diary containing contemporaneous notes relevant to Iran/contra, despite requests made in 1987 and again in early 1992 for the production of such material. Bush refused to be interviewed for a final time in light of evidence developed in the latter stages of OIC's investigation, leaving unresolved a clear picture of his Iran/contra involvement. Bush's pardon of Weinberger on December 24, 1992 preempted a trial in which defense counsel indicated that they intended to call Bush as a witness.

A STEP TOWARD NUCLEAR DISARMAMENT: SIGNING THE INF TREATY

MIKHAIL GORBACHEV

Mikhail Gorbachev became the leader of the Soviet Union in March 1985. He immediately instituted wide-ranging liberal social, political, and economic reforms known as glasnost (openness) and perestroika (restructuring). He also expressed an unprecedented resolve to cooperate with the United States in reducing the threat of nuclear weapons. At a summit in Washington, D.C., in December 1987, Gorbachev and U.S. president Ronald Reagan signed a treaty banning intermediate-range nuclear forces (INF). This agreement required the destruction of all nuclear missiles with a range of approximately 300 to 3,400 miles, including many U.S. missiles on European soil. It was subsequently ratified by both countries in 1988.

The following selection is the text of a speech delivered by Gorbachev upon signing the INF treaty at the summit in Washington, D.C., on December 8, 1987. The Soviet leader describes the treaty as a first step toward the ultimate goal of nuclear disarmament.

Mikhail Gorbachev, address to the Soviet and American Peoples, December 8, 1997.

I am addressing my fellow countrymen, the citizens of the Soviet Union, and I am addressing the American people. President Reagan and I have just signed a Treaty which for the first time in history envisages the most strictly verified destruction of two entire classes of nuclear arms.

The Treaty on the total elimination of Soviet and U.S. intermediate- and shorter-range missiles will, I am sure, become a historic milestone in the chronicle of man's eternal quest for a world without wars.

On this occasion, I would like to refer for a moment to history.

Not all Americans may know that at the height of a world war, the very first step taken by the Soviet Republic born in Russia in 1917 was to promulgate a Decree on Peace.

Its author, Vladimir Lenin, the founder of our state, said: We are willing to consider any proposals leading to peace on a just and solid basis.

This has been the cornerstone of Soviet foreign policy ever since.

We also remember another concept of his: disarmament, a world without arms. A world without violence is our ideal.

Today, regrettably, the risk of a nuclear catastrophe persists. It is still formidable. But we believe in mankind's ability to get rid of the threat of self-annihilation.

We are encouraged by the growing awareness in the world of the nature of the existing peril which has confronted mankind with the question of its very survival.

The sacred human right to live has now taken on a new, global dimension. And this is what must always be in the minds of, above all, political and state leaders invested with power by the will of their peoples.

The people is no abstract notion. It is made up of individuals and each one of them has the right to life and pursuit of happiness.

A FIRST STEP

The Treaty just signed in Washington is a major watershed in international development. Its significance and implications go far beyond what has actually been agreed upon.

Our road towards this watershed was a difficult one. It involved lengthy and heated arguments and debate, the overcoming of accumulated emotions and ingrained stereotypes.

What has been accomplished is only a beginning. It is only the start to nuclear disarmament, although, as we know, even the longest journey begins with a first step.

Moving ahead will require further intensive intellectual endeavor and honest effort, the abandonment of some concepts of security which seem indisputable today, and of all that fuels the arms race.

In November 1985, President Reagan and I declared in Geneva that nuclear war could never be won and should never be fought. We also declared that neither the Soviet Union nor the United States sought nuclear superiority.

This enabled us to take the first step up the platform of a common search.

Geneva was followed by Reykjavik [in October 1986], where a fundamental breakthrough was made in our perception of the process of nuclear disarmament. That is what made possible this Treaty and a substantive discussion of other issues pertaining to the nuclear confrontation.

We give credit to our American partners. Together, we have been gaining experience that will help seek solutions to even more challenging problems of equal and universal security.

Most important of all is to translate into reality as soon as possible agreements on radical cuts in strategic offensive arms while preserving the ABM [Antiballistic Missile] Treaty, the elimination of chemical weapons and reductions in conventional armaments.

The Soviet Union has put forward specific proposals on each of these problems. We believe that agreements on them are within reach.

We are hopeful that during next year's return visit of the U.S. President to the Soviet Union, we will achieve a treaty on the elimination of practically one-half of all existing strategic nuclear weapons.

There is also a possibility of reaching an agreement on substantial cuts in conventional troops and arms in Europe, whose build-up and upgrading causes justified concern.

Once all this is accomplished, we shall be able to say, with confidence, that progress towards a secure world has become irreversible.

The elimination of weapons of mass destruction, disarmament for development—that is the principal, and, in fact, the sole effective way to resolve other problems that mankind is having to face, as the 20th century draws to a close. Among those are environmental problems, the problems connected with the implications of the new technological revolution, energy, mass poverty, hunger and diseases, huge foreign debts and failure to balance the diverse interests and needs of scores of peoples and countries.

To cope with these problems, there will have to be, above all, fresh approaches to matters of national and universal security.

I know that with the signing of the Treaty on intermediate- and shorter-range missiles, some politicians and journalists are already speculating as to "who won." I reject this approach. It is a throwback to old thinking.

Common sense has won. True enough, it is not yet the greatest victory, but politically and psychologically it is very important. It meets the aspirations and interests of hundreds of millions of people throughout the world.

People want to live in a world in which they would not be haunted by the fear of nuclear catastrophe.

People want to live in a world in which American and Soviet spacecraft would come together for docking and joint voyages, not for "Star Wars."

People want to live in a world in which they would not have to spend millions of dollars a day on weapons that they could only use against themselves.

People want to live in a world in which everyone would enjoy the right to life, freedom and happiness, and, of course, other human rights which must be really guaranteed for any developed society to exist normally.

People want to live in a world in which the prosperity of a few is not achieved at the cost of the poverty and suffering of others. They want to have not only military, but economic security.

People want to live in a world which is democratic and free, with equality for all and with every nation enjoying the right to its own social choice without outside interference.

People want to know the truth about each other, and to feel at long last the great universal kinship of nations, ethnic groups, languages and cultures.

THE NEED FOR INTERNATIONAL COOPERATION

Can such a world be built? We in the Soviet Union are convinced that it can. But this requires a most radical restructuring of international relations.

To move towards such a world, there has to be creative courage, new thinking and a correct assessment of, and regard for, not only one's own economic capabilities and interests, but the interests of other nations as well. There has to be political will and a high sense of responsibility.

We in the Soviet Union have initiated a process of reassessing what has been achieved, and of developing a new program of action, and we are implementing it.

This is what we call perestroika. We have undertaken it without hesitation, for we realize that this is what our time demands. We have undertaken it because we want to elevate our society, speed up its development, make it even more democratic and open, and release all of its potential, so as to improve the life of our peoples materially and spiritually.

Our confidence in the future of our country and our conviction that a secure and civilized world can be built are organically interrelated.

On behalf of the Soviet leadership and of our entire people I declare that in international affairs we are acting and will continue to act responsibly and seriously. We know what our interests are, but we seek to accommodate them to the interests of others, and we are ready to meet each other halfway as equals.

The President and I have three days of intensive and important work ahead of us. Our talks are already under way. For our part, we will try to do all we can to achieve results, substantial results.

Thank you.

INTIFADA: THE PALESTINIAN UPRISING AND THE ISRAELI RESPONSE

PHIL MARSHALL

Intifada is the Arabic word for *resurgence*. It is also used to refer to the uprising of Arabs in the Israeli-occupied territories of the West Bank and Gaza Strip. As Phil Marshall explains in the following essay, the *Intifada* began on December 8, 1987, when an Israeli tank crushed four Arab workers to death in Israel. Although many commentators believe the killings were accidental, the event touched off massive protests against Israeli rule that spread throughout Gaza and the West Bank. Expressing their anger and frustration resulting from years of repressive social and economic policies, Marshall relates, youths armed with stones and Molotov cocktails battled Israeli soldiers equipped with clubs and guns. Although the government sought to put down the uprising with force, the Israeli army was ineffective against the masses of fast-moving, stone-throwing boys and young men.

As the *Intifada* continued, the political demands of the Arabs changed. Prior to the *Intifada*, Arabs had demanded the establishment of a Palestinian state in which Jews and Arabs could coexist as equals. As the *Intifada* progressed, Arabs began to seek a separate Palestinian state in the occupied territories. This goal proved elusive until the early 1990s. A peace accord reached in 1993 established Palestinian self-rule in the Gaza Strip and the West Bank town of Jericho. In 1995, Arab self-rule was extended to most of the West Bank. However, implementation of these agreements has met many obstacles, and major disagreements remain over the fate of remaining areas—especially holy sites such as the town of Jerusalem.

Phil Marshall is a journalist specializing in the Middle East. He is the author of *Revolution and Counter-revolution in Iran* and *Intifada: Zionism, Imperialism, and Palestinian Resistance*, from which this selection was excerpted.

O n 8 December 1987 hundreds of Palestinians returning to Gaza from a day's work in Israel witnessed a gruesome killing. The driver of an Israeli army tank transporter aimed his vehicle at a line of cars carrying Arab workers—four passengers were crushed to death and seven seriously injured. Three of the dead men were from nearby Jabalya refugee camp; their funerals that night turned into a demonstration of 10,000 camp residents. The *intifada* had begun.

The following day another demonstration in Jabalya was attacked by Israeli troops who killed a 20-year-old man. His funeral too became a protest against Israeli occupation; within hours marches throughout Gaza were being met by Israeli troops, repeated killings and renewed demonstrations. A tide of anger swept across the area: tens of thousands joined demonstrations that carried forbidden Palestinian flags and chanted nationalist slogans. Israeli forces declared curfews in refugee camps and closed schools. Schoolchildren took to the streets to build barricades and hurl stones and bottles at the army.

Two days into the Uprising an international relief worker described the situation in Gaza City:

> Gaza is totally closed. The roads are blocked, the streets are strewn with debris. The black smoke of burning tyres hangs over the city.

All over the area protesters defied the Israeli army. Groups of teenagers assembled at street corners, marches were organised, huge demonstrations assembled in the camps. Twenty years of frustration and bitterness at unemployment, overcrowding, poverty and repression was exploding in a collective rejection of the Israeli occupation. Everywhere Gazans demanded that Israeli troops must go and called for Palestinian rights and national independence. One young activist captured the combined sense of rage and hope that gripped the protesters: 'We were waiting to do such an uprising,' he said. 'Everyone here has a demonstration inside his heart.'

The *intifada* spread with extraordinary speed. A hundred miles away a demonstration at Balata refugee camp near Nablus in the West Bank was attacked by Israeli troops. Four Palestinian teenagers were killed and 30 people wounded. Now the cycle of protests, funerals, killings and further demonstrations began to sweep the West Bank.

Haidar Abdel-Shafi, head of the Palestinian Red Crescent Society in Gaza—the organisation which collected the dead and wounded—noted that 'the slightest spark ignites a fire'. A 'chain of confrontation' had begun in the Occupied Territories, he said.

THE IRON FIST

The Israeli government saw the protests as the work of a small minority which sought 'to disturb the peace and way of life of most residents of the territories'. Defence minister Yitzak Rabin declared that the movement was inspired by Iran, Iraq, Syria and the PLO [Palestine Liberation Organization]. He ordered reinforcements into Gaza and the West Bank with the promise that Israel would use all means to crush disruptive elements. In the first ten days of the Uprising 27 Palestinians were killed and more than 250 injured.

But already the Uprising had a momentum that could not be halted by such measures. On 21 December the Palestinian Arab population of Israel joined a general strike in solidarity with the people of the Occupied Territories. Israelis were stunned: for the first time since the 1930s all Arab communities in Palestine had mobilised to support their national rights. In towns such as Jaffa, Acre and Lod, 'Israeli' Arabs fought police during demonstrations which proved that 40 years of life under Zionist repression had not destroyed their Palestinian identity.

The evident spontaneity of the movement in Gaza and the West Bank and the reassertion of a Palestinian identity among 'Israeli' Arabs produced a first hint of official anxiety. The Israeli government had believed the PLO to be dead—crushed by Israel's 1982 invasion of Lebanon and the expulsion of Palestinian guerrillas from Beirut. Now a new wave of nationalist activity seemed capable of reviving the PLO and of threatening Israeli control over the Occupied Territories. Israeli defence minister Yitzak Rabin declared:

> Gaza and Hebron, Ramallah and Nablus [all in the Occupied Territories] are not and will never become Beirut, Sidon and Tyre [formerly PLO strongholds in Lebanon] . . . here we shall fight united and with all our strength, and it is great, against every force that tries by violent means to undermine our full control of

Judea, Samaria and the Gaza Strip.

Rabin announced a further intensification of repression in the territories: an 'iron fist' policy, similar to that which he had initiated in Lebanon, would be put into operation in Gaza and the West Bank. Israeli forces were to use 'force, power and blows' against demonstrators. 'We will make it clear who is running the territories,' Rabin insisted. 'We are adamant that the violence shall not achieve political ends.'

AN INEFFECTIVE RESPONSE

But the 'iron fist' met opposition which the Israeli army was all but helpless to resist. Trained to fight 'conventional' wars against the armies of neighbouring Arab states and PLO guerrilla fighters, Israeli forces were unable to contain mass demonstrations or the swift attacks on military vehicles or Israeli buses mounted by youths armed only with stones. By January 1988 the Israeli press was forced to admit that the army was ineffective. *The Jerusalem Post* observed:

> The streets, both in Gaza and the West Bank and in East Jerusalem, are thus in effective control of the youth. It is a situation of our 20-year-olds battling their 20-year-olds—ours using armour, helicopters and guns; theirs, clubs, rocks and primitive Molotov cocktails.

Israel's leaders tried a new tactic: they would starve the Palestinians of Gaza into submission. From mid-January long curfews were imposed on the eight Gaza camps. Soldiers were stationed at the entrances and patrolled the camps at night; no one was allowed outside. Food and water became scarce and Israeli forces increased pressure by searching houses, beating residents, firing tear-gas into homes and dropping gas canisters by helicopter. When injured Palestinians were taken to hospital they were often pursued by troops and dragged from their beds. Thousands of Palestinians were taken into detention.

The death toll mounted—by mid-January at least 50 Palestinians had been killed by gunshots or the effects of tear-gas used at close quarters. But the Uprising could not be crushed. PLO leader Yasser Arafat had already dubbed the movement 'a revolution of stones'; in the battle for the streets, stones triumphed over helicopters and guns. For the first time in a generation Palestinians had turned the tables on their Zionist enemy.

THE HISTORY OF THE TERRITORIES

The youth who battled with Israeli forces had known only occupation. Gaza and the West Bank, including East Jerusalem, had come under Israeli control in 1967 when, in the war between Israel and its Arab neighbours, the two areas had been seized from Egypt and Jordan respectively. But neither the West Bank nor Gaza were part of Arab states. They were part of historic Palestine—a country which extended from Lebanon in the north to the Sinai Desert in the south, and from the Mediterranean Sea to the River Jordan. This country had been dismembered in 1948 when the militias of the Zionist movement of settler Jews seized large areas of land while Arab armies, ostensibly fighting on behalf of the Palestinians, occupied the West Bank and Gaza.

When Israel seized these territories during the 1967 war it acquired a valuable resource. The two areas were a useful strategic asset: they provided buffer zones which, Israeli strategists argued, would help to give protection in future conflicts with the Arab states. In addition they provided land which might be used for settlement in territories the Zionist movement had long aimed to control—and which contained water resources that could be diverted into Israel. The West Bank and Gaza also contained human resources: in 1967 there were 820,000 people in the West Bank, 80,000 in East Jerusalem and 450,000 in Gaza. Tens of thousands fled the prospect of Israeli rule but the bulk of the population remained to provide the Zionist state with a valuable market for its goods and a large pool of labour which might be mobilised to serve its industries.

Israel pillaged the Occupied Territories. Its hydraulic engineers pumped water from the West Bank to the farms and towns of Israel, massively reducing local water resources. The traditional economy, based on agriculture, suffered badly; in some areas whole communities were killed off when water supplies were drained into the Israeli water system or the Israeli authorities shut off pumps.

A programme of land seizure forced tens of thousands of Palestinian peasants and labourers from areas their families had worked for generations. As part of their attempt to 'Judaise' the territories Israeli leaders initiated a new process of colonisation. Settler communities were established throughout the West Bank and Gaza with the aim of eventually integrating some or all of the territories into the Israeli state. By 1988, 55 per cent of land in the West Bank and 30 per cent of land in Gaza was in Israeli hands.

ECONOMIC CONSEQUENCES

These policies increased the large numbers of unemployed in the West Bank and Gaza. The expulsion of Palestinians from areas seized by the Zionist militias in 1948 had resulted in the establishment of refugee camps in the territories in which for 20 years many had been unemployed; after 1967 unemployment rose sharply. There was now a large pool of labour which Israeli employers were quick to exploit. Palestinians were soon being employed by Israeli industry and agriculture—but in the most menial jobs at the meanest of wages. Workers from the Occupied Territories did not enjoy the protection of Israeli trade unions and unions organised in the territories were not recognised in Israel. This employment apartheid meant that by 1977 the wages of workers from the West Bank and Gaza were on average only 40 per cent of those paid to Israelis. In 1987 the average income in Israel was ten times higher than that in Gaza and four times higher than that in the West Bank.

There were enormous benefits for the Israeli economy. Palestinian labour fuelled its industries—by 1981 more than 110,000 labourers were travelling from the Occupied Territories to work in Israel each day while the large number of those still unemployed in the West Bank and Gaza helped to keep their wages low.

Meanwhile the West Bank and Gaza became vital markets for Israeli goods. Despite limited purchasing power, their 1.3 million people provided a much-needed boost for Israel's fragile economy. By 1986 the Occupied Territories had become Israel's second largest 'export' market.

REPRESSIVE CONDITIONS

Life under occupation was a constant reminder that Israel was intent on eliminating the Palestinian identity. Israeli troops controlled movement to and from the Occupied Territories and patrolled camps and towns; Israeli administrators ran educational and legal institutions. Independent Palestinian organisations were banned. It was illegal to fly the Palestinian flag, to read 'subversive' literature, or to hold a press conference without permission.

Between 1977 and 1982 the number of incidents of Palestinian protest averaged 500 a year. Between 1982 and 1987 protests averaged 3,700 a year. They were ruthlessly suppressed. Schools and university campuses were among the key battlegrounds; here many students were killed by Israeli troops or were seriously wounded. Thousands of protesters were arrested and beaten, hundreds were placed in administrative detention (imprisonment without trial) and scores were deported. Between 1985 and 1987 alone more than 100 homes of Palestinian activists were demolished.

The situation was especially intolerable in Gaza. Close to the centres of Israeli industry, the area had been first to supply cheap labour to factories, hotels and restaurants, and to Israel's highly commercialised agriculture. By the early 1980s, 43 per cent of

Gaza's labour force worked in Israel. Banned, South Africa–style, from staying in Israel overnight, tens of thousands of labourers travelled daily to and from their homes, passing through Israeli checkpoints at the edge of the Gaza Strip. Most young Gazans knew no other routine of work. One Israeli organisation described the area as 'the labour camp of Tel-Aviv . . . the Soweto of the state of Israel'.

But jobs in Israel were often casual and many Gazans remained unemployed. As a result many families, especially new households, had no effective breadwinner. The rate of population increase was high—among the 525,000 people in Gaza by the mid-1980s, 5,000 new households were created each year. Many lived in poverty, dependent on wider family support. Employed and unemployed alike faced intolerable overcrowding. Gaza's population was crammed into an area 28 miles long and five miles wide in which population density of 3,754 people per square mile was about the same as that of Hong Kong. Though Israel could show massive economic benefits from its control of the area, it was unwilling to make any but the most basic provisions there for health, education or housing. Less than 40 per cent of new households were housed each year.

ISRAEL'S SETTLEMENT POLICY

Israel's settlement policy in Gaza increased Palestinians' anger. By 1987, 65,000 Israeli Jews had been settled in the West Bank and 2,500 in Gaza. The Jewish population of Gaza thus constituted a mere 0.4 per cent of the population of the area. But each settler had on average 2.6 acres of land; their Palestinian neighbours had on average 0.006 of an acre. And Jewish settlers, living in purpose-built accommodation and benefiting from Israeli government services, consumed, on average, 19 times more water than the slum-dwellers of the Palestinian camps, most of whom had no regular water supply and no main drainage.

For Gazans the settlement policy was an outrage which made the problems of employment, housing, education and welfare all the more unbearable. But every attempt at a response was obstructed: efforts to organise independent trade unions, university and school students' organisations and, above all, independent political parties, met with the same intimidation and violence. The Israeli approach was obsessive—even those religious and community leaders who sought to defend Palestinian rights but who sought an accommodation with the occupying power were treated with suspicion.

Israel's strategy bore a bitter fruit. As the level of resistance began to rise in 1986 it was evident that a new spirit of defiance had developed. The Israeli army's policy of arresting, beating and detaining demonstrators had less and less effect. By December 1986 Haidar Abdel-Shafi could comment that the youth were no longer retreating from Israeli troops: 'The kids are drawing different conclusions. They are becoming more daring and they are not running away,' he observed. When the *intifada* erupted in December 1987 it revealed the existence of a generation of young activists prepared to match the violence of the Israeli state with a determination to free themselves of its control.

The 'occupation generation' had grown up under Israeli rule. By 1987 it constituted the greater part of the Gazan population: the number of people aged 25–34 in the area had doubled in a decade; those under the age of 14 made up almost half of all local residents. Many of these young people had lost the fear of authority which had held back their parents. Steeled by a life under Zionist oppression and with nothing to lose, the *shabab*—'the guys' or 'the youth'—stood their ground against the Israeli army. As one middle-aged woman observed: 'Our generation failed. It is the children who now show us how to fight.'

Two months into the Uprising the reality of the new situation dawned on some Israelis. *The Jerusalem Post* admitted that a new Palestinian movement had emerged, first in Gaza, then in the West Bank. This was under the leadership of 'a young and dynamic local Palestinian leadership' which had enjoyed 'almost unbelievable success'. The paper went on:

> The Palestinians we are fighting now are not the same as the Palestinians we met 20 years ago. They have not been cowed by two decades as refugees under Egyptian and Jordanian rule, or humiliated by the defeat inflicted on the combined Arab armies by Israel in 1967. ... They are a generation who have grown up under Israeli occupation.

"I Am Still Alive": The Tiananmen Square Protests

CHAI LING

In mid-April 1989, students began a pro-democracy demonstration in Tiananmen Square in Beijing, the capital city of China. Despite government warnings of a crackdown, protests continued into May. On May 20, the government declared martial law in Beijing, but students and citizens obstructed the movement of troops into the city, and the troops pulled back to the outskirts of Beijing. In the square, protesters set up a command center and erected a scaled-down replica of the Statue of Liberty, which they dubbed the "Goddess of Democracy" or "Goddess of Liberty."

Finally, on the night of June 3–4, the government's promise to violently suppress the protests was fulfilled. Troops in tanks and armored personnel carriers entered the city and made their way to the square, opening fire on those who blocked their path, as well as on bystanders. Because most media personnel understandably fled the scene prior to their arrival, the exact story of what ensued after the troops reached Tiananmen Square is unclear. It is known that the troops surrounded the square and forced the students to leave through its southeast corner. The Chinese government insists that no one was killed in the clearing of the square; however, eyewitness accounts contradict this assertion. In any event, the number of fatalities in Tiananmen Square was likely much smaller than the number of persons killed as the troops made their way through the streets of Beijing toward the square. Reports of fatalities from the crackdown range from the hundreds to over one thousand, with hundreds of others wounded.

From "I Am Chai Ling . . . I Am Still Alive," by Chai Ling, in *Cries for Democracy: Writing and Speeches from the 1989 Democracy Movement*, edited by Han Minzhu. Copyright © 1990 by Princeton University Press. Reprinted by permission of Princeton University Press.

The following excerpt is an account of the events of June 3–4 by Chai Ling, who was the leader of the student protesters. The text is an edited version of comments taped on June 8 and broadcast in Hong Kong on June 10 after Ling was smuggled out of China. Ling stresses the nonviolent nature of the protests and condemns the brutality of the Chinese government.

Following the events in Tiananmen Square, Chai Ling traveled throughout China in disguise in order to evade capture by the government. She then spent five nights sealed in a wooden crate as she was smuggled out of China and shipped by boat to Hong Kong. From Hong Kong she made her way to France and eventually landed in the United States, where she attended Princeton and Harvard and became the CEO of an Internet start-up firm.

I t is 4:00 in the afternoon on June 8, 1989. I am Chai Ling. I am the General Commander of the Tiananmen Command Center. I am still alive.

I think I am the most authoritative commentator to speak on the overall situation in the Square during the period from June 2 to June 4. I also have an obligation to tell the true story to each of you, each and every citizen, each and every compatriot.

After around 10:00 P.M. on June 2, the first signal [of the impending repression] was that [we heard that] a police car had hit four innocent people, and three of them had already died. Then immediately following this, the second signal came: [we learned that] entire truckloads of soldiers had abandoned their guns, uniforms, and other weapons, letting them fall into the hands of the citizens and my classmates who were blocking the trucks. The students, very vigilant about this sort of behavior, immediately collected these objects and turned them into the Public Security Bureau, as our receipt proves. The third signal came at 2:10 in the afternoon on June 3, when a large force of soldiers and People's Armed Police beat students and local residents at Xinhuamen and Liubukou [the streetcorner just west of Xinhuamen]. At the time our classmates were standing on top of a bus yelling through megaphones, "the people's police love the people," "the people's police don't beat people." Just as one of our classmates was yelling out the first sentence, a soldier charged forward, kicked him in the stomach, and swore at him, "who in the hell loves you!" This was promptly followed by a truncheon, and the boy fell over immediately.

Let me explain a bit about our positions. I am the General Commander [of the Protect Tiananmen Headquarters]. We had set up a broadcast station in the Square. It was [originally] the hunger strikers' broadcast station. I always stayed there, directing the activities of all the students in the Square through broadcasts. Of course there were other students in the Headquarters, such as Li Lu, Feng Congde, and others. We frequently received emergency reports about various developments. There were continued reports of students and residents being beaten, of being cruelly injured. . . .

SACRIFICE

At precisely 9:00, all the students at Tiananmen Square rose, and raising their right hands, took an oath: "I swear that for the sake of advancing the democratization of our motherland, for the true prosperity of our nation, for our great motherland, I pledge to use my own youthful life to protect Tiananmen and defend the Republic, not to overthrow a small clique of conspirators but in order that 1.1 billion people do not lose their lives amid a white terror. Heads may be cut off and blood may flow, but the people's Square cannot be lost. We are willing to use our youthful lives to fight down to the last person."

At precisely 10:00, the Square's Democracy University officially opened for classes. The Vice General Commander [of the Headquarters], Zhang Boli, was appointed its president. People from all quarters expressed warm congratulations on the establishment of Democracy University. At the Headquarters, where emergency reports were being received continuously, the situation was extremely tense, while at another section of the Square, in the north, applause thundered for the founding of Democracy University. The university was located near the Goddess of Liberty [in the northern part of the square], and to its east and west on Changan Avenue, blood flowed like a river.

The slaughterers, the soldiers of the 27th Army, used tanks, assault weapons, and bayonets (the time for tear gas had passed) on people who had yelled only a lone slogan or only had thrown a single brick. They used automatic guns to mow them down so that the chests of all of the dead were soaked in blood. Our classmates ran to the Headquarters. Their hands, chests, and legs were covered with blood, their compatriots' last drops of blood; they had held their [dying] classmates in their own arms.

THE PRINCIPLE OF PEACEFUL PROTEST

Since April, when the movement was a student-led patriotic democratic movement, all the way to the present, when the movement has grown into a nationwide movement, our guiding principle has been [to engage in] peaceful protest; our principle for struggle has been peaceful protest. Many students, workers, and citizens came to our headquarters to tell us that since the situation had reached this state, we should take up arms. Male students were also extremely agitated . . . [but] we at the Headquarters said to everyone: "our struggle is one of peaceful protest, and the highest principle of peace is sacrifice."

In this spirit, we all emerged from our tents slowly, one by one, hand in hand, shoulder by shoulder, to the sound of the "Internationale," and walked over to the northern, western, and southern sides of the Monument to the People's Heroes. Everybody sat there quietly, awaiting with calm expressions the butcher knives of the slaughterers. We were carrying out a war of love and hate, and not a battle of military force. . . .

The students just sat there quietly, lying down to await the [moment of] sacrifice. At this time, megaphones inside the headquarters tent and loudspeakers outside played the song, "The Descendants of the Dragon" [a popular song about the Chinese race by Hou Dejian]. Our classmates sang along with the music, their eyes welling up with tears. Everybody hugged each other and held hands, for each person knew the last moment of his or her life had arrived, the moment had come to sacrifice our lives for the Chinese people. . . .

At around two or three in the morning [as troops in the Square began moving in toward us], we had no choice but to abandon the Headquarters and retreat to the broadcast station at the foot of the Heroes' Monument. As General Commander, I mobilized the students for one last time, directing them to encircle the Heroes' Monument. The students [in the first row] sat there calmly. They said to me, "We'll just sit here quietly. We in the first row are the most determined." [Behind them], other students said, "We in the back will also sit here quietly. Even if the classmates in the first row are beaten and killed, we will just sit here calmly. We will not move and we absolutely will not kill."

FOR THE LIFE OF THE REPUBLIC

I said a few words to everyone. I told them, "There is an ancient legend. According to this legend, there was once a colony of about 1.1 billion ants. One day the mountain the ants lived on caught on fire, and the ants had to escape down to the foot of the mountain if they were to live. At that point, the ants formed a ball and rolled down the mountain. The ants on the outside burned to death, but even more ants survived. . . .

"My fellow students, we in the Square, we already stand at the outermost layer of the Chinese people, for each of us in our hearts is clear: only the sacrifice of our lives will suffice for the life of the republic."

The students began singing the "Internationale," over and over again they sang it, hands clasped tightly together. Finally, our four compatriots who were hunger striking, Hou Dejian, Liu Xiaobo, Zhou Duo, [and Gao Xin] could no longer restrain themselves. They said, "Children, do not make any more sacrifices."

A PROMISE VIOLATED

Each and every one of us was utterly exhausted. The hunger strikers went to negotiate with the military and found a military representative who claimed to be responsible for the Martial Law Command Headquarters. They said, "We will withdraw from the Square, but we hope you will guarantee the safety of the students. We will withdraw peacefully." At the same time, our Headquarters was soliciting the opinions of the students, asking them whether they wanted to stay or to withdraw. We decided that all the students would withdraw. But at that moment, that bunch of slaughterers violated their promise: as the students were leaving, soldiers wearing combat helmets and armed with machine guns charged to the third tier of steps at the platform of the Monument. Before the Headquarters had a chance to announce the decision to withdraw, our loudspeakers had been strafed into shreds. This was the People's Monument! It was the Monument to the People's Heroes! They were actually shooting at the Monument. Most of the rest of the students retreated, crying as they retreated. . . .

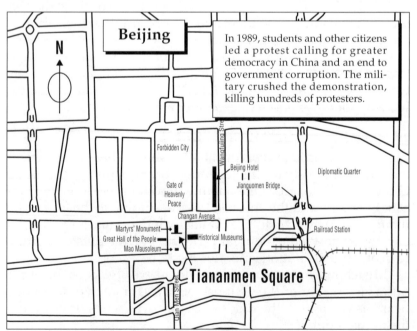

In 1989, students and other citizens led a protest calling for greater democracy in China and an end to government corruption. The military crushed the demonstration, killing hundreds of protesters.

Some say more than 200 students died; there are also others who say 4,000 have already died in the Square. Up to now, I still don't know the exact number. But every one of the people at the Workers' Autonomous Union near the [northern] edge of the Square perished. There were at least 20 or 30 of them. . . .

As we went around Mao's mausoleum [immediately south of the People's Monument] hand in hand, heading west from the south end of the Square, we saw a dark mass of some 10,000 helmeted soldiers seated at the southern side of the Monument. The students screamed at them, "Dogs!" "Fascists!" . . .

We wanted to stick out our chests and march back to the Square. But all the residents stopped us. They said, "Children, do you know, they've set up machine guns, don't make any more sacrifices." So we could only continue heading [west] toward the Xicheng District from Xidan. On the road we saw four corpses of residents. The farther north we went, the closer we got to our schools, the more citizens' eyes were filled with tears. . . .

When the last ranks of students who had withdrawn from Tiananmen Square arrived at Beijing University, this marked the forced end of our Movement, which had started on May 13 with a hunger strike and then had become a peaceful sit-in protest. Later we obtained information which said that at 10:00 on the night of June 3, Li Peng [premier of the Communist Party] had given three orders: first, army troops were permitted to open fire; second, military vehicles were to enter the city at full speed and recover the Square before dawn on June 4; and third, the organizers and leaders of the movement were to be killed, without exception.

Compatriots, this is the ruthless, crazed, bogus government that continues to deploy troops [around Beijing] and to rule China. The Beijing Massacre is happening at this very moment; massacres all over China will also slowly commence if they are not already occurring. But my dear compatriots, as the night darkens, dawn approaches. As this regime becomes increasingly fascist, crazed, and oppressive, [the Chinese people will awaken,] and a true people's democratic republic will be born. This is the final juncture for the survival of the Chinese people. Compatriots, all citizens with a conscience, all Chinese, awaken! The final victory will be yours! The day is fast approaching when the Central Committee that pretends to speak for the Party—Yang Shangkun, Li Peng, Wang Zhen, and Bo Yibo—will be annihilated!

> Down with fascism!
> Down with military rule!
> The people will be victorious!
> Long live the republic!

OBSCENITY VS. CENSORSHIP: THE DEBATE OVER ARTS FUNDING IN AMERICA

MIRIAM HORN AND ANDY PLATTNER

The National Endowment for the Arts (NEA) is an agency of the federal government that provides financial assistance to artists. In the fall of 1989, the shows of several NEA-funded artists drew protests from those who considered their work obscene. Chief among the critics was North Carolina senator Jesse Helms, who introduced legislation to deny NEA support for "obscene or indecent" art. In the following article, written in 1989, Miriam Horn and Andy Plattner describe these events and explore the issues raised by this debate. Many opposed restrictions on NEA grants as government censorship of artists, the authors note, while others insisted that refusing to provide artists with taxpayers' money in no way limits their freedom of expression. Horn is a writer for *U.S. News & World Report*. Plattner, formerly a reporter for *U.S. News & World Report*, is chairman of A-Plus Communications, a company that helps educators improve their communication with the public.

Subsequent to the writing of this article, in 1989 Congress passed legislation prohibiting the NEA from funding provocative art, but this law was eventually deemed unconstitutional. In 1990, Congress passed another law requiring the NEA to take

Miriam Horn and Andy Plattner, "Should Congress Censor Art?" *U.S. News & World Report*, September 25, 1989. Copyright, 1989, U.S. News & World Report. For additional information visit www.usnews.com.

community standards of decency into account when awarding grants. This law was upheld by the Supreme Court in 1998.

T he fight in the House of Representatives was sensational: The Champions of Child Pornography meet The Totalitarian Censors. Or so it was billed by an overheated Congress debating questions not usually heard on Capitol Hill: Can the U.S. government censor works of art if the artist is the recipient of federal funds? And should the government even be subsidizing art at all?

The immediate issue was an amendment by Senator Jesse Helms (R-N.C.) to bar federal money for "obscene or indecent art." Helms was reacting to two exhibitions financed by the National Endowment for the Arts: One included Robert Mapplethorpe's homoerotic photos and the other Andres Serrano's photograph of a crucifix submerged in urine. When the director of Washington's Corcoran Gallery, Christina Orr-Cahall, canceled the Mapplethorpe show in June 1989, the subsequent uproar gave Helms his opportunity. With the acquiescence of Democratic leaders, Helms inserted his restrictive amendment into an appropriations bill. Then Helms and his allies organized political pressure on congressmen who might defy him, including a threatening letter from 20 of the country's largest "pro-family" groups. Despite these attempts to "terrorize Congress," as Arkansas Senator Dale Bumpers called it, the House voted, 264–153, against allowing a vote on the Helms plan.

However, the battle is far from over. A House-Senate conference committee is expected to propose a commission to examine NEA grant-making procedures. Helms still promises to force a vote on his amendment when the bill comes back to the Senate. In the view of New York Shakespeare Festival director Joseph Papp, much damage has already been done. "You kill the flame of creativity with threats," says Papp. "A chill has gone down the spine of the arts community."

Museum directors and artists concede that a form of self-censorship is already under way: No arts organization wishes to be dealt the kind of punishment Helms has proposed against the institutions that organized the Mapplethorpe and Serrano shows. (Both would be barred from receiving federal funding for five years.) The NEA, too, will be more cautious, in the view of former Deputy Chairman Michael Straight, and the caliber of its grant-making panels will decline. "No first-class artist or critic is going to play this game, trying to do their work with all these vague taboos," says Straight.

FORCEFUL RESPONSE

The threat of government censorship is not limited to disturbing sexual and religious art. Controversial recent programing on public television, most notably the pro-Palestinian "Days of Rage" and the antinuclear "Dark Circle," has renewed the debate over whether the Public Broadcasting System ought to air documentaries with such strong partisan viewpoints, especially ones hostile to the U.S. government. In the classroom, the debate over appropriate books continues in almost every state.

For example, fundamentalists have repeatedly sought to ban J.D. Salinger's *The Catcher in the Rye* because of its references to adolescent sex. In September 1989, a report by the National School Boards Association argued that attempts to censor what children are exposed to are not always misguided or wrong. In April 1989, Washington's Kennedy Center turned down a satirical play on the Iran-Contra affair as "not appropriate" for a center that is dependent on federal funding.

Not surprisingly, the arts community has responded forcefully to the political pressure. Several artists withdrew from future exhibitions at the Corcoran Gallery, and one, painter Lowell Nesbitt, cut the museum out of his will. The museum's deputy director, Jane Livingston, resigned. In San Diego, artists organized a show that included a "National Condom," made out of an American flag, and a portrait of Lincoln with a swastika branded on his head. The MARS Artspace in Phoenix displayed "Piss-Helms," a photo of the senator that is submerged in what looks like urine but is actually beer. All this added to the fury of Helms's supporters and cost the arts community support of some moderates.

A MODEST TRADITION

There is now even talk in Congress of doing away entirely with federal arts funding, despite the pleas of NEA supporters, who insist that great civilizations have always relied on patronage of the arts by "enlightened princes." That tradition of patronage has endured in Europe and Japan, where public outlays for the arts today range between $1.5 billion and $3 billion a year.

But the tradition in this country is much more recent and modest. The first federal arts program, the Work Projects Administration, was scuttled in 1939 when the House Committee on Un-American Activities charged it with producing socialist propaganda. Not until 1965 was another attempt made at federal patronage, culminating in the creation of the NEA, which was allocated $169 million by Congress in 1989. One early rationale for providing public funding for art was that it would free artists from commercial and ideological restraints. But that expectation was hopelessly naive, suggests author John Updike. "The ancient law that he who pays the piper calls the tune has not been repealed even in this permissive democracy," he says. Ironically, conservatives were the first to recognize how likely Congress was to meddle in federally funded art. To buffer the NEA, they made it a semi-independent foundation with a lump-sum appropriation disbursed on the basis of peer-panel review.

DISPENSING THE SPOILS

Over the years, critics charge, these panels have degenerated into closed cabals of intellectuals dispensing spoils and gleefully flouting public taste. The charge of a spoils system is difficult to support. In 1988, some 700 panelists funded 25 percent of 18,000 applications. In fact, these elitist intellectuals are often attacked for being too democratic in their money giving, sharing the wealth too broadly, rather than singling out the best. "I see more and more undeserving recipients," says artist Helen Frankenthaler, a member of the NEA's advisory council. "There was a time of loftier minds, relatively unloaded with politics, fashion and chic."

The panels are composed of art experts, drawn from college faculties, museums and galleries, and working artists. It is probably inevitable that the American public sometimes perceives the world of modern art as elitist. John Frohnmayer, an Oregon lawyer who has been nominated by President Bush to be the new chairman of the NEA, believes that "entertainment" is accessible to everybody but adds, "I don't think art is accessible without some degree of education."

It is hardly surprising that a public that feels mocked by obscure and often intentionally provocative works of art will arrive at the same judgment on the Serrano piece as former National Endowment for the Humanities Chairman Ronald Berman: "A urine specimen is not art." Yet, as questionable as that piece might be, recent history is full of works of art initially shunned and later loved by the public. The Vietnam Veterans Memorial, an NEA project that inspired its own congressional controversy, is today Washington's most popular monument.

Some conservatives, like Hilton Kramer, editor of the art journal the *New Criterion*, have suggested that the government fund preservation programs and let living artists fend for themselves. Artists who were truly outsiders and provocateurs would not be seeking state funding anyway, Kramer says. Updike agrees. "There's nobody happier than the accepted Soviet artist," he says, "given dachas and life security. Is that really what we want?"

The language of the Helms amendment is so all-encompassing, say members of the arts community, that it puts even the classics in jeopardy. Shakespeare's *Merchant of Venice* would be banned for its insult to Jews, they say, as would Wagner's *Ring Cycle* for its depiction of incest, and countless Rubens and Rembrandt nudes.

If the Helms amendment prevails, it will surely face a constitutional challenge. Floyd Abrams, a First Amendment lawyer, argues that it violates free speech because it "would have the effect of coercing those receiving subsidies to refrain from exercising their full First Amendment rights."

The irony of the current flap is that there has been 24 years of consensus on the role of government in the arts. Of the 85,000 grants awarded since the NEA was founded, only 20 have caused dispute, a record that led columnist Michael Kinsley to complain, "Any arts-funding program that can't generate more controversy than that is a waste of money." By law, the NEA cannot ever provide more than half the funding for any project. Matching funds must be raised from private sources in the community. That system, which ensures local support for any project, may be the best guarantee of the goals Jesse Helms is trying to achieve: Guaranteeing that the American public has a hand in the art that it funds.

CRACK COCAINE AND GANGSTA RAP

NELSON GEORGE

One of the major cultural trends of the 1980s was the development of "gangsta rap" music, which grew out of the black "hip
hop" of the late 1970s. In the following essay, Nelson George explains that gangsta rap—so named because its artists portrayed
the gangster lifestyle—was a direct result of the arrival of crack
cocaine in the inner cities. Crack proved to be a highly addictive
substance, George notes, devastating the African-American community and leading to the formation of gangs that often resorted
to violence in their effort to profit from sales of the drug.

George insists that gangsta rap was unfairly blamed for promoting violence. He contends that gangsta rap took a variety of
forms; while some rap artists did adopt a gangster-like posture,
he admits, most did not participate in or advocate the gangster
lifestyle. Often their lyrics simply described the desperate and violent conditions of the urban environment of the 1980s.

George writes on black popular music and culture for various publications, including the *Village Voice*, *Esquire*, and *Essence*.
He is the author of *Hip Hop America*, from which this essay was
excerpted.

I n the "Superfly" '70s, coke was sniffed or snorted (choose
your verb) in powder form from tabletops, album covers, and
parts of other folks' bodies. In inner-city neighborhoods, coke
users wishing to socialize with those of similar appetites gathered
at after-hours clubs to separate themselves from marijuana smok-
ers and heroin junkies. Back in 1979, I interviewed a dealer who

said that "coke sniffers were Kings and Queens and heads of state"—as opposed to "the low rent people" he sold marijuana to.

By the early '80s, cocaine consumption turned toward smoking freebase, which is cocaine at its basic alkaloid level. Like many folks, I'd never heard of freebasing until Richard Pryor ran in a fiery ball out of his California home on June 9, 1980. Coke had always been an expensive drug and this "cooking" to create a smokable version just seemed another occupation of the bored rich.

In freebasing, the cocaine is boiled in water and the residue is placed in cold water where it forms "base" or "freebase." The chipped-off pieces are called "crack" because it often makes a crackling sound as it burns. The popularity of this form of cocaine coincided with a dramatic increase in the growth of coca leaves in Bolivia, Peru, and Colombia that drove down the price of manufactured cocaine.

MASS MARKET FOR CRACK

According to sociologist Terry Williams's insightful 1992 book about the crack lifestyle, *Crackhouse: Notes from the End of the Line,* the price dropped from $50,000 a kilo in 1980 to $35,000 in 1984 to $12,000 in 1992. Crack took cocaine away from high rollers and put it within reach of poorer addicts. For as little as $2, crack became available in plastic vials with red, blue, yellow, or green caps that denoted a particular dealer's territory or a particular dealer's product line. Often dealers named their brands after some pop culture artifact such as the movie *Lethal Weapon* or the band P-Funk.

The first references to mass market freebase came in two rap records—"White Lines" by Grandmaster Flash & the Furious Five, featuring Melle Mel, in 1983 and "Batterram" by Toddy Tee in 1985, which described a mini-tank the LAPD were using to break "rock houses." Soon the American media landscape would be littered with references to and discussions of crack. From those initial street reports, hip hop would chronicle, celebrate, and be blamed for the next level of drug culture development.

The crack industry became able employers of teenagers, filling the economic vacuum created by the ongoing loss of working-class jobs to the suburbs and then to poor Third World countries. Teenagers and adolescents were zealously recruited to provide the unskilled labor needed for manufacturing, packaging, and selling illegal drugs. By 1992 it was estimated that as many as 150,000 people were employed in New York City's drug trade. Similarly large numbers could be found in most major cities. MC Guru was not joking when he termed dealing "a daily operation," since the financial life of significant portions of the American economy suddenly became driven not by the stock market but by the crack industry.

THE IMPACT OF CRACK

Drug addiction has always been an equal opportunity exploiter. It strikes old, rich, white, and black. Yet there was something profoundly disheartening about crack's impact on young women. Williams estimated that 40 percent of all crackhouse denizens were female. It was maddening to see how many young mothers abandoned their children in pursuit of another hit. Often these women were forced to give sexual favors to support their dependencies.

During the eight years of Reagan's presidency, the ripple effect of crack flowed through all the social service agencies of our country—welfare, child care, medicare, you name the area of concern and crack's impact could be felt in it. At Family Court on any given day you'd see grandmothers struggling to hold families together by taking custody of their neglected or abandoned grandchildren. It was a tragedy that robbed grandparents of their rightful rest, strained their meager financial resources, and shortened their lives. In this multigenerational chaos few could raise their head above water or plan intelligently for the future.

For those who felt the fallout from crack's addictive power—the children of crackheads, their immediate families, friends, and neighbors—hope became a very hollow word. The world became defined by the 'hood, the block, or the corner where the search for drugs or their addicted loved one went on every day. As the '80s rolled on, the physical and moral decay begun by heroin [in the 1960s and 1970s] was accelerated by angel dust [PCP] and then the McDonaldization of crack.

As a consequence for many, materialism replaced spirituality as the definer of life's worth. An appreciation for life's intangible pleasures, like child rearing and romantic love, took a beating in places where children became disposable and sex was commodified. The go-go capitalism of Reagan's America (and its corporate greed) flowed down to the streets stripped of its jingoistic patriotism and fake piety. The unfettered free market of crack generated millions and stoked a voracious appetite for "goods," not good.

THE CRACK–GANGSTA RAP CONNECTION

Gangsta rap (or reality rap or whatever descriptive phrase you like) is a direct by-product of the crack explosion. Unless you grasp that connection nothing else that happened in hip hop's journey to national scapegoat will make sense. This is not a chicken or the egg riddle—first came crack rocks, then gangsta rap.

Because the intense high of crack fades quickly, crack turned ordinary drug dealers into kingpins. After shooting up or snorting heroin, an addict resides in dream land for hours; a crack addict experiences a brief, incredible rush, then five minutes later desires another rock. Crack created a fast-food economy of quick product turnover. Because it was so addictive and profitable, competition within impromptu urban enterprise zones (i.e., urban street corners) grew fierce. With the money crack generated from its increasingly ghostly clientele, bigger and more lethal guns filled our cities. Entering the '80s, the Saturday Night Special, a .45 caliber automatic, had long been America's death inducer of choice; by the end of the decade a medley of higher caliber weapons (the Israeli Uzi and Desert Eagle, the German Glock, even the good old American Mossburg 12-gauge shotgun) pushed murder totals in Washington, D.C.; Los Angeles; Detroit; Gary, Indiana; and scores of other cities to record levels.

As dealers used these guns indiscriminately, residents in the drug-ravaged communities armed themselves as well, seeking protection from dealers and crackheads, and the climate of immorality they represented. Police impotence in cleaning neighborhoods of drug trafficking and our government's failure in drug interdiction (or complicity in the trade) produced cynicism and alienation in this nation that made Nancy Reagan's "Just Say No" campaign a joke and left her husband's "Morning in America" rife with gunsmoke from the night before.

GANGSTA RAP IN THE SUBURBS

Gangsta rap first appeared in the mid-'80s. It exploded at the end of that decade and has leveled off—just like crack use—in the '90s. The majority of this subgenre's sales are made in the suburbs. A lot of this has to do with the rebel credentials of hard rappers with teenage kids and with the true nature of the contemporary teenage suburban experience.

Suburban kids—no longer just stereotypically white, but black, Asian, and Hispanic—have, since the '60s, always known a lot more about drugs than civic leaders have ever acknowledged. (Although there aren't as many drive-bys in suburban counties, they do indeed happen. Drug dealers don't necessarily all congregate on green lawns, but they have never met a mall they didn't love.) The dirty little secret of mainstream America is that kids of every age, particularly in high school and junior high, have access to a medley of controlled substances. The romance of the outlaw mystique of drugs and dealing is not foreign to young people—another reason why gangsta records, supposedly so distant to the white teen experience, is in fact quite familiar. Even the urban context of the records is not as mysterious or exotic as commentators assert, since many suburban dealers and addicts use urban 'hoods as drive-through windows.

THE INCARCERATION OF BLACK MALES

Another consequence of the crack plague was an evil increase in the numbers of incarcerated black males. In February 1990 a Washington, D.C.–based nonprofit organization, the Sentencing Project, issued a frightening report titled *Young Black Men and the Criminal Justice System: A Growing National Problem.* The report stated that one in four African-American males between twenty and twenty-nine—610,000 men in total—were either behind bars or on probation. In comparison, only 436,000 were enrolled in higher education.

The reasons for this number were legion—the crack trade, the aggressive sentencing of low-level drug offenses such as possession, the eroded economic base of urban America, a profound sense of hopelessness, ineffective school systems. The social repercussions, however, were sometimes less obvious. With so many young men in jail or monitored by law enforcement, most African-Americans had someone in their family or a friend involved with the justice system, both as perpetrator and victim. It is not surprising then that narratives dealing with crimes and its consequences—from the reality TV show *Cops* to urban movies like *Boyz N the Hood* and *Juice,* and, of course, hip hop records that talk of jail culture—have a special appeal.

More profoundly, the mentality of black culture was deeply affected. The kind of dispassionate view of violence and overall social alienation that incarceration fosters was spread by prisoners and infected the rest of the community. Jail became not a cruel punishment but a rite of passage for many that helped define one's entry into manhood. And what being a man meant could be perversely shaped by imprisonment. For many young men their sex and romantic dealings were forever altered by the sexual activity that goes on behind bars.

While homosexuality is widely condemned in the black community, the committing of homosexual acts behind bars is rarely commented on. Because they often occur through rape or psychological coercion they are not viewed as acts of sexual orientation but manifestations of control and domination, both reflections consistent with a "gangsta mental" or gangster mentality. If sex is taken, from this viewpoint, it is not an act of love but power. Whatever the justification, it suggests that there's a homoerotic quality to this culture's intense male bonding. As an example of how values shaped by prison influence behavior outside it, sex becomes about power, not affection. You bond with other men, not simply out of shared interest and friendship, but as protector and to gain predator power. For some men, in and out of jail since adolescence, jail begins to supercede the presence of all other environments.

Suspicion of women, loyalty to the crew, adoption of a stone face in confronting the world, hatred of authority—all major themes of gangsta rap—owe their presence in lyrics and impact on audiences to the large number of African-American men incarcerated in the '90s. . . .

A WIDE-RANGING GENRE

Not all rappers who write violent lyrics have lived the words. Most exercise the same artistic license to write violent tales as do the makers of Hollywood flicks. A few of those who do write violent lyrics have lived the tales or have friends who have. Within any collection of rap songs—either by those making it up or those who have lived it—a wide range of narrative strategies are employed. Many violent rhymes are just cartoons, with images as grounded in reality as the Road Runner. The outrageous words of Eazy-E and Kool G Rap fit this category. Some are cautionary tales that relate the dangers inherent to street life—Melle Mel and Duke Bootee's words in "The Message" is the prototype. Some are first-person narratives told with an objective, almost cinematic eye, by masters of the style Ice Cube and KRS-One. Some end with the narrator in bold, bloody triumph, techniques both Scarface and Ice-T employ well. A bold few end with the narrator dead and work as stories told from the grave, an approach both Tupac Shakur and the Notorious B.I.G. favored in sadly prophetic recordings.

Some violent rhymes are poetically rendered and novelistically well observed, as in the more nuanced work of Chuck D, Rakim, and Nas. Too Short and Luther Campbell can, in contrast, be as crude as the bathroom humor of Jim Carrey's *Dumb & Dumber*. Some are morally complicated by the narrator's possible insanity, which is a specialty of Houston's Scarface. Some are so empty and rote that only the most reactionary listeners would think they could incite anything beyond contempt. My point is that most MCs who've been categorized as gangsta rappers are judged thoughtlessly without any understanding of the genuine stylistic differences between them.

Besides, what's gangsta rap anyway? Listen to any of N.W.A.'s albums, as well as Eazy-E's solo efforts, Dr. Dre's *The Chronic* and Snoop Doggy Dogg's *Doggystyle*. In their celebration of gatts, hoes, gleeful nihilism, and crack as the center of their economic universe, these albums darkly display everything people fear about gangsta rap. But outside of this collection of records—most of them with brilliantly modulated vocals supervised by Dr. Dre—I'd be hard-pressed to agree to label any other major rap star a gangsta rapper. For example, the work of Ice Cube (except for his insipid West Coast Connection project) and Scarface are way too diverse and eclectic to fit a simplistic mass media stereotype.

PAC AND BIGGIE

The martyrs of '90s hip hop—Tupac Shakur and the Notorious B.I.G. (Christopher Wallace)—were quickly tagged gangsta rappers *after* their demise, though crack and crime were not their only topics. A lot of drivel has been written about these two dead young black men. Heroes for a generation. Victims of their violent recordings. Martyrs. Villains. Whatever. For a moment let's just discuss them as artists. If, over twenty years after it evolved out of the Bronx, hip hop is an artform, then these men built profoundly on that foundation. Far from being simple op-positional figures in an East Coast–West Coast soap opera, Pac and Biggie complemented each other, though outwardly they seem mismatched.

Biggie was round and spoke in a thoughtful Brooklyn-meets-the-Caribbean drawl he derived from his articulate mother, a Jamaican-born schoolteacher. Tupac was taut and spoke with an activist's urgency and an actor's sense of drama, a by-product of his mother's militant background and his theatrical training in high school. Biggie covered himself in layers of expensive cloth-ing and the regal air that led him to be dubbed the "King of New York" after the '90s gangsta film. Tupac always seemed to have his shirt off, better to expose his six-pack abdominals, wiry body, and the words "Thug 4 Life" tattooed across his belly.

But inside, both young men possessed lyrical dexterity, a writer's strong point of view, and a bitter, street-hardened sense of irony. Ultimately, Tupac and Biggie, like most of the contro-versial and best rappers who came after Public Enemy's political spiels, were both poets of negation, a stance that always upsets official cultural gatekeepers and God-fearing folks within black America. African-Americans have always been conflicted by art that explores the psychologically complex, even evil aspects of their existence, feeling it plays into the agenda of white oppres-sion. On a very direct, obvious level they have a point. Black people saying bad things about themselves can serve to reinforce racist attitudes among non-blacks.

Yet, without a doubt, political and social conditions must not, cannot, and will not circumscribe the vision of true artists. Tupac and Biggie were artists who looked at the worst things in their world and reveled in describing their meanest dreams and grossest nightmares. They embraced the evil of crack America and articulated it with style—but highlighting is not the same as celebrating. The celebrated work of director Martin Scorsese parallels this artistic impulse. His violent masterworks—*Mean Streets, Raging Bull*, and *GoodFellas*—are undeniably artful yet morally twisted and deeply troubling in what they depict about the Italian-American soul in particular and the human capacity for violence in general—yet no one accuses him of being a self-glorifying predator.

Scorsese is considered, perhaps, the greatest living American filmmaker; Tupac and Biggie were labeled gangsta rappers in their obituaries. Yet the homicidal characters depicted by Joe Pesci and Robert DeNiro in *GoodFellas* could walk into any of Tupac or the Notorious B.I.G.'s records and feel right at home. Tupac and the Notorious B.I.G. didn't make records for the NAACP; they made harsh, contemplative, graphic, deliberately violent American pulp art.

Tupac's hip hop Jimmy Cagney and the Notorious B.I.G.'s Edward G. Robinson didn't die for their sins or the ones they rhymed about; they died for their lives—the lives they chose and the lives that chose them. Rap lyrics that describe violence are a natural consequence of a world where a sixteen-year-old is shot at close range over his jacket by classmates, where a fifteen-year-old boy is fatally stabbed by another teen over his glasses, where a seventeen-year-old is stabbed to death after hitting another teen with an errant basketball pass. In a world where crack-empowered gangs run on a philosophy of old-fashioned, excessive, insatiable and unending revenge—one that is supported by the plots of American classics from *The Searchers* to *Star Wars*—gangsta rap is just further exploration of this theme.

There is an elemental nihilism in the most controversial crack-era hip hop that wasn't concocted by the rappers but reflects the mentality and fears of young Americans of every color and class living an exhausting, edgy existence, in and out of big cities. Like crack dealing, it may die down, but the social conditions that inspired the trafficking and the underlying artistic impulse that ignited nihilistic rap have not disappeared and will not because, deep in the American soul, it speaks to us and we like the sound of its voice.

Communism Falters in Eastern Europe: The Revolutions of 1989

CHAPTER 3

TEARING DOWN THE BERLIN WALL

ROBERT DARNTON

Following World War II, Germany was divided into two countries: communist East Germany, officially known as the German Democratic Republic (GDR); and non-communist West Germany, officially known as the Federal Republic of Germany (FRG). East Germany strictly prohibited egress of its citizens across its borders. As part of this strict border policy, it constructed the Berlin Wall in 1961 to prevent East Germans from fleeing to the West in that divided city. This wall quickly became a powerful symbol of the Cold War and a rallying point for protests against the communist regimes of Eastern Europe and the Soviet Union.

In the fall of 1989, East Germany experienced a quick and relatively peaceful revolution. In August, groups of East Germans began to flee to the West by crossing the border between East Germany and Austria. Once in Austria, they were granted easy access to West Germany, where they were granted asylum. Although the border was soon controlled, this event encouraged other East Germans to find ways to leave the country. It also sparked protests in many East German cities, including East Berlin, provoking violent crackdowns by government security forces. On October 9, when security forces failed to break up a massive, nonviolent protest in the city of Leipzig, the tide turned in favor of the demonstrators. The protests grew in size and culminated on November 4, when an estimated 1 million people gathered in East Berlin. On November 9, the border between East and West Berlin was opened, and citizens began to tear the wall down in a spirit of celebration.

In the following essay, written days after the collapse of the wall, Robert Darnton describes the mood in Berlin as the border opened and the Berlin Wall came down. Darnton explains that the opening of the border between East and West Berlin was both liberating and unsettling to Berliners on both sides of the border, who were now faced with the task of adapting to a new, undefined political and economic situation. The transformation of Germany continued at a rapid pace following November 1989. In October 1990, the GDR dissolved and the two Germanys were unified under one government.

Darnton is a professor of European history at Princeton University and the author of *Berlin Journal, 1989–1990*, from which this excerpt was taken.

O n the morning after, November 10, when both Berlins woke up wondering whether the first flood through the Wall had been a dream, the West Berlin tabloid *Volksblatt* ran two headlines, shoulder to shoulder, on its front page: "The Wall Is Gone" and "Bonn Demands the Destruction of the Wall."

Both were right. The Wall is there and it is not there. On November 9, it cut through the heart of Berlin, a jagged wound in the middle of a great city, the Great Divide of the Cold War. On November 10, it had become a dance floor, a picture gallery, a bulletin board, a movie screen, a videocassette, a museum, and, as the woman who cleaned my office put it, "nothing but a heap of stone." The taking of the Wall, like the taking of the Bastille, transformed the world. No wonder that a day later, in Alexanderplatz, East Berlin, one conqueror of the Wall marched in a demonstration with a sign saying simply, "1789–1989." He had helped dismantle the central symbol around which the postwar world had taken shape in the minds of millions.

To witness symbolic transformation on such a scale is a rare opportunity, and it raises many questions. To begin with the most concrete: What happened between November 9 and 12, and what does it mean?

CONQUERING THE WALL

The destruction of the Wall began in the early evening of Thursday, November 9, soon after the first wave of East Berliners, or *Ossis*, as they are called by the West Berliners here, burst upon the West. One Ossi, a young man with a knapsack on his back, somehow hoisted himself up on the Wall directly across from the Brandenburg Gate. He sauntered along the top of it, swinging his arms casually at his sides, a perfect target for the bullets that had felled many other wall jumpers, like Peter Fechter, an eighteen-year-old construction worker, who was shot and left to bleed to death a few feet in front of Checkpoint Charlie on August 17, 1962. Now, twenty-seven years later, a new generation of border guards took aim at a new kind of target and fired—but only with power hoses and without much conviction. The conqueror of the Wall continued his promenade, soaked to the skin, until at last the guards gave up. Then he opened his knapsack and poured the water toward the East, in a gesture that seemed to say, "Good-bye to all that."

A few minutes later, hundreds of people, Ossis and Wessis alike, were on the Wall, embracing, dancing, exchanging flowers, drinking wine, helping up new "conquerors"—and chipping away at the Wall itself. By midnight, under a full moon and the glare of spotlights from the watchtowers in no man's land, a thousand figures swarmed over the Wall, hammering, chiseling, wearing its surface away like a colony of army ants. At the bottom, "conquerors" threw stones at its base or went at it with pickaxes. Long slits appeared, and the light showed through from the East, as if through the eyes of a jack-o'-lantern. On the top, at the center of the tumult, with the Brandenburg Gate looming in the background, one Ossi conducted the destruction with a sickle in one hand and a hammer in the other.

By Saturday, November 11, chunks of the wall were circulating through both Berlins. People exchanged them as souvenirs of what had already taken shape in the collective consciousness as a historical event: the end of the Cold War. A sidewalk entrepreneur sold bits of wall from a table on the Ku'damm [The Kurfürstendamm, West Berlin's elegant shopping avenue]: 20 DM [deutsche marks] for a piece of the past. At one point, an East Berliner walked by and objected, with a smile on his face: "You can't sell that. It's our Wall. It belongs to us."

TWO WALLS

Like any powerful symbol, the Wall has acquired many meanings, and they differ significantly from West to East. The Wall even looks different if you study it from one side and then the other. Seen from the West, it is a prison wall that encloses the East Berliners in totalitarianism. Tourists climb on observation towers and shudder deliciously at the spectacle: the monstrous, graffiti-covered concrete structure, the no man's land beyond it—which, until 1985, was mined and rigged with rifles that fired automatically at anyone who dashed across—the barbed wire, the dog patrols, the turrets with armed guards staring back through binoculars, and the second wall or windowless buildings on the far side of the deadly, desolate space.

East Berliners see a different Wall. Theirs is painted in patterns of light and dark blue, clean, bright, and free of all graffiti. It shuts off the view of the repressive apparatus beyond it. If you lose your way or stray into outlying areas in East Berlin, you can drive along the Wall for miles without noticing that it is something more than an ordinary part of the urban landscape.

LOSS OF PROTECTION

Just after the metaphorical fall of this Wall, I visited an East Berlin friend on his side of the city. A non-Party intellectual who has supported the demonstrations and opposed the regime throughout the current crisis, he had one word of advice: "Don't tear down the Wall. We need it as a protective barrier. It should be permeable but it should stay up. One of the great mistakes in Berlin history was to tear down the customs wall in which the Brandenburg Gate was embedded in 1867. After that the tragedies of the modern age began."

A young professor from Leipzig had made a similar remark two months earlier. She described the Wall as a dike against dangerous influences from the capitalist world. I had thought she was repeating a Party line, but the same idea can be heard on East German television, in pubs, and in the streets now that the East Germans are debating their future openly and the Wall has changed its nature.

Not that they feel any nostalgia for the old police state. On the contrary, they still pour into the streets, night after night, demanding the dismantling of the Party dictatorship. But the very success of the demonstrations has created a new political consciousness, and the conquering of the Wall has raised a new question: how is the rebirth of popular sovereignty, the "We the People" of a truly democratic German Democratic Republic, to constitute itself as a viable political unit? That is the question that determines the meaning of the Wall for East Berliners.

Westerners commonly imagine that East Germans are hungering and thirsting for the chance to earn large salaries and to spend them on the consumer goods that are available in the West. This theme prevailed above all others in the media blitz surrounding the emigration of East Germans to the West, and it drowned out a more significant refrain that was chanted by the hundreds of thousands who remained home, demonstrating in the streets of Leipzig, Dresden, and a dozen other cities for weeks before the storming of the Wall: "We are the people! We're staying here!" Between 500,000 and a million people chanted that theme in the supreme demonstration of November 4 in East Berlin; not a nose was bloodied, not a window broken.

The demonstrations have operated as an Estates General in the streets, sapping legitimacy from the Communist Party and transferring it to the people. In conquering the Wall, the people brought that process to a climax. But then they faced a problem: what are they to do if nothing stands between them and the West?

To be viable, a state must define its boundaries and assert its identity in contrast to neighboring states. In the eyes of East German intellectuals, that means maintaining the Wall, but with unrestricted access to exits through it. They seem less comfortable with the idea of traffic in the other direction, however, because they know that their economy is floundering and their currency cannot stand up against the West German mark, which is officially exchanged in the GDR [German Democratic Republic] at a rate of one to one and is negotiated on the black market at one to ten. West German industrialists and financiers have declared themselves ready to pour billions of deutsche marks into the GDR, but that is not the Ossis' idea of liberation.

Ask anyone in East Berlin what he thinks of the country's economic prospects, and you will get a prophecy of doom, followed by defiance: "We do not want to be sold." In the last few days about 6 million East Germans, a third of the country's population, crossed the previously impenetrable border to the West and returned. Most of them grew up under a system that called itself socialist. They believe in socialism. They want to give it a try— by getting rid of the monopoly of the so-called Socialist Unity (i.e. Communist) Party and, if necessary, by maintaining some kind of protective wall against economic domination from the West. . . .

An Effective Barrier

To someone unfamiliar with Berlin, it may be hard to imagine how successfully the Wall had divided the city. Soon after 1961, when the Wall went up, the million or so inhabitants on the Western side and the 2 million or so on the Eastern began to lose contact. By 1989, a whole generation had come of age within the shadow of the Wall. Most of them never crossed it, even from West to East when that was allowed. They accepted the Wall as a fact of life, as something inexorable, built into the landscape—there when they were born and there when they died. They left it to the tourists, took it for granted, forgot about it, or simply stopped seeing it.

Before the fall, an old woman was interviewed on her balcony, which overlooked the Wall from the West. She spent hours every afternoon staring into no man's land. Why did she look so hard at the Wall, day after day? the reporter asked, hoping to find some expression of Berlin's divided personality. "Oh, I'm not looking at the Wall at all," she replied. "I watch the rabbits play-

A group of West Germans peer over the infamous Berlin Wall.

ing in no man's land." Many West Berliners did not see the Wall until it ceased to exist.

For the Wall enclosed the West Berliners even more thoroughly than it shut off their counterparts in the East. In 1961 it was perceived as a noose that would soon choke the life out of the western half of the city. But by 1989, West Berliners had come to regard the Wall as a source of support. Thanks to its presence, the government in Bonn poured billions into Berlin, subsidizing everything from the philharmonic orchestra to teen-age jazz groups. A whole population of underemployed intellectuals grew up around the Free University, which now has about 60,000 students. As residents of Berlin, they are exempt from the draft; they also can drink beer and talk politics in pubs throughout the night, for Berlin is the only city in the Federal Republic where the pubs are permitted to stay open past midnight, the only place where you can order breakfast in the afternoon. Many of these free-floating intellectuals became freeloaders. They lived off the Wall; and if it really falls, they may face a greater economic disaster than the Berliners in the East.

To Berliners, therefore, the Wall means something very different from what it means outside the city. But most of them realize that their local barrier is bound up with larger divisions, the Oder–Neisse line [the border between East Germany and Poland] in particular and the general dividing line between the Warsaw Pact and NATO. Having gone to bed one day in a world with clearly defined boundaries, they woke up the next in a world without firm national borders, without balanced power blocs, and even without obvious demarcations of time, because it suddenly seemed possible to produce a treaty ending World War II forty-four years after World War II had ended. They are living a truism of anthropology: the collapse of boundaries can be deeply disturbing, a source of renewal but also a threat to a whole worldview.

The mood remains euphoric, nonetheless. In East Berlin especially, the idea has spread that in conquering the Wall the people seized power. No one denies that power comes out of the barrel of a gun, but it has symbolic forms, too. The demonstrations in the streets sapped the legitimacy of the regime. Combined with the hemorrhaging of the population across the borders, they brought the government down, without a shot fired.

HOW THE WALL "FELL"

When well-informed East Berliners try to explain what happened, they sometimes produce Kremlinological accounts of splits within the Party. While Egon Krenz was occupied with purging the Politburo, his enemy, Willy Stoph, the former president of the Council of Ministers, allegedly gave word that the travel restrictions could be lifted. This tiny crack opened the way to rumors, and the first trickle of Ossis began to gather at the border crossings. Faced with questions from the border guards on one side and the press on the other, the new party spokesman, Günter Schabowski, remarked casually at the end of his daily press conference that the restrictions no longer applied. The press took it as a sign that the Party had renegotiated the terms of an agreement on liberalizing travel to the West, not as a declaration that the Wall had fallen.

But the East Berliners continued to flock to the Wall, demanding access to the West merely by showing their personal identification cards. The pressure grew in proportion to the confusion, and in the end the guards started letting a few people through. The crack became a slit, the slit a breach, and the Wall "fell"— without anyone decreeing it, least of all Egon Krenz.

We may never know the details of what happened inside the crumbling power structure of the GDR. But whatever produced the occasion, the force that broke through the Wall was there for all to see on the night of November 9. It was the people of East

Berlin. They took the Wall as they had taken to the streets for the previous two months, with nothing but their convictions, their discipline, and the power of their numbers.

When they came streaming into West Berlin, they spoke the language of liberty, but they expressed themselves by gesture, not by high-flown rhetoric. They took possession of the Wall physically, by pouring through it, climbing on it, and chipping it apart. They did the same thing in West Berlin itself. They occupied space, swarming through the Ku'damm, filling the buses and pubs, parking their tiny Trabis on the noblest sidewalks, and returning triumphantly to the East with a flower for a girl friend or a toy for an infant.

It was a magical moment, the possession of a city by its people. On Thursday, November 9, under a full moon, between the shadow of the Reichstag and the menacing bulk of the Brandenburg Gate, the people of Berlin danced on their Wall, transforming the cruelest urban landscape into a scene of hilarity and hope, and ending a century of war.

THE VELVET REVOLUTION: DEMOCRACY COMES TO CZECHOSLOVAKIA

VACLAV HAVEL

Czechoslovakia was among several European nations that over-threw their totalitarian governments in the fall of 1989. Unlike the revolutions of Hungary, Poland, and Romania, the Czecho-slovakian revolt was relatively peaceful—thus it is referred to as the "velvet revolution." The uprising began on November 17, when students led a pro-democracy demonstration in Prague, the nation's capital. Riot police beat the demonstrators, injuring over one hundred; however, their actions merely provoked wider support for the demonstrators. In the following days and weeks, massive protests were held in several major cities, and a general strike was conducted on November 27. By the end of the year, the Communist Party had been stripped of its leading role in na-tional affairs, and the country had a new president: Vaclav Havel.

Havel was a playwright and intellectual who had been jailed four times in the 1970s and 1980s for his criticism of the Com-munist regime, spending a total of five years in prison. He was one of the founders and the leader of the Civic Forum, a pro-democracy movement that was central to the 1989 revolution. As such, he was a key leader of the revolution and a natural choice for president. After being appointed president on December 27, 1989, he was freely elected president in 1990 for a two-year term. In 1992, when Czechoslovakia split into two countries—the

Vaclav Havel, New Year's address to the Czechoslovakian people, January 1, 1990.

Czech Republic and Slovakia—Havel resigned from the presidency; however, he was elected as president of the Czech Republic in 1993 and re-elected in 1998.

The following selection is the text of a speech Havel delivered to the Czechoslovakian people on January 1, 1990, just days after becoming president. Havel expresses his hope for an increasingly moral and humane society in the wake of years of totalitarian oppression.

M y dear fellow citizens,
For forty years you heard from my predecessors on this day different variations on the same theme: how our country was flourishing, how many million tons of steel we produced, how happy we all were, how we trusted our government, and what bright perspectives were unfolding in front of us.

I assume you did not propose me for this office so that I, too, would lie to you.

Our country is not flourishing. The enormous creative and spiritual potential of our nations is not being used sensibly. Entire branches of industry are producing goods that are of no interest to anyone, while we are lacking the things we need. A state which calls itself a workers' state humiliates and exploits workers. Our obsolete economy is wasting the little energy we have available. A country that once could be proud of the educational level of its citizens spends so little on education that it ranks today as seventy-second in the world. We have polluted the soil, rivers and forests bequeathed to us by our ancestors, and we have today the most contaminated environment in Europe. Adults in our country die earlier than in most other European countries.

Allow me a small personal observation. When I flew recently to Bratislava, I found some time during discussions to look out of the plane window. I saw the industrial complex of Slovnaft chemical factory and the giant Petr'alka housing estate right behind it. The view was enough for me to understand that for decades our statesmen and political leaders did not look or did not want to look out of the windows of their planes. No study of statistics available to me would enable me to understand faster and better the situation in which we find ourselves.

A CONTAMINATED MORAL ENVIRONMENT

But all this is still not the main problem. The worst thing is that we live in a contaminated moral environment. We fell morally ill because we became used to saying something different from what we thought. We learned not to believe in anything, to ignore one another, to care only about ourselves. Concepts such as love, friendship, compassion, humility or forgiveness lost their depth and dimension, and for many of us they represented only psychological peculiarities, or they resembled gone-astray greetings from ancient times, a little ridiculous in the era of computers and spaceships. Only a few of us were able to cry out loudly that the powers that be should not be all-powerful and that the special farms, which produced ecologically pure and top-quality food just for them, should send their produce to schools, children's homes and hospitals if our agriculture was unable to offer them to all.

The previous regime—armed with its arrogant and intolerant ideology—reduced man to a force of production, and nature to a tool of production. In this it attacked both their very substance and their mutual relationship. It reduced gifted and autonomous people, skillfully working in their own country, to the nuts and bolts of some monstrously huge, noisy and stinking machine, whose real meaning was not clear to anyone. It could not do more than slowly but inexorably wear out itself and all its nuts and bolts.

When I talk about the contaminated moral atmosphere, I am not talking just about the gentlemen who eat organic vegetables and do not look out of the plane windows. I am talking about all of us. We had all become used to the totalitarian system and accepted it as an unchangeable fact and thus helped to perpetuate it. In other words, we are all—though naturally to differing extents—responsible for the operation of the totalitarian machinery. None of us is just its victim. We are all also its co-creators.

Why do I say this? It would be very unreasonable to understand the sad legacy of the last forty years as something alien, which some distant relative bequeathed to us. On the contrary, we have to accept this legacy as a sin we committed against ourselves. If we accept it as such, we will understand that it is up to us all, and up to us alone to do something about it. We cannot blame the previous rulers for everything, not only because it would be untrue, but also because it would blunt the duty that each of us faces today: namely, the obligation to act independently, freely, reasonably and quickly. Let us not be mistaken: the best government in the world, the best parliament and the best president, cannot achieve much on their own. And it would be wrong to expect a general remedy from them alone. Freedom and democracy include participation and therefore responsibility from us all.

If we realize this, then all the horrors that the new Czechoslovak democracy inherited will cease to appear so terrible. If we realize this, hope will return to our hearts.

THE RECENT REVOLUTION

In the effort to rectify matters of common concern, we have something to lean on. The recent period—and in particular the last six weeks of our peaceful revolution—has shown the enormous human, moral and spiritual potential, and the civic culture that slumbered in our society under the enforced mask of apathy. Whenever someone categorically claimed that we were this or that, I always objected that society is a very mysterious creature and that it is unwise to trust only the face it presents to you. I am happy that I was not mistaken. Everywhere in the world people wonder where those meek, humiliated, skeptical and seemingly cynical citizens of Czechoslovakia found the marvelous strength to shake the totalitarian yoke from their shoulders in several weeks, and in a decent and peaceful way. And let us ask: Where did the young people who never knew another system get their desire for truth, their love of free thought, their political ideas, their civic courage and civic prudence? How did it happen that their parents—the very generation that had been considered lost—joined them? How is it that so many people immediately knew what to do and none needed any advice or instruction?

I think there are two main reasons for the hopeful face of our present situation. First of all, people are never just a product of the external world; they are also able to relate themselves to something superior, however systematically the external world tries to kill that ability in them. Secondly, the humanistic and democratic traditions, about which there had been so much idle talk, did after all slumber in the unconsciousness of our nations and ethnic minorities, and were inconspicuously passed from one generation to another, so that each of us could discover them at the right time and transform them into deeds.

THE PRICE OF FREEDOM

We had to pay, however, for our present freedom. Many citizens perished in jails in the 1950s, many were executed, thousands of human lives were destroyed, hundreds of thousands of talented people were forced to leave the country. Those who defended the honor of our nations during the Second World War, those who rebelled against totalitarian rule and those who simply managed to remain themselves and think freely, were all persecuted. We should not forget any of those who paid for our present freedom in one way or another. Independent courts should impartially consider the possible guilt of those who were responsible for the persecutions, so that the truth about our recent past might be fully revealed.

We must also bear in mind that other nations have paid even

more dearly for their present freedom, and that indirectly they have also paid for ours. The rivers of blood that have flowed in Hungary, Poland, Germany and recently in such a horrific manner in Romania, as well as the sea of blood shed by the nations of the Soviet Union, must not be forgotten. First of all because all human suffering concerns every other human being. But more than this, they must also not be forgotten because it is these great sacrifices that form the tragic background of today's freedom or the gradual emancipation of the nations of the Soviet Bloc, and thus the background of our own newfound freedom. Without the changes in the Soviet Union, Poland, Hungary, and the German Democratic Republic, what has happened in our country would have scarcely happened. And if it did, it certainly would not have followed such a peaceful course.

A New Self-Confidence

The fact that we enjoyed optimal international conditions does not mean that anyone else has directly helped us during the recent weeks. In fact, after hundreds of years, both our nations have raised their heads high of their own initiative without relying on the help of stronger nations or powers. It seems to me that this constitutes the great moral asset of the present moment. This moment holds within itself the hope that in the future we will no longer suffer from the complex of those who must always express their gratitude to somebody. It now depends only on us whether this hope will be realized and whether our civic, national, and political self-confidence will be awakened in a historically new way.

Self-confidence is not pride. Just the contrary: only a person or a nation that is self-confident, in the best sense of the word, is capable of listening to others, accepting them as equals, forgiving its enemies and regretting its own guilt. Let us try to introduce this kind of self-confidence into the life of our community and, as nations, into our behavior on the international stage. Only thus can we restore our self-respect and our respect for one another as well as the respect of other nations.

Our state should never again be an appendage or a poor relative of anyone else. It is true that we must accept and learn many things from others, but we must do this in the future as their equal partners, who also have something to offer.

Moral Politics

Our first president [Tomas Masaryk] wrote: "Jesus, not Caesar." . . . I dare to say that we may even have an opportunity to spread this idea further and introduce a new element into European and global politics. Our country, if that is what we want, can now permanently radiate love, understanding, the power of the spirit and of ideas. It is precisely this glow that we can offer as our specific contribution to international politics.

Masaryk based his politics on morality. Let us try, in a new time and in a new way, to restore this concept of politics. Let us teach ourselves and others that politics should be an expression of a desire to contribute to the happiness of the community rather than of a need to cheat or rape the community. Let us teach ourselves and others that politics can be not simply the art of the possible, especially if this means the art of speculation, calculation, intrigue, secret deals and pragmatic maneuvering, but that it can also be the art of the impossible, that is, the art of improving ourselves and the world.

A Spiritual Crossroads

We are a small country, yet at one time we were the spiritual crossroads of Europe. Is there a reason why we could not again become one? Would it not be another asset with which to repay the help of others that we are going to need?

Our homegrown Mafia, those who do not look out of the plane windows and who eat specially fed pigs, may still be around and at times may muddy the waters, but they are no longer our main enemy. Even less so is our main enemy any kind of international Mafia. Our main enemy today is our own bad traits: indifference to the common good, vanity, personal ambition, selfishness, and rivalry. The main struggle will have to be fought on this field.

There are free elections and an election campaign ahead of us. Let us not allow this struggle to dirty the so-far clean face of our gentle revolution. Let us not allow the sympathies of the world, which we have won so fast, to be equally rapidly lost through our becoming entangled in the jungle of skirmishes for power. Let us not allow the desire to serve oneself to bloom once again under the stately garb of the desire to serve the common good. It is not really important now which party, club or group prevails in the elections. The important thing is that the winners will be the best of us, in the moral, civic, political and professional sense, regardless of their political affiliations. The future policies and prestige of our state will depend on the personalities we select, and later, elect to our representative bodies.

Presidential Tasks

My dear fellow citizens!

Three days ago I became the president of the republic as a consequence of your will, expressed through the deputies of the Federal Assembly. You have a right to expect me to mention the tasks I see before me as president.

The first of these is to use all my power and influence to ensure that we soon step up to the ballot boxes in a free election, and that our path toward this historic milestone will be dignified and peaceful.

My second task is to guarantee that we approach these elections as two self-governing nations who respect each other's interests, national identity, religious traditions, and symbols. As a Czech who has given his presidential oath to an important Slovak who is personally close to him, I feel a special obligation— after the bitter experiences that Slovaks had in the past—to see that all the interests of the Slovak nation are respected and that no state office, including the highest one, will ever be barred to it in the future.

My third task is to support everything that will lead to better circumstances for our children, the elderly, women, the sick, the hardworking laborers, the national minorities and all citizens who are for any reason worse off than others. High-quality food or hospitals must no longer be a prerogative of the powerful; they must be available to those who need them the most.

As supreme commander of the armed forces I want to guarantee that the defensive capability of our country will no longer be used as a pretext for anyone to stand in the way of courageous peace initiatives, the reduction of military service, the establishment of alternative military service and the overall humanization of military life.

AMNESTY

In our country there are many prisoners who, though they may have committed serious crimes and have been punished for them, have had to submit—despite the goodwill of some investigators, judges and above all defense lawyers—to a debased judiciary process that curtailed their rights. They now have to live in prisons that do not strive to awaken the better qualities contained in every person, but rather humiliate them and destroy them physically and mentally. In a view of this fact, I have decided to declare a relatively extensive amnesty. At the same time I call on the prisoners to understand that forty years of unjust investigations, trials and imprisonments cannot be put right overnight, and to understand that the changes that are being speedily prepared still require time to implement. By rebelling, the prisoners would help neither society nor themselves. I also call on the public not to fear the prisoners once they are released, not to make their lives difficult, to help them, in the Christian spirit, after their return among us to find within themselves that which jails could not find in them: the capacity to repent and the desire to live a respectable life.

My honorable task is to strengthen the authority of our country in the world. I would be glad if other states respected us for showing understanding, tolerance and love for peace. I would be happy if Pope John Paul II and the Dalai Lama of Tibet could visit our country before the elections, if only for a day. I would be happy if our friendly relations with all nations were strengthened. I would be happy if we succeeded before the elections in establishing diplomatic relations with the Vatican and Israel. I would also like to contribute to peace by briefly visiting our close neighbors, the German Democratic Republic and the Federal Republic of Germany. Neither shall I forget our other neighbors—fraternal Poland and the ever-closer countries of Hungary and Austria.

In conclusion, I would like to say that I want to be a president who will speak less and work more. To be a president who will not only look out of the windows of his airplane but who, first and foremost, will always be present among his fellow citizens and listen to them well.

DREAMING OF A HUMANE REPUBLIC

You may ask what kind of republic I dream of. Let me reply: I dream of a republic independent, free, and democratic, of a republic economically prosperous and yet socially just; in short, of a humane republic that serves the individual and that therefore holds the hope that the individual will serve it in turn. Of a republic of well-rounded people, because without such people it is impossible to solve any of our problems—human, economic, ecological, social, or political.

The most distinguished of my predecessors opened his first speech with a quotation from the great Czech educator Komenski. Allow me to conclude my first speech with my own paraphrase of the same statement:

People, your government has returned to you!

Bringing Down Ceausescu: Revolt in Romania

Martyn Rady

Romania was one of only two communist countries remaining in Europe at the end of 1989, when it followed the lead of Poland, Hungary, East Germany, Czechoslovakia, and Bulgaria in turning away from totalitarianism. On December 16, demonstrations began in the town of Timisoara in support of Laszlo Toekes, a Catholic priest who had been removed from his post for speaking out against the country's dictatorial leader, Nicolae Ceausescu. The army and the *securitate* (secret police) were brought in to quell the unrest. Despite Ceausescu's orders to put down the protests with force, the army and *securitate* initially attempted to control the demonstrations with clubs. Then, on December 17, they shot, bayoneted, and ran over the crowds with armored vehicles, killing about seventy.

As Martyn Rady explains in the following selection, Ceausescu's downfall followed swiftly as news of the events in Timisoara spread. On December 21 in the capital city Bucharest, Rady recounts, a carefully staged appearance by Ceausescu was disrupted by protesters, who continued their demonstrations into the evening. While forces attempted to break up the crowds, Rady writes, a full-scale crackdown was avoided due to the refusal of high-ranking officers to comply with Ceausescu's orders to shoot to kill. By December 22, large elements of the army and *securitate* had defected to the side of the demonstrators, and Ceausescu and his wife Elena were forced to flee by helicopter as a mob of protesters broke into the main government building

Excerpted from "The Revolution in Bucharest," by Martyn Rady, in *Romania in Turmoil*. Copyright © 1992 by Martyn Rady. Reprinted with permission of IB Tauris & Co. Ltd.

where they resided. The ruler and his wife were subsequently arrested, secretly tried for murder and embezzlement of government funds, and executed on December 25.

In the wake of Ceausescu's ouster, Ion Iliescu, a former high-ranking Communist Party member, took over as president. He was elected president in 1990 and has subsequently overseen the country's gradual, turbulent transition to democracy.

Martyn Rady is senior lecturer at the School of Slavonic and East European Studies, University of London. He is the author of several books on Eastern Europe, including *Romania in Turmoil: A Contemporary History*, from which this essay was excerpted.

'Television made the Revolution; television is the Revolution.' With these words, the first director of Free Romanian Television, Aurel Munteanu, identified the critical role played by the media in the making of the Christmas Revolution. Throughout the preceding autumn, Romanians had followed the fall of the communist dominos in Eastern Europe through the Romanian language services of foreign radio stations and, where possible, on Bulgarian, Hungarian and Yugoslav television. The symbol of the national flag with its communist emblem ripped out and the chant, first heard in Bucharest on 21 December, of 'We are the people', both derived from media accounts of recent events in Prague, Berlin and Leipzig. Importantly also, Romanians were able to draw the conclusion that the Soviet Union would not intervene to save Nicolae Ceausescu should his regime run into difficulties.

In December 1989, Romanians followed the events happening in their own country through these same foreign channels and they learned the truth of what had passed in Timisoara. [On December 17, the government violently suppressed demonstrations in Timisoara, killing about 70 citizens.] Both inspired and appalled by the news coming from the city, Romanians took to the streets in Tirgu Mures, Arad, Cluj and Constanta, taunting the government and demanding an end to bloodshed. Once reports of these secondary disturbances had reached the media stations abroad, they were promptly relayed back through the airwaves to Romania, thus setting in train further protests. On 21 December, the tide of protest spilled uncontrollably on to the streets of Bucharest and swiftly brought down the Ceausescu government.

EXPOSING CEAUSESCU'S VULNERABILITY

Television and radio did not just maintain the impetus of the revolution but acted as the channel through which Ceausescu's vulnerability was first made plain. On the official service of Romanian television and radio, broadcasting before the revolution on 21 December, a breach in the facade of the Ceausescu regime was suddenly exposed at a decisive moment and projected around the country. Ceausescu's public humiliation on this occasion emboldened the opposition to his rule and speeded his own demise.

Ceausescu, of course, had not planned it thus. With typical bravado, he intended on the morning of 21 December to make a media display of the strength and resolve of his government in the face of the continuing disorder in Timisoara. In factories throughout the countryside, employees were summoned to attend meetings to deplore the demonstrations in Transylvania. For nine hours, workers were bussed continuously into the centre of the capital itself, ready for a rally which the president had scheduled for midday. Once they had disembarked, the crowd was handed out such typical posters as 'Long live the Party; Long live Ceausescu', as well as more pertinent placards condemning hooliganism and calling for discipline. By late morning approximately 100,000 persons were crammed into the Square of the Republic in front of the Central Committee Building ready to hear Ceausescu's address which was to be carried live on Bucharest radio and television.

A few minutes after midday, Ceausescu appeared on the first floor balcony of the Central Committee Building and began to speak. He never was an impressive orator nor a telegenic performer. His speeches comprised slogans strung together to make sentences and he made his points more by repeated assertion than by reasoned argument. To add cogency to his words, he customarily pounded his fist or gesticulated into the air. The fatuity of the cult of personality stood never more starkly revealed than in the actual presence of the object of worship.

LIVE HUMILIATION

Typically, Ceausescu began his speech by offering 'revolutionary greetings' to the crowd gathered before him; and the crowd equally typically responded with orchestrated chants of 'Ceausescu; Romania: Our Esteem and our Pride'. Suddenly however, the president was interrupted. Shouts of 'Murderer', 'Timisoara' and screams were heard. The live television transmission was interrupted, but not before viewers had caught the blank look of confusion and disbelief on the president's face. Over the next few minutes, militia-men sought to restore order among the crowd, sections of which were already engaged in tearing up posters and in improvising new chants against the government. During the delay, listeners to the radio and television heard only the prere-corded songs of a patriotic choir.

With a semblance of order restored, Ceausescu reappeared on the balcony and transmission of his speech recommenced. After a few empty phrases about strength and unity, and the indepen-dence and integrity of Romania, the president adopted a more placatory tone. He announced a string of improvements in wages, pensions and allowances in the hope of mollifying the crowd. This only confirmed, however, the impression that the ini-tiative lay no longer with the president and that popular discon-tent was forcing him to make concessions. Throughout the re-mainder of his speech, Ceausescu was continually interrupted by agitated shouting and he was able to watch the failure of the militia to restore order in the main body of the rally. Later that day, Ceausescu's speech was rebroadcast with loud chants of support dubbed over the original soundtrack. It is unlikely, how-ever, that this remedy proved at all convincing to those who had previously witnessed Ceausescu's humiliation live on Romanian television and radio.

Once assembled, the crowd gathered in the Square of the Re-public proved hard to dislodge. Armoured cars were brought into the city centre and water cannon and tear gas were used to disperse the protesters. When these failed to have effect, armed units opened fire on the crowd from street corners and from rooftops. The demonstrators, however, broke up into small, run-ning groups of several hundred and evaded all attempts to bring them to order. When the police received reinforcements from units of the army and *securitate* [secret police], protesters built barricades across the streets. As in Timisoara, a few days earlier, bookshops were broken into and armfuls of the president's col-lected works were consigned to flames. Ceausescu's posters were defaced and the walls of the capital were covered with slogans denouncing his rule. Of these, the most popular proved to be, 'Today Timisoara, tomorrow the whole country'. By that evening, Magheru Boulevard, the university quarter and the nearby In-tercontinental Hotel had been taken over by the protesters. By all accounts, most of the demonstrators consisted of young people and students.

ATTEMPTING TO REGAIN CONTROL

Following his humiliation before the crowd, Ceausescu ordered a meeting of the Permanent Bureau of the Polexco [Political Ex-ecutive Committee of the Communist Party]. At an extended ses-sion, its members sought out ways to contain the unrest. As a first step, the president confirmed the wage increases he had announced during his recent speech. Realizing the futility of this gesture, he instructed the patriotic guard units in factories to be put on full alert, commanded the army to shoot on demonstrators as necessary, and ordered the military reinforcement of the Central Committee Building and of the inner quarter of the capital. That evening he held a teleconference with local party secretaries, advising them of the new measures he was putting in train to counter the unrest. On this occasion, Elena Ceausescu [Nicolae's wife] repeatedly intervened in the conference, imploring her husband to be more decisive in his instructions.

Reports from eyewitnesses actually within the Central Committee Building at this time tell of the considerable confusion among officials and party functionaries. The overwhelming consensus of opinion was that the Ceausescu government was on the verge of collapse and was sure to be replaced within the next 24 hours, if not sooner. This conviction was supported by reports that individual units of the army were failing to obey instructions to shoot and that some indeed had already defected to the side of the demonstrators. The belief that the collapse of the regime was imminent prompted a number of important groups within the political and military elite to move towards forming a successor government. The full details of these events have yet to be revealed, while conjecture and deliberate disinformation on the part of the main actors have served to confuse the historical record still further. The rapidity with which the new government of the National Salvation Front was formed, strongly suggests that close discussions between members of the party 'old guard', the army and the *securitate* may already have been underway by the time of Ceausescu's flight. It has yet to be shown, however, that these groups had worked out in advance 'a carefully prepared blueprint for taking power', as stated by Michael Shafir.

In the immediate wake of the revolution, members of the newly constituted government took pains to establish that they had not plotted the President's downfall. Indeed, at the time a certain amount of regret was expressed that no such conspiracy had existed since this would have added to the new government's legitimacy and revolutionary credentials. Over the course of 1990, however, it was gradually divulged that a major 'breach' in the army and *securitate* had been achieved, which involved some 20 generals gathered in a Military Resistance Committee. The membership and affiliation of this committee continues to vary according both to the informant and to the political score he is endeavouring to settle. Suffice it to say that had the generals been as committed to despatching Ceausescu as is now commonly maintained, they would surely have turned against him with rather more alacrity and purpose than they in fact displayed. Still, on 21 December, the army was shooting civilians in Cluj, Sibiu, Brasov, Tirgu Mures and Arad as well as in the capital itself. In fact, responsibility for the army's eventual defection probably owed less to the alleged work of any Military Resistance Committee as to the endeavours of the Defence Minister Vasile Milea, the memory of whose deeds has been deliberately effaced by the apologists of the 'military conspiracy' school.

MILEA'S DISOBEDIENCE

Already on 17 December General Milea had experienced Ceausescu's wrath on account of his failure to issue live ammunition to his troops in Timisoara. On this occasion, he had only narrowly kept his job. Milea's continued reluctance to issue unequivocal instructions to the units of the Ministry of National Defence apparently resulted in a fresh outburst from the president on the evening of 21 December. Evidently by this time, Milea's exasperation with Ceausescu was complete. During that night, he issued instructions to various commanders both inside and outside the capital to hold their fire and not to shoot on demonstrators. A further uncorroborated report also tells that Milea deliberately failed to implement Ceausescu's instruction to reinforce the Central Committee Building. Instead, he simply ordered vehicles to parade through the centre of the city to give the impression that something really was being done. Later on, Ceausescu was apparently to complain that he had spent a sleepless night on account of the noise created by all these manoeuvres.

When daybreak came, the extent of Milea's disobedience became clear. The Central Committee Building was only lightly guarded and the streets leading up to it were inadequately protected. At the same time, the earliest reports began to come in from local party secretaries and *securitate* offices that the army was no longer taking any action to put down demonstrations in the provinces. Thus whereas the previous day, the army had shot down six demonstrators in Tirgu Mures, it had now assumed a passive position, simply guarding the party headquarters and leaving the streets to the crowds.

In view of this worrying information, Ceausescu urgently summoned Milea to his conference rooms on the third floor of the Central Committee Building. He instructed Milea to order the army to recommence active operations immediately and to open fire on such units as proved recalcitrant. General Milea refused Ceausescu's order. Accordingly, at about 9:30 A.M. he was taken out of the room and shot by members of the president's personal protection squad. (In some accounts, he was murdered by the president's brother, Ilie Ceausescu.) In what would turn out to be its last lie for Ceausescu, Bucharest radio reported that Milea had committed suicide.

Throughout the night, there had been running battles between demonstrators, the army and units of the *securitate*. The latter were able to make full use of their highly sophisticated radio communications and their network of command centres to surprise and harass the crowds. In a few places they detonated bombs in the hope of spreading panic. The morale of the demonstrators remained, however, firm. They lit candles to the memory of those slain in the fighting and continued improvising songs against the government. Their spirits were kept up by news from the rest of the country telling of demonstrations and strikes for, remarkably, telephone contact between the capital and the provinces had not been lost. During the night of 21–22 December, several shops opened to allow the purchase of fresh supplies of bread. In university halls of residence and in a number of work places, committees were formed to coordinate the swelling movement of protest.

DEFECTIONS

At daybreak, the confusion within the ranks of the army was plain. It seems that the last firm order which the commanders on the spot had been given was Milea's command not to fire. Already the earliest reports of the death of the Minister of Defence had been received, adding to rumour and sapping the army's resolve. One officer later reported, 'As soon as the news of Milea's death broke, the army was in rebellion. That was the turning point. Milea was a true army man and a good commander who had come up through the ranks.' Other accounts tell of how exchanges of news between soldiers and demonstrators led to open fraternization and of how officers looked on uncomprehendingly as Christmas trees were planted on gun turrets.

The bewilderment in the army was matched by equivocation among the security forces. By the morning of 22 December, sections of the *securitate* had plainly defected to the side of the revolution. Whether these groups were acting on their own initiative or on the order of their superiors, who saw which way the tide was turning, is uncertain. It seems probable, however, that a part of the *securitate* USLA [an anti-terrorist arm of the *securitate*] changed sides at a very early stage in the revolution and may even have been manipulating some of the crowd on the morning of 22 December. It is certainly the case, as photographic evidence records, that unidentified persons in plain clothes were directing the demonstrators and exercising an unusual level of control in the events immediately preceding the storming of the Central Committee Building.

Conceivably, these were *securitate* men belonging to the USLA group deputed to guard the building, for their commander, Vasile Ardeleanu, is known to have changed sides at an early stage in the revolution.

CEAUSESCU'S DEPARTURE

From about 9 A.M. on Friday 22 December, the centre of the city began once more to fill up with demonstrators; on this occasion, however, the army took no ostensible measures to control the crowd. Gradually emboldened, and shouting cries of 'The army is with us', a vast throng pushed its way towards the Central Committee Building. Shortly before midday, groups eventually broke into the party offices, climbing through the ground floor windows. As they made their way up the staircases inside, Nicolae and Elena Ceausescu appeared briefly on a balcony. For a moment, it seemed as if the president might address the crowd laid out along the square before him. But he was pulled inside by his wife. A few minutes later, a helicopter landed on the roof of the building and the Ceausescus clambered inside, pulling in after them Manea Manescu and Emil Bobu, two of their closest collaborators. As it turned out, the inclusion of Manescu and Bobu overburdened the helicopter, forcing it shortly afterwards to descend. In the meantime, a second helicopter dropped leaflets, advising the citizens of Romania of the imminent threat to the independence and integrity of the country. Even as the Ceausescus made their undignified flight from the capital, the president hoped that he could rally support behind his regime by repeating the outworn appeal to national unity.

Within a few minutes of Ceausescu's departure, students appeared on the balcony of the Central Committee Building. They proclaimed the fall of the Ceausescu government, and shouted out the names of those they would like to see serving in its successor. Over the next few hours, a bewildering succession of speakers variously denounced Ceausescu, sang revolutionary songs, and announced the formation of new democratic governments.

Throughout those final 24 hours, Romanian television had devoted itself to playing martial music and to relaying the latest statistical information on the country's economic performance. Only in response to a state of martial law, proclaimed by Ceausescu an hour before his flight, did the official media suggest that anything unusual was happening in the country. Shortly afterwards, a group of young people broke into the television and radio studios. At just before one o'clock, television transmission was interrupted by a crowd headed by the dissident poet, Mircea Dinescu. With the words, 'Brothers, thanks to God, we have won', Dinescu announced the fall of the Ceausescu government and that Romania was free. A few minutes later, Bucharest radio declared in a formal communique that after 23 years the door of the Romanian media had been opened to the people and proclaimed the triumph of the revolution in Bucharest. As news of the events in Bucharest flashed on television screens throughout Romania, crowds poured out into the streets of the country's villages and towns, ransacking party offices and holding huge celebratory processions.

The Early 1990s: Competing Forces for Liberation and Aggression

CHAPTER 4

FREEDOM IN SOUTH AFRICA

NELSON MANDELA

From 1948 to the early 1990s, black South Africans lived under a system of apartheid, or legal segregation, which barred them from politics and strictly controlled where they lived, worked, and went to school. One of the system's harshest critics was Nelson Mandela, a black lawyer and member of the African National Congress (ANC), a civil rights group that was banned by the government. Mandela was arrested for his anti-apartheid activities in 1962 and was subsequently sentenced to life imprisonment for sabotage and treason. As a prisoner, Mandela became an internationally recognized symbol of apartheid repression and a rallying point for critics of the system.

In 1990, the new South African president, F.W. de Klerk, legalized the ANC, released Mandela from prison, and promised a new constitution granting political power to the nation's black majority. By the end of 1991, all apartheid laws had been repealed. In 1993, Mandela and de Klerk shared the Nobel Prize for their actions toward peace and racial harmony in South Africa. Mandela was elected president of South Africa in the nation's first multiracial elections in May 1994 and remained in that office until 1999, when he retired from public life.

The following selection is the text of a speech Mandela delivered to a joint session of the U.S. Congress on June 26, 1990, four months after his release from captivity. In his comments, he stresses the commitment of the ANC to the abolishment of apartheid and urges U.S. leaders to keep economic sanctions against South Africa in place until this goal is achieved.

Nelson Mandela, address to the Joint Session of the U.S. Congress, June 26, 1990.

We have come here to tell you, and through you, your own people, who are equally noble and heroic, of the troubles and trials, the fond hopes and aspirations, of the people from whom we originate. We believe that we know it as a fact that your kind and moving invitation to us to speak here derived from your own desire to convey a message to our people, and according to your humane purposes, to give them an opportunity to say what they want of you, and what they want to make of their relationship with you.

Our people demand democracy. Our country, which continues to bleed and suffer pain, needs democracy. It cries out for the situation where the law will decree that the freedom to speak of freedom constitutes the very essence of legality and the very thing that makes for the legitimacy of the constitutional order.

It thirsts for the situation where those who are entitled by law to carry arms, as the forces of national security and law and order, will not turn their weapons against the citizens simply because the citizens assert that equality, liberty and the pursuit of happiness are fundamental human rights which are not only inalienable but must, if necessary, be defended with the weapons of war.

We fight for and visualize a future in which all shall, without regard to race, colour, creed or sex, have the right to vote and to be voted into all effective organs of state. We are engaged in a struggle to ensure that the rights of every individual are guaranteed and protected, through a democratic constitution, the rule of law, an entrenched bill of rights which should be enforced by an independent judiciary, as well as a multi-party political system.

SERIOUS WORDS

Mr Speaker, We are actually conscious of the fact that we are addressing an historic institution for whose creation and integrity many men and women lost their lives in the war of independence, the civil war and the war against Nazism and Fascism. That very history demands that we address you with respect and candour and without any attempt to dissemble.

What we have said concerning the political arrangements we seek for our country is seriously meant. It is an outcome for which many of us went to prison, for which many have died in police cells, on the gallows, in our towns and villages and in the countries of southern Africa. Indeed, we have even had our political representatives killed in countries as far away from South Africa as France.

Unhappily, our people continue to die to this day, victims of armed agents of the state who are still determined to turn their guns against the very idea of a non-racial democracy. But this is the perspective which Congress will feel happy to support and encourage, using the enormous weight of its prestige and authority as an eminent representative of democratic practice.

ECONOMIC OBJECTIVES

To deny people their human rights is to challenge their very humanity. To impose on them a wretched life of hunger and deprivation is to dehumanise them. But such has been the terrible fate of all black persons in our country under the system of apartheid. The extent of the deprivation of millions of people has to be seen to be believed. The injury is made that much more intolerable by the opulence of our white compatriots and the deliberate distortion of the economy to feed that opulence.

The process of the reconstruction of South African society must and will also entail the transformation of its economy. We need a strong and growing economy. We require an economy that is able to address the needs of all the people of our country, that can provide food, houses, education, health services, social security and everything that makes human life human, that makes life joyful and not a protracted encounter with hopelessness and despair. . . .

The political settlement, and democracy itself, cannot survive unless the material needs of the people, the bread and butter issues, are addressed as part of the process of change and as a matter of urgency. It should never be that the anger of the poor should be the finger of accusation pointed at all of us because we failed to respond to the cries of the people for food, for shelter, for the dignity of the individual.

We shall need your support to achieve the post-apartheid economic objectives which are an intrinsic part of the process of the restoration of the human rights of the people of South Africa. We would like to approach the issue of our economic cooperation not as a relationship between donor and recipient, between a dependent and a benefactor.

MUTUAL BENEFIT

We would like to believe that there is a way in which we could structure this relationship so that we do indeed benefit from your enormous resources in terms of your capital, technology, all-round expertise, your enterprising spirit and your markets. This relationship should, however, be one from which your people should also derive benefit, so that we who are fighting to liberate the very spirit of an entire people from the bondage of the arrogance of the ideology and practice of white supremacy, do not build a relationship of subservient dependency and fawning gratitude.

One of the benefits that should accrue to both our peoples and to the rest of the world, should surely be that this complex South African society, which has known nothing but racism for three centuries, should be transformed into an oasis of good race relations, where the black shall to the white be sister and brother, a fellow South African, an equal human being, both citizens of the world. To destroy racism in the world, we, together, must expunge apartheid racism in South Africa. Justice and liberty must be our tool, prosperity and happiness our weapon.

PEACE, PROCESS AND PRESENT REALITY

You know this more than we do that peace is its own reward. Our own fate, borne by a succession of generations that reach backwards into centuries, has been nothing but tension, conflict and death. In a sense we do not know the meaning of peace except in the imagination. But because we have not known true peace in its real meaning; because, for centuries, generations have had to bury the victims of state violence, we have fought for the right to experience peace.

On the initiative of the ANC, the process towards the conclusion of a peaceful settlement has started. According to a logic dictated by our situation, we are engaged in an effort which includes the removal of obstacles to negotiations. This will be followed by a negotiated determination of the mechanism which will draw up the new constitution.

This should lead to the formation of this constitution-making institution and therefore the elaboration and adoption of a democratic constitution. Elections would then be held on the basis of this constitution and, for the first time, South Africa would have a body of law-makers which would, like yourselves, be mandated by the whole people.

Despite the admitted commitment of President F.W. de Klerk to walk this road with us, and despite our acceptance of his integrity and the honesty of his purposes, we would be fools to believe that the road ahead of us is without major hurdles. Too many among our white compatriots are steeped in the ideology of racism to admit easily that change must come.

Tragedy may yet sully the future we pray and work for if these slaves of the past take up arms in a desperate effort to resist the process which must lead to the democratic transformation of our country. For those who care to worry about violence in our country, as we do, it is at these forces that they should focus their attention, a process in which we are engaged.

We must contend still with the reality that South Africa is a country in the grip of the apartheid crime against humanity. The consequences of this continue to be felt not only within our borders but throughout southern Africa which continues to harvest the bitter fruits of conflict and war, especially in Mozambique and Angola. Peace will not come to our country and region until the apartheid system is ended.

SANCTIONS MUST CONTINUE

Therefore we say we still have a struggle on our hands. Our common and noble efforts to abolish the system of white minority domination must continue. We are encouraged and strengthened by the fact of the agreement between ourselves, this Congress as well as President George Bush and his administration, that sanctions should remain in place. The purpose for which they were imposed has not yet been achieved.

We have yet to arrive at the point when we can say that South Africa is set on an irreversible course leading to its transformation into a united, democratic and non-racial country. We plead that you cede the prerogative to the people of South Africa to determine the moment when it will be said that profound changes have occurred and an irreversible process achieved, enabling you and the rest of the international community to lift sanctions.

We would like to take this opportunity to thank you all for the principled struggle you waged which resulted in the adoption of the historic Comprehensive Anti-Apartheid Act which made such a decisive contribution to the process of moving our country forward towards negotiations. We request that you go further and assist us with the material resources which will enable us to promote the peace process and meet other needs which arise from the changing situation you have helped to bring about.

TRIBUTE TO THE UNITED STATES

The stand you took established the understanding among the millions of our people that here we have friends, here we have fighters against racism who feel hurt because we are hurt, who seek our success because they too seek the victory of democracy over tyranny. And here I speak not only about you, members of the United States Congress, but also of the millions of people throughout this great land who stood up and engaged the apartheid system in struggle. The masses who have given us such strength and joy by the manner in which they have received us since we arrived in this country.

We went to jail because it was impossible to sit still while the obscenity of the apartheid system was being imposed on our people. It would have been immoral to keep quiet while a racist tyranny sought to reduce an entire people into a status worse than that of the beasts of the forest. It would have been an act of treason against the people and against our conscience to allow fear and the drive towards self-preservation to dominate our behaviour, obliging us to absent ourselves from the struggle for democracy and human rights, not only in our country but throughout the world.

We could not have made an acquaintance through literature with human giants such as George Washington, Abraham Lincoln and Thomas Jefferson and not been moved to act as they were moved to act. We could not have heard of and admired John Brown, Sojourner Truth, Frederick Douglass, W.E.B. DuBois, Marcus Garvey, Martin Luther King Jr., and others, and not be moved to act as they were moved to act. We could not have known of your Declaration of Independence and not elected to join in the struggle to guarantee the people life, liberty and the pursuit of happiness.

We are grateful to you all that you persisted in your resolve to have us and other political prisoners released from jail. You have given us the gift and privilege to rejoin our people, yourselves and the rest of the international community in the common effort to transform South Africa into a united, democratic and non-racial country. You have given us the power to join hands with all people of conscience to fight for the victory of democracy and human rights throughout the world.

We are glad that you merged with our own people to make it possible for us to emerge from the darkness of the prison cell and join the contemporary process of the renewal of the world. We thank you most sincerely for all you have done and count on you to persist in your noble endeavours to free the rest of our political prisoners and to emancipate our people from the larger prison that is apartheid South Africa.

The day may not be far when we will borrow the words of Thomas Jefferson and speak of the will of the South African nation. In the exercise of that will by this united nation of black and white people it must surely be that there will be born a country on the southern tip of Africa which you will be proud to call a friend and an ally, because of its contribution to the universal striving towards liberty, human rights, prosperity and peace among the peoples.

Let that day come now. Let us keep our arms locked together so that we form a solid phalanx against racism to ensure that that day comes now. By our common actions let us ensure that justice triumphs without delay. When that has come to pass, then shall we all be entitled to acknowledge the salute when others say of us, blessed are the peacemakers.

OPERATION DESERT STORM: WAR IN THE PERSIAN GULF

GEORGE BUSH

In August 1990, Iraq, led by President Saddam Hussein, invaded the neighboring country of Kuwait. In the ensuing months, various United Nations resolutions, sanctions, and diplomatic efforts by the United States and other nations failed to persuade Hussein to withdraw his troops. Finally, on January 16, 1991, a multinational coalition of forces led by the United States began an aerial attack on targets in Iraq and Kuwait. The air war continued until mid-February, when ground troops were added to the attack, quickly bringing the conflict to an end.

The following selection is the text of a speech delivered by U.S. president George Bush just hours after the air war commenced. Bush outlines the objectives of the attack and articulates the U.S. interests at stake in the conflict, including the security of the Middle East and the political stability of "the new world order."

Just 2 hours ago, allied air forces began an attack on military targets in Iraq and Kuwait. These attacks continue as I speak. Ground forces are not engaged.

This conflict started August 2nd when the dictator of Iraq invaded a small and helpless neighbor. Kuwait—a member of the Arab League and a member of the United Nations—was crushed; its people, brutalized. Five months ago, Saddam Hussein started this cruel war against Kuwait. Tonight, the battle has been joined.

George Bush, televised address to the American people, January 16, 1991.

This military action, taken in accord with United Nations resolutions and with the consent of the United States Congress, follows months of constant and virtually endless diplomatic activity on the part of the United Nations, the United States, and many, many other countries. Arab leaders sought what became known as an Arab solution, only to conclude that Saddam Hussein was unwilling to leave Kuwait. Others traveled to Baghdad in a variety of efforts to restore peace and justice. Our Secretary of State, James Baker, held an historic meeting in Geneva, only to be totally rebuffed. This past weekend, in a last-ditch effort, the Secretary-General of the United Nations went to the Middle East with peace in his heart—his second such mission. And he came back from Baghdad with no progress at all in getting Saddam Hussein to withdraw from Kuwait.

Now the 28 countries with forces in the Gulf area have exhausted all reasonable efforts to reach a peaceful resolution—have no choice but to drive Saddam from Kuwait by force. We will not fail.

OBJECTIVES

As I report to you, air attacks are underway against military targets in Iraq. We are determined to knock out Saddam Hussein's nuclear bomb potential. We will also destroy his chemical weapons facilities. Much of Saddam's artillery and tanks will be destroyed. Our operations are designed to best protect the lives of all the coalition forces by targeting Saddam's vast military arsenal. Initial reports from General Norman Schwarzkopf are that our operations are proceeding according to plan.

Our objectives are clear: Saddam Hussein's forces will leave Kuwait. The legitimate government of Kuwait will be restored to its rightful place, and Kuwait will once again be free. Iraq will eventually comply with all relevant United Nations resolutions, and then, when peace is restored, it is our hope that Iraq will live as a peaceful and cooperative member of the family of nations, thus enhancing the security and stability of the Gulf.

WHY NOW?

Some may ask: Why act now? Why not wait? The answer is clear: The world could wait no longer. Sanctions, though having some effect, showed no signs of accomplishing their objective. Sanctions were tried for well over 5 months, and we and our allies concluded that sanctions alone would not force Saddam from Kuwait.

While the world waited, Saddam Hussein systematically raped, pillaged, and plundered a tiny nation, no threat to his own. He subjected the people of Kuwait to unspeakable atrocities—and among those maimed and murdered innocent children.

While the world waited, Saddam sought to add to the chemical weapons arsenal he now possesses an infinitely more dangerous weapon of mass destruction—a nuclear weapon. And while the world waited, while the world talked peace and withdrawal, Saddam Hussein dug in and moved massive forces into Kuwait.

While the world waited, while Saddam stalled, more damage was being done to the fragile economies of the Third World, emerging democracies of Eastern Europe, to the entire world, including to our own economy.

The United States, together with the United Nations, exhausted every means at our disposal to bring this crisis to a peaceful end. However, Saddam clearly felt that by stalling and threatening and defying the United Nations, he could weaken the forces arrayed against him.

While the world waited, Saddam Hussein met every overture of peace with open contempt. While the world prayed for peace, Saddam prepared for war.

I had hoped that when the United States Congress, in historic debate, took its resolute action, Saddam would realize he could not prevail and would move out of Kuwait in accord with the United Nations resolutions. He did not do that. Instead, he remained intransigent, certain that time was on his side.

Saddam was warned over and over again to comply with the will of the United Nations: Leave Kuwait, or be driven out. Saddam has arrogantly rejected all warnings. Instead, he tried to make this a dispute between Iraq and the United States of America.

A NEW WORLD ORDER

Well, he failed. Tonight, 28 nations—countries from 5 continents, Europe and Asia, Africa, and the Arab League—have forces in the Gulf area standing shoulder to shoulder against Saddam Hussein. These countries had hoped the use of force could be avoided. Regrettably, we now believe that only force will make him leave.

Prior to ordering our forces into battle, I instructed our military commanders to take every necessary step to prevail as quickly as possible, and with the greatest degree of protection possible for American and allied service men and women. I've told the American people before that this will not be another Vietnam, and I repeat this here tonight. Our troops will have the best possible support in the entire world, and they will not be asked to fight with one hand tied behind their back. I'm hopeful that this fighting will not go on for long and that casualties will be held to an absolute minimum.

U.S. ground troops were deployed to the Persian Gulf to help oust Saddam Hussein's military forces from Kuwait.

This is an historic moment. We have in this past year made great progress in ending the long era of conflict and cold war. We have before us the opportunity to forge for ourselves and for future generations a new world order—a world where the rule of law, not the law of the jungle, governs the conduct of nations. When we are successful—and we will be—we have a real chance at this new world order, an order in which a credible United Nations can use its peacekeeping role to fulfill the promise and vision of the U.N.'s founders.

We have no argument with the people of Iraq. Indeed, for the innocents caught in this conflict, I pray for their safety. Our goal is not the conquest of Iraq. It is the liberation of Kuwait. It is my hope that somehow the Iraqi people can, even now, convince their dictator that he must lay down his arms, leave Kuwait, and let Iraq itself rejoin the family of peace-loving nations.

Thomas Paine wrote many years ago: "These are the times that try men's souls." Those well-known words are so very true today. But even as planes of the multinational forces attack Iraq, I prefer to think of peace, not war. I am convinced not only that we will prevail but that out of the horror of combat will come the recognition that no nation can stand against a world united, no nation will be permitted to brutally assault its neighbor.

THE VOICES OF THE TROOPS

No President can easily commit our sons and daughters to war. They are the Nation's finest. Ours is an all-volunteer force, magnificently trained, highly motivated. The troops know why they're there. And listen to what they say, for they've said it better than any President or Prime Minister ever could.

Listen to Hollywood Huddleston, Marine lance corporal. He says, "Let's free these people, so we can go home and be free again." And he's right. The terrible crimes and tortures committed by Saddam's henchmen against the innocent people of Kuwait are an affront to mankind and a challenge to the freedom of all.

Listen to one of our great officers out there, Marine Lieutenant General Walter Boomer. He said: "There are things worth fighting for. A world in which brutality and lawlessness are allowed to go unchecked isn't the kind of world we're going to want to live in."

Listen to Master Sergeant J.P. Kendall of the 82nd Airborne: "We're here for more than just the price of a gallon of gas. What we're doing is going to chart the future of the world for the next 100 years. It's better to deal with this guy now than 5 years from now."

And finally, we should all sit up and listen to Jackie Jones, an Army lieutenant, when she says, "If we let him get away with this, who knows what's going to be next?"

I have called upon Hollywood and Walter and J.P. and Jackie and all their courageous comrades-in-arms to do what must be done. Tonight, America and the world are deeply grateful to them and to their families. And let me say to everyone listening or watching tonight: When the troops we've sent in finish their work, I am determined to bring them home as soon as possible.

Tonight, as our forces fight, they and their families are in our prayers. May God bless each and every one of them, and the coalition forces at our side in the Gulf, and may He continue to bless our nation, the United States of America.

THE COLLAPSE OF THE SOVIET UNION

BERNARD GWERTZMAN

One of the most momentous international political events of the early 1990s was the sudden breakup of the Soviet Union in 1991. In the following essay, Bernard Gwertzman writes that the nation's collapse was partly a result of the liberal reforms instituted by Soviet president Mikhail Gorbachev in the mid- to late 1980s. By relaxing government control of economic and social life, Gwertzman contends, Gorbachev gave the green light to prodemocracy and nationalist movements within the Soviet Union as well as the Soviet bloc countries of Eastern Europe. After watching the Eastern European nations overthrow communism in 1989, according to Gwertzman, many of the fifteen republics that made up the Soviet Union—including Latvia, Estonia, and Lithuania—began to demand their own independence.

As Gorbachev prepared to grant the republics more power over governmental affairs, a group of hard-line communists staged a coup in August 1991. Their attempt to take over the government failed, according to Gwertzman, in part because the army did not support them. With the communists discredited, the Union quickly unraveled. Gorbachev announced his resignation as president on December 25, effectively declaring the Union dead. Since that time, the fifteen republics—which are now independent nations—have made the transition to democratic governments and free market economies to varying degrees and at varying rates.

Gwertzman is editor of *New York Times on the Web* and co-editor (with Michael T. Kaufman) of *The Decline and Fall of the Soviet Empire*.

After delaying the inevitable for several days, Mikhail S. Gorbachev announced over television on the evening of December 25, 1991, that he was giving up trying to hold the Soviet Union together. "I hereby discontinue my activities at the post of president of the Union of Soviet Socialist Republics," he said.

"I am making this decision on considerations of principle," he explained, saying that he could not support a policy of "dismembering this country and disuniting the state."

And so, at 7:32 P.M., the red flag with hammer and sickle, which had flown over the Kremlin for most of the twentieth century, was lowered, and the white-blue-and-red flag of the Russian federation rose in its place. It marked not only the breakup of one of the world's superpowers, but also the early retirement of one of this era's most interesting political figures. What emerged from the wreckage of the Soviet Union are 15 separate national states, whose future association is still uncertain, and whose overall political, economic, and military power has been dramatically reduced. . . .

THE COUP ATTEMPT

The catalyst for his resignation, of course, was the ill-planned effort by some of his top aides in August 1991 to carry out a coup, which collapsed within days. The Gorbachev appointees, who ran the K.G.B., the police, and the defense forces and included the vice president and former prime minister, had hoped by their plot to stem the disarray in the central authority, to block the plan to grant more authority to the national republics, and to prevent the demise of the Communist Party. In the aftermath, of course, not only did the disarray continue, but the national republics, one after another, all broke with finality from the Soviet Union, and both the Communist Party and Gorbachev were discredited.

Boris N. Yeltsin, Gorbachev's chief political rival, since he had the effrontery to criticize Gorbachev in late 1987, zoomed in popularity for his courage during the brief coup when he stood outside his "White House" Russian republic headquarters and rallied the opposition. As these words are written in the spring of 1992, Yeltsin remains the most prominent public figure in the former Soviet Union, but it is uncertain whether his economic reforms, meant to shock the Russians out of their lethargy, will succeed.

UNDERLYING FORCES

Of course, the underlying reasons for the U.S.S.R.'s collapse are many—a broken-down economy, a political system based largely on fear, and the bankruptcy of the Communist ideology which for a time in this century had attracted millions to its banners. What Gorbachev did was loosen the controls enough to end the decades of fear and unleash a Soviet equivalent of the popular will; which was, very simply, that the Soviet Union should die. It was similar to what had happened in 1989 in Eastern Europe, and in 1979 in Iran. It recalled the words of Alexis de Tocqueville about the French Revolution:

"Thus it was precisely in those parts of France where there had been most improvement that popular discontent ran highest. This may seem illogical—but history is full of such paradoxes. For it is not always when things are going from bad to worse that revolutions break out. On the contrary, it oftener happens that when a people which has put up with an oppressive rule over a long period without protest suddenly finds the government relaxing its pressure, it takes up arms against it."

GORBACHEV'S RULE

But Gorbachev's distinct personality also played a major part in his own downfall. Like the last czar, Gorbachev tried to conciliate and shied away from brutal force. In Eastern Europe, he almost seemed to support the downfall of Communist regimes in 1989, and shocked the West by doing nothing to prevent the collapse of the Berlin wall, something which had stood as a fortress symbol of the dividing line between East and West for nearly 30 years, and which Western leaders had been convinced would have been defended by nuclear arms if they had tried to breach it. At home, Gorbachev wavered between trying to invigorate the society with freedoms totally lacking in the Soviet Union, with constant talk of reforms and democratization, while at the same time trying to reassure the Communist Party that he would not undercut its well-established interests as the ruling force. The effort to be both a good democrat and a good party man in the end proved impossible.

And on one issue he seemed absolutely insensitive: the historic grievances of the peoples of the non-Russian republics for more independence. Adam Ulam of Harvard University believes that if Gorbachev had moved with a concrete plan of increased autonomy for the Baltics and others earlier in his term he could have avoided the rapid slide to independence that occurred at the end, and which ultimately forced Gorbachev to acknowledge the Soviet Union no longer could exist.

What was so surprising about the fall of the Soviet Union was not only that it was so rapid, but also that it went so gently into the night. As Ulam has noted, both German Nazism and Italian fascism died after catastrophic military defeats. The common wisdom for years had been that the Soviet system, with its centralized totalitarian wings, the Communist Party, the K.G.B., the enormous military, and the controlled media would never topple from within, and that any attempts from the outside to bring about the collapse of the empire would lead to nuclear war. The common wisdom proved to be utterly wrong. . . .

NATIONALIST MOVEMENTS

August 1989 marked the fiftieth anniversary of the Hitler-Stalin secret agreement to carve up separate areas of influence, which included Hitler's allowing Stalin to absorb Lithuania, Latvia, and Estonia. Over a million people in the Baltic states were reported to have joined in a 400-mile human chain linking Estonia, Latvia, and Lithuania in a symbol of solidarity and a call for their independence. Other nationalist movements were reported in Central Asia. Even the Ukraine was not immune from the nationalist movements. Keller reported in March that one of Gorbachev's nightmares should be the evident nationalism in the Ukraine. One leader told him in Lvov that "here we're not talking about 1.5 million people, as in Estonia, but 50 million, a nation the size of France or Italy. We think the question of the Soviet Union, whether it survives or not, will be resolved not in Estonia, but in the Ukraine." But Gorbachev seemed to think that these were transitory developments and did not appear to realize the dangers the separatist forces were for his government.

In addition to his frequent travels to the West, Gorbachev also paid the expected visits to the Communist states of Eastern Europe, whose leaders were completely dependent on the Soviet Union for their existence. In the past, Soviet armed forces had been used to quell liberal moves in Hungary in 1956 and Czechoslovakia in 1968, and it was Soviet pressure that forced the imposition of martial law in Poland in 1981. Nevertheless, to the disquiet of the Eastern European Communists, Gorbachev's message on his visits was to hasten reform. He acted, not as the head of an empire, but as one foreign leader to another. It seemed evident that Gorbachev would have easily countenanced the kind of Prague spring of 1968 that led Leonid Brezhnev to send in troops. But Brezhnev realized what Gorbachev apparently didn't, that once Eastern Europeans were allowed to choose freely, they would choose to break with Communism and with the Soviet Union.

THE LOSS OF EASTERN EUROPE

The changes at first were gradual—elections in Poland and Hungary, the two most "liberal" states in Eastern Europe. But starting in August and September, thousands of East Germans were fleeing via Hungary and Czechoslovakia to the West. When nothing was done to stop this, people took to the streets in Czecho-slovakia, East Germany, and Bulgaria. By the end of the year, all the former members of the Soviet bloc had in one way or other done away with the ruling Communist Party and their close links to Moscow. Rumania, which was independent of Moscow, also came apart. Gorbachev's response was almost nonchalant. While in Helsinki on October 25, Gorbachev's spokesman jok-ingly declared that Moscow had adopted the "Sinatra doctrine," in Eastern Europe. "You know the Frank Sinatra song, 'I did it my way,'" said Gennadi I. Gerasimov. "Hungary and Poland are doing it their way."

"I think the Brezhnev doctrine is dead," he added, referring to the armed intervention to stifle liberalism in Eastern Europe which had been used in the past. In trying to answer why Gor-bachev was so relaxed about the loss of Soviet domain, Bill Keller speculated that the Soviet Union had drastically redefined its se-curity interests, recognizing that halting its own economic de-cline was more important to the ultimate survival of Soviet power than enforcing an unpopular Communist gospel. And to some extent, Gorbachev made a policy of the inevitable, realiz-ing that even if he wanted to stop the transformations of Eastern Europe he could not do so without endangering his support at home and abroad. Better to claim the initiative, winning admi-ration in his own bloc and credibility in the West.

NATIONALISM WITHIN THE UNION

With Moscow's acquiescence toward Eastern Europe's indepen-dence, it was perhaps inevitable that this would only fan the na-tionalists within the Soviet Union who had even larger griev-ances. The Eastern Europeans, after all, never were incorporated into the Soviet Union. But virtually every one of the non-Russian republics had a past history of independence, even if for only a few years, before being incorporated into the Soviet Union.

At the start of 1980, Gorbachev went to Vilnius to implore Lithuanians to remain within the Soviet Union, warning that se-cession would mean economic calamity for this tiny republic, while weakening Soviet security and endangering his own posi-tion and program. But his words had no impact on the crowds, who continued to foment for independence. There were new re-ports of moves for independence in Moldavia and in Azerbaijan, where there were mob killings of Armenians, which the Soviet forces could not prevent. Lithuania on March 11 proclaimed it-self a sovereign state and named a non-Communist government headed by Vytautas Landsbergis to negotiate their future rela-tions with Moscow.

On April 13, Gorbachev issued an ultimatum to Lithuania saying that if the republic did not rescind its strongest independence measures within 48 hours, he would order other republics to start cutting off needed supplies. But in the end, Lithuania withstood the boycotts, and the actions only made Gorbachev less popular overseas and in other parts of the country. . . .

SECESSION IN LITHUANIA

However important the developments in the Soviet Union, world attention in January 1991 was on the looming war in the Persian Gulf, caused by Iraq's occupation of Kuwait the preceding summer. Moscow had quickly backed the United States' moves to send troops to Saudi Arabia, and had fully supported the Security Council warnings to Iraq. But if Gorbachev had no problems with the West, the same could not be said of the growing pressures on him brought about by Lithuania's continuing secessionist moves.

For reasons not altogether clear even as these words are written, Gorbachev either ordered or agreed to the intervention of Soviet troops in strength in Lithuania and Latvia, where they seized buildings and in doing so caused many casualties. Yeltsin flew to Vilnius to show support for the independence-minded government. He said that the fate of democratic movements in Russia and elsewhere hinged on the outcome of the confrontation in the Baltics. Sensing that the future was being decided now, 100,000 people marched in Moscow in support of Lithuania, putting Gorbachev clearly on the spot to either reaffirm his democratic moves or continue a crackdown.

President Bush, who was supposed to meet with Gorbachev in Moscow in February, postponed his visit on January 28, ostensibly to direct the war effort; but it was clear that concern about the Baltics also contributed. The issue was even further drawn when Lithuanians voted overwhelmingly on February 10 for independence. On February 19, Yeltsin on television called for Gorbachev's resignation for amassing "absolute personal power" and "deceiving the people." In mid-March, the Soviet people voted in a referendum sponsored by Gorbachev on the question: "Do you support the preservation of the union as a renewed federation of sovereign republics in which the rights of a person of any nationality are fully guaranteed?" The results favored Gorbachev, but Yeltsin, who put his own question on the ballot, also won a strong mandate for a direct election for the Russian presidency.

Meanwhile, on March 28, defying a ban by Gorbachev, and despite a show of military force, some 100,000 Muscovites rallied in support of Yeltsin. Serge Schmemann reported that "as the day

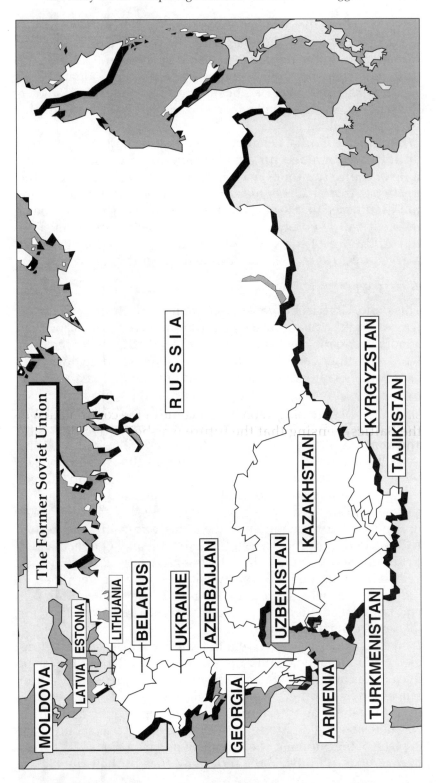

The Former Soviet Union

RUSSIA

MOLDOVA

LATVIA ESTONIA

LITHUANIA

BELARUS

UKRAINE

AZERBAIJAN

GEORGIA

UZBEKISTAN

KAZAKHSTAN

ARMENIA

TURKMENISTAN

KYRGYZSTAN

TAJIKISTAN

drew to a close, the consensus was that Mr. Gorbachev had suffered a serious political setback." By the spring, Gorbachev was
reaching out to the republics to fashion some kind of union accord, but meanwhile Yeltsin in June was elected president of Russia, the first time there had been a popularly elected leader in
Russian history. Gorbachev by comparison was elected only by
his parliament.

On July 24, Gorbachev announced that he had worked out a
draft treaty for a decentralized system of power sharing with
nine of the 15 republics, including Russia. He was to sign the
treaty on August 20. On July 25, Gorbachev told the party Central Committee that to survive it would have to jettison some of
its most hallowed principles, even Marxism–Leninism. This
paved the way for a visit at the end of July by Bush, a visit
marked by an agreement on scaling down nuclear arsenals.

AUGUST 1991

This done, Gorbachev went on vacation in the Crimea, where he
was when the coup occurred against him on August 18 and was
announced to the Soviet people on August 19. It was evident that
whatever other complaints the main plotters had against Gorbachev, they wanted to ensure he did not sign the treaty giving
the republics more power. By August 21, the coup had failed.
With Yeltsin preaching defiance, the military did not back the
coup, and the seemingly inept plotters gave in to public pressure
and allowed Gorbachev to return to the capital.

As Schmemann noted, "It was evident that the balance of
power and the course of the Soviet Union's history had shifted,
that the Communists, who had fought a rearguard action against
change, had suffered a potentially fatal blow, that Mr. Gorbachev
himself was now beholden to the anti-Communist forces that
had rescued him, and above all, to Mr. Yeltsin." Gorbachev did
not improve his situation by refusing on August 22 to join with
Yeltsin in condemning the party. He said he was determined to
remain as party leader; but on August 24, he reversed himself
and issued a statement quitting as party leader and calling for
the seizure of party property.

By August 25, it was evident that the Soviet Union had crum-
bled and Gorbachev could not put the U.S.S.R. back together.
Byelorussia and the Ukraine both announced independence; and
one by one, the other republics followed suit. Gorbachev still
tried to fashion another union treaty to replace the one which
was never signed on August 20. A State Council was set up to act
in place of the Supreme Soviet. One of its first actions was to recognize on September 6 the independence of the three Baltic

states, and the Russian republic officially accepted the name change of the city of Leningrad back to St. Petersburg.

FROM UNION TO COMMONWEALTH

The coup de grace to the Soviet Union followed on December 8, when without any prior warning, the heads of the three Slavic states—Russia, Byelorussia, and Ukraine—announced in Minsk that the Soviet Union had ceased to exist and that they had formed a new "Commonwealth of Independent States." Because only three republics signed that statement, it was repeated on December 21 by 11 of the remaining 15 republics—only Georgia, caught up in its own civil conflict, did not sign—which formally issued a new statement proclaiming the end of the Soviet Union and the formation of the Commonwealth of Independent States. But it was clear that the commonwealth was only a handy title to allow some form of united army to remain and for an Olympic team to be formed. There was no central organizing force behind it, and as the former Soviet Union entered into 1992, there were indeed many questions as to how such neighbors as Russia and Ukraine were going to coexist.

The decline and fall of the Soviet Union was a breathtaking story of enormous consequence. Mikhail S. Gorbachev had come to power determined to help save Communism from itself. In the end, it would be his fate to preside over its demise. The manner of its dissolution occurred in a way that no one had predicted. History, it turned out, was still full of surprises, and had in no sense ended. Indeed, for the peoples of the former Soviet Union, it may have just begun.

THE WAR IN BOSNIA

CAROLE ROGEL

From 1918 to 1991, the country of Yugoslavia consisted of six republics: Bosnia and Herzegovina (often shortened to "Bosnia"),
Croatia, Macedonia, Montenegro, Serbia, and Slovenia. In 1991,
following decades of communist control, the nation began to
break up as the republics expressed competing demands for autonomy versus continued central authority. In June, Croatia and
Slovenia declared their independence, and the Yugoslav National
Army (JNA)—dominated by Serbs—went to war to prevent their
secession. The Serbs were defeated in ten days in Slovenia, but
gained one-third of Croatian territory after seven months of fighting in that republic. Nevertheless, Slovenia and the remainder of
Croatia were recognized as independent nations in January 1992.
Macedonia declared itself autonomous in September 1991 and
made a relatively peaceful transition to independence.

In March 1992, Bosnia and Herzegovina declared its independence. Ethnic Serbs within Bosnia—about one-third of the republic's population—opposed this action and went to war with
the government, which was made up of Serbs, Croats, and Muslims. In the following selection, Carole Rogel describes the gen-
esis of this war and efforts to bring it to an end. The war was particularly disturbing, Rogel notes, due to the Bosnian Serbs'
deliberate targeting of civilians and its tactic of "ethnic cleansing"—ridding Bosnian territories of Muslims and Croats by forcing them from their homes, raping the women, killing the men,
and setting their towns on fire.

Efforts to negotiate a peace were futile until 1995, when all parties to the conflict signed the Dayton Agreement declaring Bosnia
a sovereign nation composed of two states—one controlled by
Serbs, the other by Muslims and Croats. In the end, the war had
resulted in over 200,000 deaths, had produced over 2 million

The Breakup of Yugoslavia and the War in Bosnia, by Carole Rogel. Copyright © 1998 Carole
Rogel. Reproduced with permission of Greenwood Publishing Group, Inc., Westport, CT.

refugees, and had left the infrastructure of many areas in ruins.

Carole Rogel is associate professor emeritus of history at Ohio State University and the author of *The Slovenes and Yugoslavia, 1890–1914* and *The Breakup of Yugoslavia and the War in Bosnia,* from which this selection was excerpted.

I n November 1990 the Bosnians held a multiparty election, a half year after Slovenia and Croatia and a month before Serbia. The communists were ousted, and members of three national parties replaced them in Bosnia's assembly. The three winning parties were all nationalist and won seats in approximate proportion to the size of their respective national groups. They were the Party of Democratic Action (PDA) (Muslim), the Serbian Democratic Party (SDP), and the Croatian Democratic Party (CDU-BH), a branch of the CDU of Croatia. The three also won all the seats on the presidency, and Alija Izetbegovic (PDA) was chosen to head it. For Bosnia to hold together, all the parties would have to remain committed to Bosnian unity. But events had overtaken Bosnia, and maintaining unity was to prove difficult. Slovenia had already held its referendum for independence (December 1990); Bosnian Croats were being drawn toward Croatia, which was also considering separation; and the Bosnian Serbs were being swayed by the Greater Serbia rhetoric of Radovan Karadzic of the SDP, who would ultimately lead them into war. When Slovenia and Croatia declared independence (June 1991) and war with the JNA [Yugoslav National Army] ensued, President Izetbegovic rejected suggestions that Bosnia cantonize so that its national communities might have autonomy. Thus in September 1991, the Bosnian Serbs acted, as had the Croatian Serbs the previous year, by declaring enclaves of Bosnia to be Serbian autonomous regions (SARs). On October 24, 1991, the assembly's Serbian deputies proclaimed a separate assembly of the Serbian nation.

TOWARD WAR

For the next six months Bosnia was pulled in two directions: it could remain part of a rump Yugoslavia, which Bosnian Serbs favored in a referendum of November 1991, or it could declare independence, which Bosnian Croats and Muslims voted for on February 29/March 1, 1992. The independence vote, which tallied 99.4 percent positive responses from 63 percent of the electorate, had been prompted by an international community proposal that offered all Yugoslav republics the option of being independent. But by spring 1992 Bosnia was damned if it remained in Yugoslavia, and damned if it declared independence. Left in Yugoslavia, it would become another Kosovo or Vojvodina, a part of Greater Serbia and subject to Slobodan Milosevic's political will. Committed to independence, it was certain to face military force, particularly since the JNA was available for war, having stopped fighting in Croatia in January. Izetbegovic tried to keep his republic free of Serbia and free of war, but in the end it was clear he could not do both. Tragically, the mild-mannered and somewhat naive Izetbegovic would not believe war could come and was unprepared to deal with it when it did. At a mid-March meeting in Lisbon the European Community (EC) attempted to head off a confrontation by proposing to create a Bosnia with three constituent parts. All parties, even Izetbegovic, agreed, although he reversed his position a week later. The Bosnian Serbs countered by declaring a Serbian Republic of Bosnia-Hercegovina on March 27. War began ten days later, a day before the EC recognized Bosnia-Hercegovina as an independent state.

Something not known at the time was that both Serbia and Croatia had express designs on Bosnia. Presidents Milosevic and Franjo Tudjman had met in September 1991 and secretly agreed to divide their neighboring republic. Memoirs and interviews with key players in the Yugoslav breakup have confirmed this collusion. Croatia's Tudjman, moreover, conceded as much when he drew the former Yugoslavia's new boundaries on a napkin for a British statesman at a dinner party in London in May 1995. Wartime developments (both Serbs and later Croats, too, fought against the Bosnian army) and the various proposed peace agreements would all stipulate a division of Bosnia in some manner or other. In general, the agreements, including the peace treaty produced in Dayton in November 1995, had the support of Milosevic and Tudjman (some were even proposed by them), and all diminished the multinational unity and strength of Bosnia while providing Serbia and Croatia with opportunities for expansion. It will be easier to understand some of the complexities of the Bosnian war if one keeps in mind the political ambitions of the republic presidents of the former Yugoslavia.

The war in Bosnia began in April 1992 and ended in October 1995. During the first year of fighting, until about May 1993, the leading combatants were the Bosnian Serbs and the Bosnian government. The government, although multinational (Croat, Muslim, and Serb), was usually misleadingly identified as Muslim, partly because its president, Izetbegovic, was Muslim. It had a small (50,000), poorly armed and poorly organized fighting force. (By summer 1994 it had 110,000 troops and was much better organized; the Bosnian Croats, at times allies of the Bosnian army, had 12,000 national defense troops in 1992 and 50,000 by mid-1994.) The Bosnian Serbs were led by Radovan Karadzic, head of the Serbian Democratic Party, and had an army of 80,000, a number that remained constant. These were troops that technically had been released from the JNA but continued to be supported and supplied by Belgrade (rump Yugoslavia or FRY [Federal Republic of Yugoslavia]). They concentrated their attacks in eastern and northern Bosnia with the goal of creating a continuous arc of Serb-held territory that would link Serbia with Serbs in western Bosnia and western Croatia (the Krajina area). Karadzic's forces also repeatedly targeted Sarajevo, Bosnia's capital, with an eye to establishing postwar headquarters there. The Bosnian government, unprepared for war, appealed to the United Nations for assistance. The UN responded by recognizing Bosnia-Hercegovina as an independent state on May 22; on May 30 it imposed sanctions against the aggressor, the FRY (Serbia and Montenegro), for its involvement in the conflict.

In spite of the UN actions, the war continued, and in the late summer and autumn of 1992 reports of concentration camps and crimes against civilians began to fill the media. That summer Bosnians fleeing "ethnic cleansing" and genocide caused refugee numbers to swell, so that by November the figure for all national groups reached 1.5 million (a third of Bosnia's population). When the International Red Cross obtained access to the camps, its investigators concluded that the Serbs were most to blame for the human rights violations, including at least 20,000 rapes. In September the EU and the UN established a permanent Geneva conference to deal with the Bosnia problem. By November 6,000 UNPROFOR [United Nations Protection Force] forces were dispatched to the area to process war prisoners and refugees and to dispense humanitarian aid. The previous month the UN Security Council had attempted, rather lamely, to deal with Serb aerial attacks by declaring Bosnia a "no-fly zone." Early the following year the UN had also established an international court to try war criminals. It passed a resolution to allow NATO to fire on violators of the no-fly zone, and it declared six cities, Sarajevo, Bihac, Gorazde, Srebrenica, Tuzla, and Zepa, "safe areas" under UN protection. For the most part the UN pronouncements were empty gestures that were not enforced and were regularly defied and brazenly violated by Karadzic's Serbs.

ETHNIC CLEANSING

Ethnic cleansing, as a Serbian war policy, had first been implemented in late summer 1991 in eastern Croatia. It aimed at Serbianizing certain Croatian territories by ridding them of non-Serb inhabitants, primarily Croats. The policy of ethnic cleansing, however, was most rigorously applied in Bosnia, beginning shortly after that state's independence was proclaimed in April 1992. Muslims became the primary target of the policy, which active perpetrators have maintained was prepared well in advance and carried out calmly and systematically. Ethnic cleansing became a defining factor in Radovan Karadzic's newly proclaimed Serbian Republic of Bosnia, and Bosnian Serbs became its agents. However, the first "cleansers" were Serbs from Serbia, many of whom belonged to special paramilitary forces (Arkan and Vojislav Seselj led such units), who had refined their cleansing techniques in Croatia the previous year. The policy in Bosnia, implemented first in Muslim villages, began with harassing and terrorizing local inhabitants (civilians), many of whom, fearing for their lives, left voluntarily. The less fortunate were tortured, raped, mutilated, and murdered; their homes and other property were confiscated. By the fall of 1992, the policy was extended to towns and cities, where systematic destruction of Muslim culture and history was undertaken. Mosques, libraries, schools, and public places important to Muslims were all targeted for destruction. Anti-Muslim propaganda played an important role in implementing the policy.

Western governments and the UN were already aware of what was happening in Bosnia in April 1992, but they chose not to reveal it or to intervene on behalf of the victims. The Western media

The Bosnian Serbs' war policy of "ethnic cleansing" forced thousands of Muslim and Croat civilians to flee their homes.

discovered the detention and death camps of Omarska, Trnopolje, and Manjaca in July of that year and widely publicized the horrors, which they compared to the Holocaust against the Jews during World War II. Genocide was occurring again in Europe, and no one was doing anything about it. Yet in spite of a massive media exposé, little would be done to stop the anti-Muslim genocide. As late as summer 1995, when Srebrenica was "cleansed" of its Muslims (6,000 men were executed, while the rest of the town's inhabitants were forced to flee), the powers still failed to act. They continued to treat the Bosnian situation as a humanitarian crisis, sending food to feed the hungry, while looking the other way when it came to identifying and punishing those responsible for the crime. Granted, it might have been difficult to determine exactly who was behind ethnic cleansing. But even Vojislav Seselj, one of ethnic cleansing's boastful agents in Croatia and Bosnia, admitted that the policy was planned in Belgrade and suggested a connection with the Serbian Ministry of Interior. The finger of responsibility pointed ominously to President Slobodan Milosevic of Serbia. But even in late 1995, at the Dayton peace conference (discussed below), the great powers would conveniently relegate the issue of genocide to a virtually powerless war crimes tribunal. The great powers at the end of the twentieth century would prove unwilling to act on behalf of universally held moral principles when it was clearly not in their basic self-interest.

PEACE PROPOSALS

By January 1993 the international community produced a first comprehensive peace proposal, the Vance-Owen plan. It proposed dividing Bosnia into ten provinces—three for each national community and a separate UN-supervised province for Sarajevo. It was difficult to sell the plan to the combatants and their supporters. The negotiators, Cyrus Vance, who represented the UN, and Lord David Owen, who acted on behalf of the EU, traversed the former Yugoslavia seeking compliance while peace talks and truces came and went. In May 1993 the assembly of the Bosnian Serbs, who were the key combatants and in control of about two-thirds of Bosnia, decisively rejected the Vance-Owen proposal.

The next phase of the Bosnian war lasted nearly a year, until March 1994. It began with a new peace proposal—the Owen-Stoltenberg plan—on the table. (Owen had continued as EU envoy, while Thorvald Stoltenberg, a former Norwegian foreign minister, took over Vance's UN job.) The new plan proposed that Bosnia be reconfigured into a confederation of three ethnic units. Serbia's Milosevic and Croatia's Tudjman encouraged adoption of the plan; they had in fact been its coauthors. Bosnia's Izetbegovic, still hoping to maintain a united multinational state (one which the UN, after all, had recognized), boycotted the peace talks; he was firmly opposed to dividing Bosnia along ethnic lines. Until the spring of 1993 the Bosnian government chiefly had the Serbs to worry about, but for the rest of that year Izetbegovic also had to deal with hostile Bosnian Croats, renegade Muslims in the Bihac area, and civil disorder among Muslim crime lords in Sarajevo. The criminals of the capital were dealt with in the autumn in an effective crackdown executed by Bosnia's new prime minister, Haris Silajdzic. The Muslims in northwestern Bosnia (adjacent to Croatia), led by Fikret Abdic, a popular local figure and rival of Izetbegovic, who proposed an autonomous province for the Bihac area, were a more complicated issue. Abdic, who also favored an agreement with Karadzic's Serbs and the Bosnian Croats, continued to be a problem for Bosnian unity until the end of the war.

Izetbegovic's greatest problem in 1993 was the Bosnian Croats, led by Mate Boban. By July 1992 they had established an autonomous Croat state—Herceg-Bosna—centered in southwestern Bosnia. (Tudjman's Croatia later admitted to supporting this move.) In spring 1993, with the Owen-Stoltenberg peace plan on the table, the Bosnian Croats decided to enlarge the territory of their proposed ethnic unit through military action and at the Muslims' expense. This meant ending a formal alliance with the Muslims and fighting against the Bosnian government. Many Croats left Izetbegovic's government at this time, and fierce combat raged between former allies who had until then fought together against the Serbs. The Croat-Muslim war was most vicious in the area of Mostar, a city whose elegant sixteenth-century bridge—a symbol of ethnic and religious harmony—was destroyed by Croat fire in November 1993. Mostar was almost totally destroyed and became a divided city. Civilians on both sides, Croat and Muslim, were killed, "ethnically cleansed," terrorized, or forced to flee. The refugee flow surged again, and the Owen-Stoltenberg plan collapsed.

A Turning Point

At the beginning of 1994 prospects for peace were slimmer than ever. Fighting continued and took on the character of a civil war. All parties engaged in ethnic cleansing and atrocities against civilians. The early victims adopted the aggressors' tactics in dealing with the enemy. Representatives of the international community, working through EU bodies and the UN, scurried about, hoping that diplomatic means would bring about an end to the fighting. In February 1994 there was yet another Serbian bombing of the marketplace in Sarajevo, a bloody massacre filmed by ABC television crews who were in the city at the time.

That bombing marked a turning point in the handling of the Bosnian situation. NATO was brought in to frighten the Serbs, who were given an ultimatum to vacate a twenty-kilometer exclusion zone around Sarajevo. In late February, NATO shot down four Serbian planes near Banja Luka. It should be noted, however, that NATO's move was made in defense of UN personnel only. Bosnian victims of aggression were still without a defender, a situation all the more exasperating because the Serbs, who had inherited the arsenal of the JNA, had the military advantage. The September 1991 UN ban on sale of weapons to the republics of the former Yugoslavia still held. It had been imposed by the UN at the request of the Yugoslav federal government—still headed at the time by Prime Minister Ante Markovic—in hopes of saving a united Yugoslavia. Only in 1994 were the Muslims and Croats able to smuggle in adequate weapons to challenge the Serbs. . . .

RENEWED DIPLOMATIC EFFORTS

By December 30, 1994, Bosnia had been at war for 1,000 days. The estimated number of deaths was 200,000; there were 2 million refugees, 1. 1 million of whom now lived abroad. The Bosnian Serbs appeared to be the victors. The year 1995, however, brought a reversal of fortunes for the Bosnian Serbs, and it also produced a peace agreement. Three interlocking developments determined the course of events: military action in Croatia, NATO bombing in Bosnia, and diplomatic efforts of the Contact Group as orchestrated by the United States. . . .

Diplomatic efforts to end the war in Bosnia heated up in spring and summer 1995. All members of the Contact Group were engaged, although the Americans led the mission. In mid-August three U.S. diplomats who had been involved in shuttling between Serb, Muslim, and Croat factions were killed in an accident on Mt. Igman (between Sarajevo and Pale) while hurrying to meet with a Bosnian government delegation. After their deaths, the peace mission went into even higher gear and became the preserve of Richard Holbrooke, who managed through determination and a forceful personality to accomplish what had been undoable for four years. On September 8 the warring parties agreed to participate in peace talks, based on an accord issued in Geneva. Its broadly drawn basic provisions were (1) that Bosnia-Hercegovina would continue to exist as a legal entity within its existing borders, and (2) that it would consist of two parts—the Muslim-Croat federation that had been established in March 1994, and the Serbian Republic (Republika Srpska) of Bosnia-Hercegovina—each having its own constitution and the right to establish separate relationships with neighboring states.

It is important to stress that in the accord the Serbian Republic, Karadzic's renegade self-proclaimed state within Bosnia, was granted recognition for the first time. The fact that each of the two entities would have separate institutions and the right to separate foreign policies, implying that they would be closely linked to different neighboring states, is also notable. In the future the federation and the Serbian Republic might well become satellites of Croatia and the FRY, respectively, opening the door for a possible division of Bosnia—a fulfillment of the Milosevic-Tudjman agreement of September 1991 to divide it. The warring parties also accepted the accord's general provisions about establishing commissions to deal with elections, human rights, refugees, joint public corporations (e.g., for transportation systems), preservation of national monuments, and an arbitration system for the resolution of current and future disputes.

THE DAYTON AGREEMENT

In October, while preparation for peace talks proceeded in earnest, isolated fighting continued. In mid-October Wright-Patterson Air Force Base, near Dayton, Ohio, became the venue for the deliberations. The talks, which began on November 1,

lasted three weeks and were subject to a news blackout. Anxious journalists busied themselves with human interest stories about the local community or hung around outside the air force base "waiting for the white smoke"—an allusion to the smoke that appears from a Vatican chimney when a new pope has been elected. The representatives of the warring factions were housed separately (and virtually held captive during what were referred to as "proximity talks") while the international community's spokespeople went from delegation to delegation seeking agreement on specific points. It was an arduous three weeks for the negotiators, but Holbrooke and Secretary of State Warren Christopher of the United States, who shuttled back to Dayton from remote parts of the world whenever reluctant Serbs, Croats, or Muslims required additional arm-twisting, were unrelenting. Agreement was finally reached and initialed in Dayton on November 21. Official signing took place on December 14 before an imposing array of world leaders at the Elysée Palace in Paris. . . .

The Dayton agreement confirmed the sovereignty and independence of Bosnia-Hercegovina, now a dual or two-part state. The Muslim-Croat federation would control 51 percent, and the Serbian Republic 49 percent of Bosnian land. There would be a central government and a collective presidency, while each of the two component states would have its own legislative and executive bodies, all to be chosen through internationally supervised free and democratic elections, to be held within six to nine months. The Dayton document also spelled out a military settlement to be supervised by IFOR (Implementation Force), headed by NATO and commanded by a U.S. general. Troops were to withdraw behind cease-fire lines within 30 days, and both heavy weapons and troops were to be removed to their barracks within 120 days, both of which were accomplished within the allotted time. The agreement also guaranteed refugees the right to return to their homes or to be compensated for losses of property. IFOR's mission was to last one year, until December 1996. The implementation of the civilian aspects of Bosnian reconstruction was assigned to a joint civilian commission headed by Carl Bildt, a former conservative prime minister of Sweden. The task of this body was rather vaguely defined, yet its duties (economic reconstruction, restoring law and order, promoting human rights, and holding free elections) were crucial to the success of the Dayton peace. Implementation of auxiliary provisions of the treaty, such as facilitating the work of The Hague war crimes tribunal, was also going to be extremely difficult.

THE LOS ANGELES RIOTS AND THE PLIGHT OF THE INNER CITY

MAXINE WATERS

On March 3, 1991, a group of Los Angeles police officers were videotaped beating African-American motorist Rodney King. The footage, aired repeatedly on television news broadcasts nationwide, outraged the public. Four of the officers involved in the beating were tried for the use of excessive force. On April 29, 1992, when a mostly white jury found the four officers not guilty, riots broke out in Los Angeles. Over the next six days of violence, fire-setting, and looting, at least 42 people were killed and more than 700 businesses were burned, resulting in more than $1 billion in property damage.

While most commentators condemned the rioters, many social critics insisted that the rioting resulted not from a lack of personal responsibility among participants, but from underlying social and economic conditions. Specifically, they argued that years of government neglect of the inner cities had led to widespread poverty and unemployment, giving rise to hopelessness and rage. Among these critics was Maxine Waters, congresswoman for the 35th Congressional District, which includes South Central Los Angeles. The following selection was excerpted from testimony Waters delivered before the U.S. Senate Banking Committee on May 14, 1992, about two weeks after the riots erupted. She contends that during the Reagan-Bush years, reduced gov-

From Maxine Waters's testimony before the U.S. Senate Banking Committee, May 14, 1992.

ernment funding for job programs, along with discrimination in housing and employment, had increased poverty and despair in the inner city, setting the stage for the civil unrest of 1992.

T
he riots in Los Angeles and in other cities shocked the world. They shouldn't have. Many of us have watched our country—including our government—neglect the problems, indeed the people, of our inner-cities for years—even as matters reached a crisis stage.

The verdict in the Rodney King case did not cause what happened in Los Angeles. It was only the most recent injustice—piled upon many other injustices—suffered by the poor, minorities and the hopeless people living in this nation's cities. For years, they have been crying out for help. For years, their cries have not been heard.

I recently came across a statement made more than 25 years ago by Robert Kennedy, just two months before his violent death. He was talking about the violence that had erupted in cities across America. His words were wise and thoughtful: "There is another kind of violence in America, slower but just as deadly, destructive as the shot or bomb in the night. . . . This is the violence of institutions; indifference and inaction and slow decay. This is the violence that afflicts the poor, that poisons relations between men and women because their skin is different colors. This is the slow destruction of a child by hunger, and schools without books and homes without heat in the winter."

What a tragedy it is that America has still, in 1992, not learned such an important lesson.

UNEMPLOYMENT AND HOPELESSNESS

I have represented the people of South Central Los Angeles in the U.S. Congress and the California state Assembly for close to 20 years. I have seen our community continually and systematically ravaged by banks who would not lend to us, by governments which abandoned us or punished us for our poverty, and by big businesses who exported our jobs to Third-World countries for cheap labor.

In LA, between 40 and 50 percent of all African-American men are unemployed. The poverty rate is 32.9 percent. According to the most recent census, 40,000 teenagers—that is 20 percent of the city's 16 to 19 year olds—are both out of school and unemployed.

An estimated 40,000 additional jobs were just lost as a result of the civil unrest the last two weeks. The LA Chamber of Commerce has said that at least 15,000 of these job losses will be permanent. This represents another 10 to 20 percent of South Central LA's entire workforce permanently unemployed. Keep in mind, our region had one of the country's highest unemployment rates before the recent unrest. It is hard to imagine how our community will cope with the additional devastation.

We have created in many areas of this country a breeding ground for hopelessness, anger and despair. All the traditional mechanisms for empowerment, opportunity and self-improvement have been closed.

A DEVASTATING EXPERIMENT

We are in the midst of a grand economic experiment that suggests that if we "get the government off people's backs," and let the economy grow, everyone, including the poor, will somehow be better off. So what have we done the last 12 years?

• We eliminated the Comprehensive Employment Training Act (CETA) and replaced it with the Job Training Partnership Act. In this transition, the federal commitment to job training has shrunk from $23 billion in 1980 to $8 billion now.

• General Revenue Sharing, a program designed to assist local governments to cope with their own problems, was eliminated entirely. Another $6-billion abandonment.

• Community Development Block Grants (CDBG), a building block program for local economic development, was also severely cut. In 1980 the program sent $21 billion to localities; it's now less than $14 billion.

In housing, the federal government virtually walked away from the table. Overall federal support for housing programs was cut by 80 percent.

And Reagan-Bush tried to do more—by trying to eliminate the Job Corps, VISTA [Volunteers in Service to America] and Trade Adjustment Assistance.

The results of this experiment have been devastating. Today, more than 12 million children live in poverty, despite a decade of "economic growth," the precise mechanism we were told would reduce poverty. Today, one in five children in America lives in poverty.

The number of children in poverty increased by 2.2 million from 1979 to 1989. This was true for every sub-group of America's children. White child poverty increased from 11.8 percent to 14.8 percent. Latino children's poverty went from 28 percent to 36.2 percent. And black child poverty increased from 41.2 percent to 43.7 percent.

While the budget cuts of the eighties were literally forcing millions of Americans into poverty, there were other social and economic trends destroying inner-city communities at the same time.

I'm sure everyone has read the results of the Federal Reserve Board's study on mortgage discrimination that demonstrates African-Americans and Latinos are twice as likely as whites of the same income to be denied mortgages.

High-income blacks are more likely to be turned down for a mortgage than low-income whites. These trends were true in all regions of the country and in every bank surveyed.

In Los Angeles, a group called the Greenlining Coalition did its own study of the Bank of America—the area's largest bank and the primary financial institution in South Central Los Angeles. As you know, the Fed recently approved the merger of Bank of America and Security Pacific—the largest bank merger in history. One of the criteria for approval of that merger was the CRA [Community Reinvestment Act] rating of the Bank of America. BofA had earned an "outstanding" CRA rating. Despite this, the Greenlining Coalition's study revealed some startling figures:

• Only 2 percent of all of BofA's loans were made to California's 2.5 million African-Americans.

• Of these, only a trivial number, 156 loans, were made to low-income African-Americans. That comes to only one-fifth of 1 percent of all loans for low-income African-Americans.

• It is estimated that as little as $8 million was loaned to low-income African-Americans, or one-tenth of 1 percent of the $8 billion in home mortgages lent by the bank.

• Only $20 million was loaned to low-income Latinos, and one-fourth of 1 percent of Bank of America's loans went to low-income Asian-Americans.

• In total, only 4 percent of all Bank of America loans were made to low-income Californians.

DISCRIMINATION IN LAW ENFORCEMENT

In law enforcement, the problems are longstanding and well-documented as well:

• In a system where judges and lawyers remain overwhelmingly white, blacks account for a share of the prison population that far outstrips their presence in the population as a whole. According to The Sentencing Project, black men make up 6 percent of the population, but 44 percent of inmates.

• A USA Today analysis of 1989 drug-arrest statistics found that 41 percent of those arrested on drug charges were black, although blacks are estimated to be only 15 percent of the drug-using population.

• A San Jose Mercury News investigation last year of almost 700,000 criminal cases found that "at virtually every stage of pre-trial negotiation, whites are more successful than non-whites." Of the 71,000 adults with no prior criminal record, one-third of the whites had their charges reduced, compared to only one-fourth of blacks and Hispanics.

• A Federal Judicial Center study this year of federal sentences for drug trafficking and firearms offenses found that the average sentence for blacks was 49 percent higher than for whites in 1990, compared to 28 percent in 1984.

Is it any wonder our children have no hope?

The systems are failing us. I could go on and on. All we can hope for is that the President, his Cabinet and Congress understand what is happening. We simply cannot afford the continued terror and oppression of benign neglect—the type of inaction that has characterized the federal government's response to the cities since the late 1970s.

TONI MORRISON WINS THE NOBEL PRIZE

GAIL CALDWELL

Author Toni Morrison was awarded the 1993 Nobel Prize for Literature, becoming the first African American and the eighth woman to receive the award. By 1993, Morrison had authored six novels that chronicled the experience of black Americans throughout U.S. history. In the following essay, *Boston Globe* staff writer Gail Caldwell argues that Morrison's greatness lies in her ability to tell the painful stories of African Americans in a resonant language derived from the black oral tradition. After learning she had won the award, Morrison stated, "Winning as an American is very special—but winning as a black American is a knockout."

T oni Morrison, the acclaimed novelist and critic, has been awarded the 1993 Nobel Prize for Literature. She is the first black American and the eighth woman to be cited for the prestigious award since its inception in 1901.

In its citation, the Swedish Academy lauded Morrison for the "visionary force and poetic import" of her six novels, which include *Song of Solomon* and the Pulitzer Prize–winning *Beloved*. The Academy further praised the 62-year-old professor of humanities at Princeton for the "epic power" of her fiction, for its "unerring ear for dialogue and richly expressive depictions of black America."

Morrison is the 11th American writer to win the Nobel, which last went to an American in 1987 when the prize was awarded to

Joseph Brodsky. Speaking through her publisher, Alfred A. Knopf, Morrison expressed gratitude that a black American had been named by the Academy. "I am outrageously happy," she said. "But what is most wonderful for me, personally, is to know that the prize at last has been awarded to an African-American. Winning as an American is very special—but winning as a black American is a knockout."

BREAKING NEW GROUND

Born Chloe Anthony Wofford in Lorain, Ohio, in 1931, the daughter of Alabama sharecroppers who had migrated north, Morrison began her career of letters in academe and publishing. After teaching stints at Howard and Yale, she became an editor at Random House in 1967. Her first novel, *The Bluest Eye*, was published in 1970, followed by *Sula* and *Song of Solomon*, which won the National Book Critics Circle Award in 1978. *Tar Baby* followed in 1981; in 1983, Morrison resigned from Random House in order to write full-time. She spent five years working on the novel that would become *Beloved*, the story of an ex-slave, Sethe, and her children, which won the Pulitzer Prize in 1988.

By now acknowledged as a cornerstone in African-American literature, Morrison's work broke new ground during a critical time for black writers, particularly black women writers. If they had only a handful of superlative black role models in the literary mainstream—Langston Hughes, Ralph Ellison, Richard Wright, James Baldwin, Zora Neale Hurston—they had even fewer open avenues to literary success. Morrison's early fiction not only authenticated the black experience by delivering the painful stories of a modern dispossessed, it also imbued those tales with a language so resonant it seems to belong as much to myth as to memory. In Morrison's hands, the starkest of tragedies comes transported with the hushed force of gospel singing.

For this singular, magical vocabulary that would soon define her voice, Morrison turned to her childhood and ancestry: to the ghost stories she had heard as a girl, the songs and preaching that were part of the black oral tradition. All her novels are rich with supernatural lore, from the dream imagery of *Sula* to the ghostly narrators of *Beloved* and her most recent novel, *Jazz*. If Gabriel Garcia Marquez had his yellow butterflies and levitating priest to make the enduring mark of the Latin American magic realists, Toni Morrison, too, has her omniscient imagery—her melancholic cadences from the other side of the grave.

But it is the terrible beauty of Morrison's fiction that, above all else, grants it such abiding elegance. Her first novel, *The Bluest Eye*, contains such precisely rendered sorrow that it seems astounding as a first novel; in the black girl Pecola's stagger into madness, one sees "all the waste and beauty of the world." *Song of Solomon*, a rhapsodic epic where a man's determination to fly takes him home again, offers as much celebratory promise as it does grief; the novel solidified Morrison's reputation as a writer of perfect-pitch dialogue and lyrical description. A decade later, Morrison turned to one of the great agonies of history, capturing the ravages of slavery through the story of what a woman would do to save her children.

The tragedy of *Beloved* is almost unendurable; only a voice as sinewy and faithful as Morrison's could have mastered so wrenching a narrative. The novel secured a kind of grand stature for Morrison, assuring her a permanence beyond the capricious reach of literary fame. Far more important, *Beloved* broke tens of thousands of hearts and delivered truths that even history sometimes fails to convey. Such is the job of literature, and rarely in contemporary fiction has it been achieved with such anguished grace.

In 1992 came the publication of *Jazz*, Morrison's sixth novel, as well as a critical work, *Playing in the Dark: Whiteness and the Literary Imagination*. Set in 1920s Harlem, *Jazz* is a lush, sensual prose riff that mirrors its name, while *Playing in the Dark* displays a formidable grasp of the contours and hidden sentiments of American literature—what Morrison calls "the rhetoric of dread and desire." The text of *Playing in the Dark* was originally presented as the Massey Lectures at Harvard; with *Jazz*, it represents a creative intelligence as fluent as it is far-flung.

"A BLACK WOMAN NOVELIST"

Throughout her career, Morrison has embraced her heritage and acknowledged her creative debt to her experience as a black female. In 1986, addressing an international literary congress in New York, she spoke to the obstacles she had overcome: "Had I lived the life that the state planned for me from the beginning," she said, "I would have lived and died in somebody else's kitchen, on somebody else's land, and never written a word.

"That knowledge is bone deep, and it informs everything I do."

Two years later, in an interview with the [Boston] *Globe*, Morrison said that she had wrestled with the difficulty of being known as a black writer, or a woman writer, rather than simply a member of the international community of letters. "So I've just insisted—insisted!—upon being called a black woman novelist," she said. "And I decided what that meant, because I have claimed it. I have claimed what I know. As a black and a woman, I have had access to a range of emotions and perceptions that were unavailable to people who were neither.

"So I say, 'Yes, I'm a black woman writer.' And if I write well enough, then maybe in about five years—or 10, or 15 . . ." Morrison left the sentence unfinished. What she couldn't have known was that, six years later, it would simply be: Toni Morrison, Nobel laureate.

GENOCIDE IN RWANDA

In April 1994, a civil war between two ethnic groups in Rwanda, Africa, became extremely violent when the radical elements of one group, the Hutus, began an all-out slaughter of their enemies, the Tutsis, as well as moderate Hutus. Gradually, Western news agencies began to report that Hutu militias all across the country were hacking Tutsi men, women, and children to death with machetes and other primitive killing tools. In the end, the estimates of the number of people killed ranged from 500,000 to 1 million.

In the following passage, Alain Destexhe argues that although this killing initially appeared to be a sudden, chaotic outbreak of violence, it was in fact a systematic, planned attempt by the Hutus to completely exterminate all Tutsis. As such, he contends, it was an act of genocide on a par with Hitler's attempt to exterminate the Jews during World War II. Destexhe is a Belgian senator and the author of *Rwanda and Genocide in the Twentieth Century*, from which this essay was excerpted.

I t took exactly 50 years for Primo Levi's prediction that 'it could all happen again' to be realised. Even if the circumstances of the Jewish genocide are different in regard both to the scale of the killings and in the methods used, *it* or something very like *it* has indeed happened again. Although it is true that previous massacres of Hutus in Burundi and Tutsis in Burundi and Rwanda seemed very like acts of genocide, they were never part of a concerted plan aimed at what might be called a Final Solution to the Tutsis 'problem' in Rwanda (although there are instinctive reservations about making this kind of comparison). Just as Hitler's grand plan was founded on an engrained European anti-semitism which he played on by singling out the Jews as the source of all Germany's ills, the Hutu radicals are inheritors of the colonial lunacy of classifying and grading different ethnic groups in a racial hierarchy. While the Jews were described by the Nazis as 'vermin', the Tutsis were called *invenzi* ('the cockroaches that have to be crushed'). Anti-Tutsi propaganda presented them as a 'minority, well-off and foreign'—so similar to the image developed to stigmatise the Jews—and thus an ideal scapegoat for all Rwanda's problems. The radicalisation of the Hutu began around 1990, when their monopoly of power was first seriously challenged by the army of the Rwandan Patriotic Front (RPF). This was reinforced by the power-sharing conditions of the 1993 Arusha Accords which offered credible possibilities for national reconciliation and peace for the majority of Rwandans at the expense of the ruling Hutu parties. At that point, the Hutu extremists decided on the relentless pursuit of Tutsis and moderate Hutus.

INCREASING VIOLENCE

The plot was devised within the close circle surrounding President Juvénal Habyarimana. From 1990, at the instigation, and with the active complicity of Habyarimana and his government, massacres of Tutsis increased and went unpunished. Two Hutu parties—a wing of the Movement Républican National for Development (MRND), the only party to have held power since independence, and the Coalition for the Defence of the Republic (CDR), a more recently created, extremist group—increasingly promoted a racist ideology. With the complicity of the army and those in power, they developed a simple strategy for retaining control through the formation of militias and the manipulation of the media, both of which later became tools of the genocide itself.

The militias were set up in order to spread terror. The *Interhamwe* ('those who attack together') and the *Impuzamugambi* ('those who only have one aim'), the youth wings of the MRND and CDR respectively, soon claimed 50,000 members between them. They carried out intimidation raids and 'punitive expeditions' against the terrorized Tutsi population as well as Hutus who supported democracy and negotiations with the RPF. It is not as well-known as it should be that for the previous two or three years an impressive movement in favour of a multi-party system, the rule of law and a respect for human rights had grown up in Rwanda. There were a large number of individual initiatives, the monopoly of one-party power had been broached and independent human rights organisations set up. In the eyes of the CDR and MRND these democrats were traitors who only merited the fate of all traitors. Although there were certainly many obstacles, political change seemed inevitable and reconciliation hovered on the horizon, but only at the expense of the racist parties who had the most to lose from them—and everything to gain by preventing them.

Between 1991 and 1994, alarm bells were ringing and signs were there to be read, in the form of massacres that went unpunished. These warning signals were even reported by the UN Human Rights Commission. In 1993 and 1994, thousands of militia members were given arms and military training by the Rwandan Armed Forces (the FAR) which, thanks to French generosity, grew from 5000 to 40,000 men, thus enabling it to take on both the RPF and the internal opposition. In September 1992, a document originating from FAR headquarters established the distinction between the principal enemy and their supporters. The first is defined as:

> Tutsis inside the country or outside, extremists and longing to return to power, who have never recognised and never will recognise the reality of the 1959 social revolution [when the Tutsi were thrown out of power], and who would take back power in Rwanda by any means possible, including the use of arms.

The second is described as: 'anybody who gives any kind of support to the main enemy' (the Hutu opposition).

ANTI-TUTSI PROPAGANDA

In a country which receives virtually no information from the outside world, local media, particularly the radio, play an essential role. For a large part of the population, a transistor radio is the only source of information and therefore has the potential for exerting a powerful influence. Rwandan radio broadcasts are in two languages, French and the national language, Kinyarwanda, which is spoken by all Rwandans. Less than a year before the genocide began, two close associates of President Habyarimana (his brother-in-law Alphonse Ntimavunda and Félicien Kabuga, a businessman married to his daughter) set up the 'private' radio station, popularly known as Radio Mille Collines. Assured of a large audience thanks to regular programmes of popular music, the programmes in Kinyarwanda broadcast unceasing messages of hate, such as 'the grave is only half full. Who will help us to fill it?' Christened 'the radio that kills' by its opponents, it was the basic instrument of propaganda for the Hutu extremists, and the militias rallied in support of its slogans.

The monthly journal *Kangura* also contributed to spreading

anti-Tutsi racism. Two months after war broke out in October 1990, it published a 'Call to the Conscience of the Bahutu Peoples' accompanied by the 'Ten Bahutu Commandments'. The eighth of these ten commandments pronounced, 'The Hutus should stop feeling any pity for the Tutsis', and the tenth ordered, 'regard as a traitor every Hutu who has persecuted his brother Hutu for reading, spreading and teaching this [Hutu] ideology'. Intent on bringing the ethnic question into the political process, the journal called for all available means to be used to prevent a successful conclusion to the negotiations with the RPF. For the racist Hutu parties, the President had betrayed his people by signing the Arusha Accords, which he had been obliged to accept as a result of international pressure.

THE START OF THE GENOCIDE

On 6 April 1994, the plane carrying President Habyarimana and President Cyprien Ntariyamira of Burundi was shot down by rocket-fire. Although it is not yet known who was behind this assassination, it is clear that it acted as the fuse for the eruption of the violence which led to the greatest tragedy in the history of the country. Even before the national radio station announced the death of the President, death lists were being circulated to facilitate the identification of Hutu opponents, mostly those who supported the democratic movement or promoted human rights. Several ministers in the transition government were assassinated, including members of the democratic opposition such as Prime Minister Agathe Uwilingiyima. These extensive killings veiled the essential fact that although Hutu intellectuals and opponents were being killed, the intention was to systematically eliminate every single Tutsi. As this fundamental distinction was not immediately obvious, neither was it clear at the beginning that a genocide was underway, especially in the growing confusion caused by a new RPF attack.

As the stereotypes of physical characteristics do not always provide sufficient identification—and can even be totally misleading—it was the identity cards demanded at the roadblocks set up by the militias that acted as the signature on a death warrant for the Tutsis. As control of the road could not alone ensure that no Tutsi escaped, the militia leaders divided up the territory under their control so that one man was allocated for every ten households in order to systematically search for Tutsis in their immediate localities. In this way every Tutsi family could be denounced by somebody who knew the members personally: pupils were killed by their teachers, shop owners by their customers, neighbour killed neighbour and husbands killed wives in order to save them from a more terrible death. Churches where Tutsis sought sanctuary were particular targets and the scene of some of the worst massacres: 2800 people in Kibungo, 6000 in Cyahinda, 4000 in Kibeho, to give just a few examples. In Rwanda, the children of mixed marriages take the ethnic group of the father and, although many of the Hutu killers—including some militia leaders—had Tutsi mothers, so effective was the indoctrination programme, that even this apparently counted for nothing. Radio Mille Collines encouraged the violence with statements such as that made at the end of April 1994, 'By 5 May, the country must be completely cleansed of Tutsis.' Even the children were targeted: 'We will not repeat the mistake of 1959. The children must be killed too.' The media directly influenced Hutu peasants, convincing them that they were under threat and encouraging them to 'make the Tutsis smaller' by decapitating them. In the northern areas occupied by the RPF, the peasants were astonished that the Tutsi soldiers did not have horns, tails and eyes that shone in the dark as they had been described in radio programmes.

MEDIA MISPERCEPTIONS

The genocide spread rapidly to cover the whole country under the control of the government army. By the end of April, it was estimated that 100,000 people had been killed. Africa had never known massacres on such a scale, yet the world was blind to the reality of events. Reviewing headlines in the French and English language press in those first weeks, there is a clear attempt to present the massacres as part of a civil war: 'Rwanda on Fire', 'Fierce Clashes', 'Slaughter', 'Massacre', 'Civil War', 'Bloody Horror', 'Rwanda Anarchy', 'Fall of Kigali Imminent'. It is rare to find a newspaper that made a distinction between the assassinations of specifically targeted Hutus and the systematic elimination of all Tutsis. It took three weeks from 6 April—a long time in the world of CNN-style news—before editorials finally began comparing the situation in Rwanda with Germany under Nazism and referring to it as a genocide. Overall, however, the word genocide rarely appeared in the main headlines—certainly not often enough to raise the awareness of the general public to the extraordinary event that was taking place. Conversely, 'genocide' and 'Holocaust' were frequently and quite incorrectly applied, even by the most widely respected journalists, in reference to the subsequent cholera epidemic in Goma.

Most commentators in the written press highlighted the political objectives of the crime and resisted the temptation to treat the situation as a 'tribal conflict', as if Hutu and Tutsi were two sides of the same coin. But therein lies both a contradiction and a problem: if the aims were political and not tribal in any way, there was, nonetheless, a clear intention to exterminate a group of people on the basis of their ethnic identity. It was not easy to identify what was at stake here, particularly when those who misused the word genocide were, blinded by the extent of the carnage, unable to recognise the characteristic intentionality of the crime.

There are aspects of this genocide which are new and contemporary; others we have seen before. The use of propaganda, the way control was exercised over the population via the militias, the use of the machinery of local administration: these are all reflections of the modem era. So too are the extreme racist ideology and the radical determination to exterminate all Tutsis in one all-encompassing blow. It would be a mistake to think that the killings were carried out in an anarchic manner: the reality is that they were meticulously well organised. However, the means used to accomplish them were primitive in the extreme: for example, the use of machetes and *unfunis* (wooden clubs studded with metal spikes). Unfortunately, the media eclipsed the first aspect in its preoccupation with the second.

The Voice of a Generation Is Lost: The Suicide of Kurt Cobain

Robert Hilburn

Kurt Cobain, the lead singer of the post-punk rock band Nirvana, gave voice to the feelings of alienation, cynicism, and despair of many American young people in the early 1990s. In April 1994, at the age of twenty-seven, Cobain committed suicide with a shotgun. In the following selection, written days after Cobain's death, Robert Hilburn describes the sadness and grief of the fans who gathered to mourn the singer's passing. Hilburn, the pop music critic for the *Los Angeles Times*, equates the sense of loss to that experienced at the death of Elvis Presley in 1977 and John Lennon in 1980.

The mood of broken teen spirit hangs over this citadel of '90s rock [Seattle] in the aftermath of the suicide of rock star Kurt Cobain.

The words most often heard as you passed through the crowd of 5,000 who gathered in the chill on Sunday evening for a public memorial at the Seattle Center were "why" and "sad."

Courtney Love, Cobain's widow and a rock singer herself, tried to explain the "why" in a message taped for the memorial. It contained excerpts from the suicide note found next to Cobain's body Friday at the couple's lakefront house here.

Reprinted from "In Seattle, a Mood of Teen Dispirit," by Robert Hilburn, *Los Angeles Times*, April 12, 1994. Reprinted with permission.

"I haven't felt the excitement for so many years," Love read from the note, her voice trembling on the tape. "I feel guilty beyond words about these things. . . . When we are backstage and the lights go out and the manic roar of the crowd begins, it doesn't affect me. . . ."

To many of the young people listening to his words, Cobain's lyrics of alienation and anguish were reflections of their own lives. They found comfort in songs such as "Smells Like Teen Spirit" and "All Apologies" that made them turn to Cobain's music with the band Nirvana the way earlier generations turned to John Lennon or Bob Dylan.

Yet Cobain, who often spoke about his own difficult childhood, felt inadequate when people looked to him as a spokesman for his generation. He hated the corruption he saw in mainstream rock and worried that he might be adding to that corruption by assuming the role of a spokesman.

"The fact is," Love continued reading Cobain's note, "I can't fool you, any of you. It simply isn't fair to you or to me. . . . The worst crime I can think of would be to (trick) people by faking it and pretending as if I were having 100% fun."

He ended the note by quoting Neil Young's lyric: "It's better to burn out than to fade away."

An emotional Love followed the line with a bittersweet aside, calling that philosophy "a (expletive) lie."

Tearfully, she added a personal note. "I'm really sorry and I miss him the way you do. . . . I don't know what else I could have done."

But neither Cobain's nor Love's words of explanation eased the sadness in the crowd, most of which was dressed in the loose-fitting flannel shirt and pants identified with the city's grunge rock movement.

THE VOICE OF A GENERATION

"I think the hard part for me is that he really was the voice for most of us," said Rusty Reichert, 18, sitting beside six candles friends had placed on the ground. "He was the one who let the world know that we were here . . . that we were alive and how we felt."

Realizing the degree of disillusionment, memorial organizers invited representatives of the city's Crisis Clinic help group to attend the memorial to counsel youngsters. The first speaker on the program opened with the words, "We're going to get through this. It's OK."

"The hard part is that my folks just don't understand what he meant to me," said another teen-ager, who asked that his name not be used. "The night he died, my dad yelled at me for moping around the house. That just makes it all hurt all the more."

Indeed, the mood around Seattle was far different from similar memorials to earlier, more established rock heroes. At tributes in Memphis following the death of Elvis Presley in 1977 and in New York City after the murder of John Lennon in 1980, you could sense the entire cities in mourning.

You'd hear people of all ages talking tenderly about the singers wherever you went, and see messages on business marquees saying, "We miss you, John" or "R.I.P., Elvis."

Here on Sunday, however, only the young people mourned. For most of the city, it was business as usual on a weekend—shopping, relaxing in the parks or riding bicycles in the exclusive Madrona area where Cobain lived. There were no messages spotted in the downtown area or along the route to Cobain's house.

Despite all the publicity about the suicide, people living as close to the house as three blocks didn't recognize the name Cobain when asked for directions to the house. The only signal of recognition was when Cobain was identified as the rock star who had committed suicide.

"Oh, him. Three blocks down and turn to your left," a man said before resuming his walk.

AN UNDERGROUND FORCE

The generation gap was only natural.

Cobain didn't live long enough for his fans to grow up and be able to look upon him with affection, the way Lennon's and Presley's did.

Even though his band sold an estimated 15 million records around the world, he was still, in terms of the mass pop market, an underground force.

One of the local newscasts underscored the point.

"Before this weekend, you may not have known much about Kurt Cobain . . . ," said the Channel 4 newscaster in the star's hometown.

The fans at the Seattle Center, however, spoke of Cobain with much the same intensity and passion as fans spoke in 1977 about Presley or in 1980 about Lennon.

Jon Ballard, a disc jockey on one of the rock radio stations sponsoring the memorial, said that the station was flooded by calls from despondent Nirvana fans after news of Cobain's death was learned. He equated the reaction to "what it must have been like when Kennedy died."

By the end of the public memorial, some fans turned unruly and ignored police instructions as they crowded into a giant fountain on the grounds of the center.

While the media attention was directed at the public memorial, about 200 of Cobain's family and friends gathered privately a few blocks away at Unity Church of Seattle for their own, unannounced funeral services. (Cobain's body was to be cremated and Love, his mother Wendy O'Conner and Nirvana bassist Krist Novoselic were to decide where the ashes would be spread.)

At the funeral, soft chamber music was played over the sound system as mourners, including R.E.M.'s Peter Buck, who now lives here, took their place in pews, which were lined with childhood photos of Cobain.

Novoselic led off a series of spoken tributes. Dressed all in black, Love read from the Bible and then read again from the suicide note.

At the end, mourners listened to a tape of some of Cobain's favorite music. One selection offered a clue to what the man who brought comfort to a generation of young people turned to himself in times of need.

The song on the tape was John Lennon's Beatles song "In My Life," a comforting celebration of life that opens "There are places I'll remember all my life, though some have changed. . . ."

Before returning home, Love stopped by the Seattle Center with a few friends, but the area was largely deserted by then.

Nearby, however, some fans stood around a car listening to Nirvana music blaring from the tape player. The song from the *In Utero* album seemed to offer a final benediction to the long, draining weekend:

> *Hate, hate your enemies*
> *Save, save your friends*
> *Find, find your place*
> *Speak, speak the truth.*

THE GROWTH OF THE INTERNET AND THE WORLD WIDE WEB

J. NEIL WEINTRAUT

One of the most significant technological developments of the early 1990s was the rapid growth of the Internet and the emergence of the World Wide Web. In the following essay, J. Neil Weintraut traces the history of these changes and explores their impact on society. He argues that the Internet will benefit the world by altering the nature of business, improving communication, and allowing new avenues for creativity. Weintraut is a founding partner of 21st Century Internet Venture Partners, a business that assists in the start-up of new information technology companies.

T hrough a combination of foresight, intuition, and mostly luck, I was one of a then relatively small number of people who grabbed onto the tail of the commercial Internet tiger when it was a mere cub in mid-1994, launching my career from a technology industry analyst to an Internet industry insider and spokesman. Since late 1994 the Internet has been all-consuming for those—including myself—in its vortex.

"All-consuming" is not meant casually. Indeed, I have yet to hear of a description that encapsulates the surreal hyper-speed/happening/different virtual world of the virtual world. Its speed, scope, and scale—plus its uncanny and intrinsic nature to warp or obviate experienced-built knowledge, principles, and concepts—is unlike anything mankind has experienced at least in this century, if not in all time. And for us in the Internet vor-

Excerpted from J. Neil Weintraut's introduction to *Architects of the Web: One Thousand Days That Built the Future of Business,* by Robert H. Reid. Copyright © 1997 by Robert H. Reid. Reprinted by permission of John Wiley & Sons, Inc.

tex, we even get *paid* to do this. As Rick Adams, the founder of UUNET Technologies, described it in December 1994: "We haven't spent a cent on marketing, the phone never stops ringing, and every time we answer it, it's another new customer." This was a precursor, an understatement, of what was to come; in Rick's case, his company went on to be the largest Internet service provider, growing to a size in the subsequent two years like what it normally takes the fastest-growing non-Internet technology companies five to seven years to reach—that's Web time. Put another way, the transformations brought forth by the technology industry over the past 20 years, exemplified by the invention of the microprocessor, the advent of the personal computer, the rise of Microsoft and fall of IBM, are mere gusts of wind compared to the tornado, the hurricane, and the tsunami wave of the Internet.

Furthermore, the Internet is becoming *more* intense. Remember those nonstop customer calls Rick Adams was fielding in 1995? It has gotten even headier; many Internet companies cannot respond to all of the calls and opportunities—jammed switchboards may be the best symbol of the spiraling white-hot intensity of the Internet of 1997. It is appropriate to say that the Internet has gone nuclear.

WHAT IS THE INTERNET?

The Internet—and this is important—is a lot of things. Important because although the Internet is prima facie a technology, it is most significant as the stimulus and means to a new—and better—world, ultimately touching virtually every facet of our lives. Furthermore, for all of the attention and impact of the Internet to date, it's about to get more exciting. The Internet is more important in what it enables than what it is; more phenomenon than fact. Yes, the Internet is networks, software, computers, and other technologies; but more so, it is a catalyst of change, a new mass medium, a culture, a mindwarp, new things never before imagined. In the same manner that the world we live in is attributable to a major meteorite collision with the earth (which transformed our world from its previous era of the dinosaur), the Internet is a modern-day meteorite noteworthy not only because of itself, but rather because of the new world resulting from its aftermath.

It's one thing to "online-ize" a business; it is another to unleash pent-up forces of change that existed long before and are bigger than the Internet, that shatter, upset, revolutionize, and reformulate entire industries and even change the products that they sell. The former is a boring half-step of progress, while the latter is profound, tremendously beneficial, and opportunity-rich—this is the Internet. Similarly, rather than being yet another technology that widens the chasm between affluent and poor schools and students, the Internet promises to equalize the opportunity to be technology-fluent, due to the intrinsic nature of the Internet to provide everyone and anyone—regardless of economic class or geographic circumstance—with access to resources far beyond anything most of us have ever experienced. Additionally, just when conventional media such as print, radio, television, and film have run their course, the Internet provides a profoundly different medium that is spawning a new era of creativity. Indeed, the Internet will even recover great things now lost; notably, writing as an art form, a communications medium, and a lubricant within our society—lost for the past 40 years—is rapidly resurging on Internet E-mails and chat forums.

Transforming the fundamental structure and nature of business, equalizing and empowering us as individuals and as a society, providing a new and better medium both for communicating and for enabling creativity, and challenging our conventional thoughts . . . these are aspects of the Internet. Thus, just as the word "Hollywood" is really a metaphor (films, stars, lifestyle, creativity, and mass-influencer) rather than a location, the Internet is really a metaphor and stimulus to a new world (i.e., its consequences are what's really important, not its substance) rather than just a thing. And yes, the Internet is also a profound collection of computer and network technologies that are revolutionizing computers and communications. . . .

INTERNET: THE TECHNOLOGY

Technologically, the Internet is a network of computers. Not just a few special computers, but millions of all types of computers. Similarly, it is not just a network, but a network of networks—internetworks—and hence, its name.

This borderline technogobble, however, does not identify the key values that lead to the Internet's profoundness. There are many other networks, including the technology, online service, and private networks such as those used on Wall Street or within major companies. Each of these, however, is expensive, constrained in its functionality, and/or limited to private—and hence small—communities of subscribers or employees. In contrast, due to both its technology and philosophical underpinnings, the Internet is trivially inexpensive, can be used for seemingly any type of communication, and—most importantly—is open equally to *everyone*. These factors make the difference between the Internet being just yet another computer network and being the platform for the most phenomenal event and (virtual) thing during our lifetime.

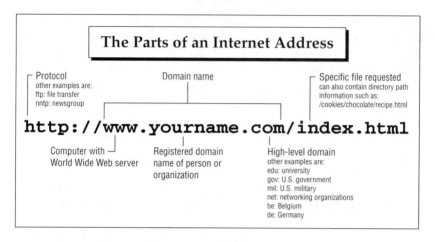

A comparison to the telephone network will help here. With a telephone network, you connect to a single point (e.g., your grandmother), and you communicate with a simple device such as a telephone (or to a lesser extent a facsimile machine or computer, albeit in a cumbersome fashion). With the Internet, you or more specifically your computer connects to the Internet of *millions* of computers (as opposed to a single end-point), and you communicate, well, with just about anything in any way. Each computer is the technological agent representing and maintaining interaction with a company, activity, or individual. Simply put, you can do far more things on the Internet that are either cumbersome or not possible to do with plain old telephones (of course the Internet is cheaper too).

With no more than a point-and-click hyper-link, you can entertain yourself at a Walt Disney site, send electronic mail to Grandma, check employment opportunities at a French winery, get real-time stock quotes at Quote.com or have them effortlessly broadcasted to your home via PointCast, track a Federal Express package, or participate with many other individuals simultaneously in a chat forum in topics ranging from sex to multiple sclerosis. . . .

NUCLEAR PACKETS

No discussion of the Internet would be complete without mentioning its roots in the age of nuclear defense. Indeed, despite its potential as the most significant phenomenon during our lifetime, the Internet shares some background with other technological innovations such as the integrated circuit (invented in 1956 and flourished in the late '70s), and the personal computer (prototyped in 1977 and flourished in the mid '80s); it is one of the longest overnight successes.

The Internet's roots trace back 27 years to a project of the Defense Agency Research Projects Administration (known as DARPA). The project, appropriately enough christened ARPAnet, was to prototype a communications infrastructure for the U.S. military that could withstand a nuclear attack. Indeed, some of the best attributes of the Internet—its architecture, technology, and gestalt—are all legacies of this unwitting nuclear parent.

The design goal of nuclear resilience inspired a network architecture and technology unlike any other, and certainly unlike the standard telephone network. Where the telephone network architecture requires connection through a central switch (which by virtue of its centralization makes thousands of connections vulnerable to a single nuclear strike), the ARPAnet, and hence Internet, allows any computer to tap in anywhere, analogous to tapping many holes down the length of a garden hose. Furthermore, whereas the telephone network architecture is predicated on transferring information along logically-fixed and defined pathways between two points, the Internet instead slices information into small "packets," and each one then bounces around from computer to computer across the nation until it lands on its destination computer, where the collection of packets is reassembled into the original message. This packet technology again complements nuclear resilience; if a nuclear attack compromises one path to a destination, each packet will just keep being rerouted between computers until it finds a path that still exists. Most importantly, the packet-based architecture of the Internet enables many of its fundamental capabilities: Packet communication is far better suited to computer communication—which is of course what the Internet is, namely a network of networks of computers—than the point-to-point technology of telephone networks, and the packet and distributed architecture engenders the openness that sets apart the Internet from all other networks and underlies much of its mass utility. . . .

WEBBING THE INTERNET

For all of its technological wonder, the Internet was an obscure scientific endeavor. This would be changed and changed markedly by the innovation of an idea and technology called the World Wide Web—or the Web—in 1993.

Prior to the Web, the Internet was a world that only a technologist could love, much less use. It required adeptness at painfully cryptic computer programs, and even if one mastered these, other than E-mailing your buddies, where to go or what to do on the Internet was, well, a mystery. The Internet was a massive library of some of the most advanced information and discussion forums in the world from the leading research institutions, but locating and getting the information was obtrusively difficult. It was akin to walking down each aisle of a library, scanning each book just to figure out what is there, but doing all of this in the dark! Furthermore, once you found something relevant to your needs, you then had to read (i.e., download) the entire book, rather than skim or browse parts of it. Worse still, once found, one piece of information often referred to other valuable information but provided no means for locating it, thrusting you into a seemingly endless cycle of hunting in the dark to browse and gather information that was all but impossible to aggregate. Enter the World Wide Web.

Tired of the hunt-and-peck process for locating and obtaining information, a researcher named Tim Berners-Lee at the CERN atomic research center in Switzerland proposed software and networking protocols (protocols are sets of commands and sequences that computers use to communicate over a network) in 1989 that any computer could use to browse—rather than find information by brute force. This effort gained momentum by 1993, culminating in the development of the critical piece of software called a Web browser—and the rest, as they say, is history. (Quoting a report by Matthew Gray of MIT in 1994: Technically, "the World Wide Web was originally proposed in 1989 and the first implementation appeared in 1990. The Web, however, did not gain any widespread popular use until NCSA Mosaic [browser software] became available in early 1993.")

HYPER-LINKING

Berners-Lee's software and protocols created the ability to browse documents and navigate among not only different documents but among different computers—and in fact throughout the Internet—with simple point-and-click commands. Key to the technology was the concept of "hyper-links," which are highlighted words or symbols within documents that when clicked on, cause your computer to automatically and instantaneously jump (in a virtual sense) to, well, anywhere, ranging from the next page in the same document to a different report on a different computer, located, perhaps, halfway around the world. Clicking on a highlighted (i.e., hyper-link–enabled) name of a team in a sports article, would, for example, change the screen to details about the team, recent games, players and positions, and upcoming events. In turn, clicking on a player's name presents a detailed biography of the player, including education, statistics, and commentaries.

This hyper-linking functionality spun the Internet from an information terra incognita into a web of information spanning the world; hence, the moniker World Wide Web.

The Web is the Rosetta stone of the Internet for the masses. The Web makes the Internet ubiquitous, easy, and useful—useful in particular by the masses versus only the technologically elite. Notably, Web software has become easier to use than even the Apple Macintosh computer, a computer long heralded for its ability to be used by almost anyone, yet the Web offers more power, more information, and more services to just about anyone for anything. Not even the most sophisticated computer networks on Wall Street or within major businesses like IBM, or American Airlines' SABRE reservation system, have the power of the Web—and the Web is accessible by anyone for $19.95 a month or less.

Within months of the release of an early version of a Web browser developed by Berners-Lee, Web software spread like wildfire throughout the research community; by June 1993 more than 130 server computers (i.e., the computers where information is stored and served to client computers such as yours and mine) were Web-enabled. As a tipoff of what is to come, the number of Web-enabled server computers grew a thousandfold—yes, 1000 times—to over 150 thousand server computers by July 1996! The statistics of the Web also mirror the transformation of the Internet from academic to commercial, as only 1.5 percent of Web servers (i.e., 2 out of 130) were ".com" addresses in June 1993, whereas that fraction transformed into 90 percent of a markedly higher number, namely 200 thousand, by the end of 1996.

One of the places where the primordial Web software spread during 1993 was the University of Illinois, where it engaged a small group of students including one named Marc Andreessen. They took it upon themselves to rectify many of the shortcomings of the very primitive prototypes then floating around the Internet. Most significantly, their work transformed the appeal of the Web from niche uses in the technical area to mass-market appeal. In particular, these University of Illinois students made two key changes to the Web browser, which hyper-boosted its appeal: they added graphics to what was otherwise boring text-based software, and most importantly, they ported the software from so-called Unix computers that are popular only in technical and academic circles, to the Microsoft Windows operating system, which is used on more than 80 percent of the computers in the world, especially personal and commercial computers. Marc's team circulated a version of the NCSA Mosaic browser that ran on the Microsoft Windows operating system in October 1993. . . .

BETTERING OUR WORLD

The transformation, technology, and prosperity brought about by the Internet will be on a scale unmatched during our lifetime, yet the ultimate value of the Internet lies in its potential for it to better our society, culture, and indeed our world, both for us to benefit from in the immediate future, and for our children tomorrow.

The Internet obviates physical impediments of geography and cost, and empowers the masses with automation and information greater than even the most powerful company or government. Amongst the many ramifications of these subtle but key capabilities will be to make the 21st century the century of equality, creativity, and time. Specifically, the Internet promises to equalize many opportunities across our society, unleash creativity on a scale never before imaginable, and enable us to optimize our ultimate asset, namely, our time.

Following are a few examples to underscore these grand hopes:

• *Equalization.* The Internet promises to equalize the opportunity for everyone to become technology-literate, particularly within our schools.

Historically, computers in schools have mostly been a failure, except in the rare instances where they were successful in favored affluent schools. Why? Because the stand-alone nature of computers (i.e., versus networked computers) necessitated very high and costly efforts to keep them current, and even when they were kept up, they still offered only a spartan collection of useful things to do, all done by isolated users—hardly the makings of an educational tool.

In contrast, the Internet fundamentally obviates these structural problems, thereby both equalizing the ability for anyone or any school of almost any economic means to have use of computer technology, but moreover to gain access to more power and information than has ever been available to anyone, including even the most affluent of schools. Specifically, rather than requiring the latest and most costly computer and software, essentially any computer of recent means can gain access via the Internet to, well, anything, ranging from national magazines to E-mailing to the President of the United States. That's equal opportunity.

CREATIVITY AND TIME

• *Creativity.* Except for the limits of human imagination and resources, the Internet has removed essentially all barriers to being creative—a profound capability that will likely take decades for us to exploit, but when we do, it will be tremendous.

What a refreshing change. Unrelenting broadcast media over the past half-century has inculcated our society into being passive observers rather than making any effort to develop and capture our own sense and opinions about life. Furthermore, even if one could retain sufficient motivation to create, how and to whom would such creativity be distributed beyond the confines of our home and family? Meanwhile, the advent of convenient and relatively low-cost telephone communication has caused the art of writing—including its thoughtful process and resulting insights, as well as command of the language as a skillful tool—to be all but lost in our society.

The Internet changes this predicament. The Internet provides essentially anyone with electronic canvas—be it audio, graphical, textual, animated, or video content—and a means to make available creative work to the masses. Similarly, E-mail and chat forums promise to restore the lost arts of writing and debate— talents that both better us as a culture and become increasingly important in smoothing the increasing factionalization of our society at the same time that the world is getting smaller. Most importantly, the creativity-enabling capabilities of the Internet promise to empower our children to be more creative, expressive, and intelligent than ever before.

• *Time.* The Internet at once is potentially the greatest means of preserving significant amounts of time to spend at our discretion, as well as the greatest threat to consuming even more of our time. Indeed, time more than anything else will be the resource of the next century.

The Internet obviates space as a consideration in our world, leaving only time, and hence amplifying its significance. For example, by eliminating geographic constraints that inherently and conveniently introduced minimum amounts of elapsed time—that could be used, for example, to think—the Internet is making our world instantaneous. This is not necessarily all good. On the positive side, however, in both the automation and the ability to better understand our world and do so more efficiently and conveniently (i.e., select the best product that matches individual needs), the Internet promises to recoup significant amounts of time wasted on geographic "overhead" (i.e., driving to and from stores).

Forecasting the future is difficult. Accordingly, it is amusing to think how naive the grand projections previously discussed will sound five years hence—naive not in the fundamental idea but in the interpretation of the consequences.

CHRISTO WRAPS THE REICHSTAG

WIELAND SCHMIED

In the 1960s, the Bulgarian-born artist known as Christo and his wife and artistic partner Jeanne-Claude became well-known around the world for their large-scale public art projects, which usually involved the use of often brightly colored fabric to wrap or accentuate large objects—both natural and manmade. Most notably, in 1976 they created a 39.5-kilometer-long "Running Fence" out of white nylon fabric in California; in 1983 they surrounded eleven islands in Florida with pink floating fabric; and in 1985 they wrapped the Pont Neuf in Paris in nylon fabric and ropes.

In 1995, Christo and Jeanne-Claude completed one of their most ambitious and controversial projects—wrapping the German Reichstag, a large building that was the home of Germany's parliament in Berlin prior to World War II and again beginning in 1999. The artists had been considering this idea since 1971, when Germany was divided by the Cold War. In the following essay, written in 1977 in anticipation of the action, Wieland Schmied explains that one of the purposes of wrapping the Reichstag would be to encourage the German people to confront their painful and turbulent history and its impact on their contemporary lives. Schmied is the author of numerous books on art and art history.

Christo and Jeanne-Claude's personality and development must be appreciated before one can enter into a discussion of the validity of their project to wrap the Reichstag. Only then can one confine oneself to the project itself. For me there is no question of their seriousness and the objective chance to real-

Excerpted from "Eight Aspects and a Summary," by Wieland Schmied, in *Christo: Reichstag and Urban Projects*, edited by Jacob Baal-Teshuva. Copyright © Prestel Verlag, Munich and New York, 1994. Reprinted with permission.

ize this project. To characterize and understand the work, eight aspects seem to be absolutely essential.

The Philosophical Aspect. The ancient Greeks said that wonder was the beginning of all philosophy. A sense of wonder at trivialities and what is habitual and seemingly self-evident triggers off prolonged thinking about what seems obvious. Christo and Jeanne-Claude's art is always directed toward this philosophical dimension, to further meditation on what is familiar and habitual and aims to bring to our notice things which are near at hand and well-known, and which we easily overlook for just this reason. Christo and Jeanne-Claude achieve this sensibility by either veiling or unveiling. They deprive us of familiar objects by wrapping them, and thus making them strange and mysterious; they make us curious. Rediscovering them from their wrappings, we see them with a new awareness, new eyes.

The Aesthetic Aspect. The state of a wrapped object not only has the negative aspect that the object is withdrawn, estranged from us; it also contains its own formal qualities. The wrapped object—tree, house, tower, whatever, can also be beautiful in its wrapping, can be an aesthetic object. We discover its special outline, form, and volume. The wrapping reflects light, sun, clouds, gleams in many colors, plays an unusual, fascinating game, raises expectations about the wrapped object.

The Technical Aspect. Christo and Jeanne-Claude have great experience in realizing utopian projects; they are fascinated by the magnitude of the task. This fires their imagination and also makes their helpers enthusiastic. Christo and Jeanne-Claude have a host of helpers who have learned from past projects: engineers, technical personnel, experienced and skilled workmen, and helpers who are already familiar with Christo and Jeanne-Claude's work and who can advise them on the choice of materials, fixing, strengthening, etc. The role of the artists lies in the concept and idea for the project, which should at the same time be non-utilitarian, but also sensible. The technical details are given over to professionals—Christo and Jeanne-Claude only supervise the various phases of the realization.

INCLUDING THE PUBLIC

The Social Aspect. Christo and Jeanne-Claude's art seeks the public. It is not feasible without publicity or the participation of the public. It requires active, not only passive, public participation. It is constructed in such a way as to give rise to lasting reflections on it. The process which leads to the realization of a work by Christo and Jeanne-Claude is part of the work of art itself and is the social dimension of the work. The public, regularly confronted with Christo and Jeanne-Claude's plans and ideas at hearings, seems to be included, with all its reactions, within Christo and Jeanne-Claude's work. It is important for Christo and Jeanne-Claude that the public is not only represented through the technicians, workmen, professionals, and students who take part in the project, but also through the general public, which is represented by its members of parliament, politicians, press, and television. Public and official opinions and statements about any of Christo and Jeanne-Claude's projects are for them an integral part of their work. Especially in the case of the *Wrapped Reichstag* project, public opinion—if possible in all districts of Berlin, but also in other German towns—should be prepared and made familiar with Christo and Jeanne-Claude's project through lectures, discussions, films, etc. The artists themselves would be available to the public for questions.

The Financial Aspect. The following fact is decisive. The project will not cost the German taxpayer one penny. Christo and Jeanne-Claude are not interested in subsidies. They finance their own projects—not through a personal fortune (which they do not possess), but through their work. With a project in mind, they sell high-quality collages and drawings to collectors, galleries, and museums. They use the revenue from these sales to realize their project. In this way, their work is self-sufficient.

The Urban Aspect. Christo and Jeanne-Claude's biggest projects have been based on landscape—accentuating, strengthening, or changing the definite impression of a landscape (a rocky coastal strip, a valley in Colorado), they become part of this landscape. Now Christo and Jeanne-Claude are returning to the urban space with which they began. However, this is a much bigger project than the previous wrappings of houses or monuments. The *Wrapped Reichstag* is going to draw attention to the isolated urban situation of this building on the fringe of the vital life-stream of West Berlin, and perhaps it may provoke later architectural and planning ideas.

THE MEANING OF THE REICHSTAG

The Historical Aspect. The Reichstag is part of German history, and in a certain sense its symbol. Do we still possess the Reichstag? Or have we only retained the empty shell, which is filled with the glories and miseries of the past and its controversies and conflicts? Why is the Reichstag so precious to us as a national monument, on the one hand, and on the other so irrevocably burdened with painful memories? Is it only because the building was left without a vital function, a few yards away from the Berlin Wall which separates a city, a country and a people without mercy? Or is it because this empty Reichstag is itself a symbol of the partition, the tragic development of German history—and guilt? When Christo and Jeanne-Claude wrap the Reichstag—for however short a time—they will be putting a finger into a deep wound. This, however, is their intention. Christo and Jeanne-Claude are not looking for thoughtless acclaim from gallery visitors. Their art leads them into confrontation with the present day—into discussions about ecology (as with the *Running Fence* project in California), and now (1977) they are drawing attention to German partition. We should accept this.

The Political Aspect. From the historical aspect, the political one follows. This is, it seems to me, the decisive one. How will the people—and here, the people become the public—react? Will they realize that the example of the wrapping—and therefore the emphasis on a historical building—not only touches a chapter of our history, but touches present-day Germany, our everyday life, in which we live quite comfortably and without too much thought? Are people aware that Christo and Jeanne-Claude are only veiling something which we have missed for a long time and which we only possess as an empty shell? Are they going to react with sensitivity, humor, courage, ingenuity, and spontaneity, the qualities which are specially attributed to the people of Berlin? Are thoughts being activated or only emotions provoked? Here lies the risk in this artistic experiment, but at the same time its importance and its chance.

Summing up, I would like to say that we should have the daring to carry out the project *Wrapped Reichstag.* But it should not be done without being explained to people sufficiently in advance. This seems to me imperative. Against the background of the intense media interest that can be expected, the problematic nature of the project should be discussed in all its aspects and dimensions. Only when there is a general understanding of the project—not of course an undivided consensus, which can never be obtained for any artistic work, and which perhaps is not even desirable—should it be implemented. For the *Running Fence* project in California, Christo and Jeanne-Claude progressed in just this manner. In contrast to California, this project rests not only on the numbers attending meetings, but on a qualitative weighing up of the arguments and a critical examination of the hoped-for result.

Only when the expected (and welcome) controversial debates have arrived at the crucial points, can the realization of the project be most effective. The project will not only make us conscious of our situation at this point in time, historically and politically, but also of our existence between the past and the future. The *Wrapped Reichstag* was realized in 1995.

Toward a New Millennium: The Late 1990s

CHAPTER 5

AFGHANISTAN IN TURMOIL: THE RISE OF THE TALIBAN

PETER MARSDEN

Soviet troops withdrew from Afghanistan in 1989, ending their ten-year campaign against Islamic guerrilla rebels (the Mujaheddin). Despite the Soviet withdrawal, civil war continued as various rebel groups fought the Soviet-backed central government. In the following essay, Peter Marsden describes the emergence of a new Islamic guerrilla group—the Taliban—in 1994. The Taliban quickly made surprising military gains, Marsden writes, taking over the capital city Kabul in September 1996.

The Taliban's goal, according to Marsden, was to disarm the country and establish an Islamic republic. To that end, Taliban leaders imposed strict requirements regarding dress, religious practices, and work roles. Specifically, they required women to wear the *burqa*, a garment that covers them from head to toe, forbade women from working, closed girls' schools, and banned games and music. The Taliban were harshly criticized by many Westerners, including Amnesty International, for these actions, which critics believed violated the human rights of women. Amnesty International also reported that the Taliban beat and tortured citizens, including women and children, who did not comply with their edicts.

Marsden is the information coordinator for the British Agencies Afghanistan Group. He is the author of *The Taliban: War, Religion, and the New World Order in Afghanistan*, from which this essay was excerpted.

T he Taliban appeared to emerge out of nowhere when they first came to the world's notice in October 1994. Their arrival on the Afghan military scene coincided with an initiative by the government of Pakistan to dispatch a trade convoy through Afghanistan, via Kandahar and Herat, to Turkmenistan. As the convoy entered Afghanistan, travelling north from Quetta, it was attacked by an armed group. Immediately, another group came to the rescue and fought off the attackers. These were the Taliban.

After allowing the convoy to proceed, the Taliban moved on Kandahar and took the city with almost no resistance. Kandahar had witnessed virtual anarchy for the previous two years, as a number of Mujahidin [Islamic fundamentalist guerrillas of Afghanistan] groups fought for control. The Taliban were able to seize the faction leaders, killing some and imprisoning others. Having taken the city, they called on the population to surrender their weapons at a designated place and to cooperate with the new authorities in bringing peace to the area. The people duly complied.

The Taliban simultaneously announced that it was their mission to free Afghanistan of its existing corrupt leadership and to create a society that accorded with Islam. They issued decrees in which they required men to wear turbans, beards, short hair and *shalwar kameez* [a loose-fitting, pajama-like garment] and women to wear the *burqa*, a garment that covers the entire body, including the face. Men were strongly encouraged to pray five times a day, ideally in the mosque. Women were advised that it was their responsibility to bring up the next generation of Muslims. To this end, they were prohibited from working. It was also made clear that the education of girls would have to await the drawing up of an appropriate Islamic curriculum by religious scholars, and that this process could start only when the Taliban had control of the whole country. Other decrees banned music, games and any representation of the human or animal form. In order to enforce these bans, televisions and tapes were symbolically displayed in public places.

MOVING WESTWARD

The remarkable success of the Taliban in bringing order to Kandahar earned them considerable popularity and this, building on popular superstition and combined with their distinctive white turbans and obvious religious fervour and purity, lent them an almost supernatural aura. When they moved westwards from Kandahar, their reputation had already travelled before them and they were able to clear the main road of armed groups and bandits with great ease. As they captured positions they seized abandoned weaponry, some of it left in great haste, and encouraged people to join the ranks of their fighters.

Over the winter of 1994–95, the Taliban were able to repeat this pattern many times over and, by February 1995, they were positioned on hilltops overlooking the southern suburbs of Kabul, having taken almost half of Afghanistan. They had even managed to secure the speedy evacuation of Charasyab, to the south of the capital. . . . As they approached Kabul from the south-west they captured the western suburbs at the invitation of the Shi'a group, Hisb-e-Wahdat. . . . In the course of the military operation the Shi'a leader, Abdul Ali Mazari, was taken by the Taliban and he died a few days later in their custody, for reasons that remain unclear.

The occupation of western Kabul proved to be short-lived, however. Government troops launched a major offensive and were able to retake the area within a month of its capture by the Taliban. They were also able to push the Taliban out of Charasyab to positions out of rocket range of Kabul. Thereafter, there was a virtual stalemate between the forces of the Taliban and those of the government, at least in relation to Kabul, until September 1996. During the intervening 18 months, the capital experienced a period of relative calm until the Taliban were able to recover Charasyab and also capture new positions in October 1995. . . .

The winter of 1995–96 was a particularly harsh one for Kabul as food and fuel shortages and spiralling inflation took their toll on a highly impoverished people. Humanitarian agencies pulled out the stops to get relief supplies to the capital, but the task was far from easy. Memories of this hardship were a factor in the relative ease with which the Taliban subsequently took Kabul in September 1996.

THE TALIBAN TAKE HERAT

While the Taliban were endeavouring to take Kabul, there was also intense military activity in western Afghanistan. The city of Herat was under the control of Ismail Khan, who was allied to the government. . . .

Over the ensuing months, there was a stand-off between the forces of the Taliban and Ismail Khan at Delaram, on the border between the provinces of Farah and Helmand. Then, in August 1995, Ismail Khan's forces took the initiative and advanced towards Kandahar. They moved with remarkable speed at first and posed a serious threat to the city. However, they were halted by the Taliban at Girishk, about 120 km west of Kandahar, and then pushed back. The Taliban kept going and, within a relatively short space of time, had taken Shindand and walked into Herat without a fight, entering it on 5 September 1995. . . .

There has been much speculation as to why Ismail Khan gave in so easily to the Taliban and effectively handed over Herat to them. Rumours at the time that there had been differences between Ismail Khan and the central government in Kabul, which had led to Ismail Khan's resignation or dismissal from the post of governor, cannot be substantiated. Another rumour in circulation was that Ismail Khan wished to avoid the destruction of a city he had taken three years to rebuild and that he may not have felt able to count on the support of the population who, having enjoyed a period of peace, were reluctant to take up arms again. The fact that the Taliban had a reputation for behaving relatively well when taking new areas—they did not engage in looting, rape or mindless destruction—may have strengthened an assessment that resistance by the population on any scale could not be relied upon.

THE IMPACT ON HERAT

When the Taliban took Herat they issued edicts on the dress and behaviour of the population, as they had done in Kandahar, ordered the closure of all the girls' schools, and placed a ban on women working. The statue of a horse in the city centre was decapitated because, by representing the animal form, it was seen as being inconsistent with Islam. The Taliban conducted house-to-house searches to disarm the population.

The edicts relating to female access to education and employment had a greater impact than they had had in Kandahar. In Kandahar, the administrative infrastructure had effectively collapsed by the time the Taliban arrived and there were few girls' schools in operation. There were also very few opportunities for women to seek employment outside the home. However, in Herat city in 1994 there was a reported school population of 21,663 girls and 23,347 boys. By contrast, in the rural areas, 1,940 girls were attending school as compared with 74,620 boys. A significant proportion of the teachers were women and it proved necessary to close many boys' schools as a result. Further, much of the population of Herat had lived as refugees in Iran, where female access to education had been provided as a right. The bans on girls being educated, pending the introduction of a new and more appropriate curriculum, and on women working, therefore had a significant impact.

The capture of Herat by the Taliban was felt to be a military occupation, not only because of the restrictions placed on female access to education and employment but also because, culturally and linguistically, the predominantly Pushtun [a traditional tribe] and rural Taliban were very different from the Persian-speaking

Heratis, with their long aesthetic and liberal traditions.

During the early months of Taliban rule in Herat, long queues were reported outside the Iranian consulate as large numbers applied for visas for Iran. Many of these were educated professionals, a proportion of whom had been working in the various government ministries. There was obviously a slowing down in the construction sector, reducing the opportunities for people to engage in daily labouring work and accelerating the process of return to Iran. The repatriation programme from Iran to western Afghanistan ground to a standstill.

Humanitarian agencies sought to engage in dialogue with the Taliban in Herat as they had done in Kandahar. In the latter city, it had proved possible to secure authority for women to work in the health sector and this authority had been extended when the Taliban took Herat. However, the agencies in Herat were not able to achieve any modification of the ban on women working in non-health-related posts or a reversal of the closure of girls' schools.

WALKING INTO KABUL

Following the capture of Herat the Taliban made few gains until, a year later, they suddenly marched into Jalalabad, on 11 September 1996. Again, there was minimal resistance as the Mujahidin leaders who had composed the Nangarhar *shura* [group] opted to leave without much of a fight. The Taliban then surprised all observers by forcing themselves through the apparently impenetrable Sarobi Gorge. After a few days of intense fighting in the eastern suburbs of Kabul, they walked into the capital on 26 September with scarcely a shot being fired. Shockwaves were then felt throughout the world when ex-President Muhammad Najibullah and his brother, who was visiting him, were seized from the protection of the UN compound, within a few hours of the Taliban entering the city, and hanged in a public place. It is still not known whether this hanging was authorised by the Taliban leadership or carried out spontaneously by enthusiastic followers, or whether others, with old scores to settle, took the opportunity created by the situation to wreak their revenge. It was rumoured that the atrocity arose from old antagonisms within the PDPA [People's Democratic Party of Afghanistan]. Others wondered whether Najibullah's years as head of the secret police had played a part.

The population of Kabul would, by this stage, have been apprehensive of a further prolonged siege of the capital. Many had already sold even their most basic possessions and were nearing destitution. When the Taliban entered there was therefore considerable relief and a hope that there might, at last, be peace and the possibility of an improvement in the local economy. It is likely that Rabbani and Masoud were aware of this view amongst the population, and this may have been a factor in their decision not to fight for every last inch of Kabul. The aura of invincibility held by the Taliban may have created an additional concern that the government forces would be unwilling to put up a fight. The government may also have calculated that opposition to the Taliban would grow once they had taken the capital, and Masoud made this view explicit in a number of subsequent statements. . . .

THE IMPACT ON KABUL

In Kabul, the Taliban proceeded to issue the same edicts as they had done in Kandahar and Herat. However, it soon became clear that there was to be a greater degree of enforcement of the Taliban requirements, particularly that men should pray at their local mosques rather than individually and that the dress codes for men and women, including long beards, *shalwar kameez* and turbans for men and the *burqa* for women, should be strictly observed.

There was also a downturn in the economy as there had been in Herat. This was in spite of easier access for trade than there had been during the previous siege of Kabul, and in contrast to the mushrooming of the Kandahar economy during the post-Taliban period. In the case of Kabul, this may have been a consequence of many government servants suddenly losing their jobs or being paid only very irregularly when the Taliban took control. The departure, with the ousted government, of what little was left of the more affluent element of Kabul society may have accelerated this process. Certainly the Kabul money market, which provides a good indicator of the health of the economy, responded very positively to the Taliban takeover during the first week or so, but the afghani then fell in value again. Subsequent problems, with Dostam printing his own banknotes and the ousted government flooding the market with newly printed notes, caused spiralling inflation and a virtual collapse of the afghani.

Whether for economic reasons or fear of renewed conflict, there was a significant outward flow of people from Jalalabad and Kabul following the arrival of the Taliban. Ten thousand people left for Pakistan from Jalalabad in September 1996, some in direct response to a bombing raid launched by government forces. A further 50,000 fled to Pakistan from Kabul between October and December 1996. Provision was made for the new arrivals at Nasirbagh camp near Peshawar. As in Herat, this departure further weakened the government and reduced the pool of skilled professionals able to run an administration.

During the early months after the takeover of Kabul, the Taliban gave every indication of having overextended themselves. It proved difficult for outside organisations and diplomatic missions to be clear as to the nature of the internal decision-making process. There were inconsistencies in some of the public statements made, which created concern and confusion. Some of the soldiers in the streets appeared to be acting in the absence of any clear chain of command.

It was also evident that the Taliban regarded the population of Kabul as being very different from those living in other conquered areas. Many of them had their roots in rural traditions and gave the impression of seeing Kabul as corrupt and decadent. The behaviour of the footsoldiers at times reflected this attitude, and led to a number of incidents on which Amnesty International reported. The Taliban leadership gave every indication that they regretted these early excesses and Mullah Omar, the Taliban leader in Kandahar, issued an appeal on Radio Voice of Shari'a for his followers to treat the population of Kabul kindly.

There were also tensions in Kabul arising from Ahmed Shah Masoud's statements that he hoped the population would rise up against the Taliban. The Taliban were reported to have conducted house-to-house searches for those rumoured to be sympathetic to Masoud, and a number of people were arrested. Because of the absence of records as to who was held where, there was concern over apparent disappearances.

A SCIENTIFIC BREAKTHROUGH: THE CLONING OF AN ADULT MAMMAL

NATIONAL BIOETHICS ADVISORY COMMISSION

In February 1997, scientists in Scotland astounded the world when they successfully cloned a mammal from a single cell for the first time. In order to accomplish this feat, the scientists transferred the cell of an adult sheep into the egg of another sheep, then transplanted the egg into a third animal and brought it to fruition. The resulting animal was an exact genetic replica of the original adult sheep.

This event immediately touched off a wave of speculation about the possibility of cloning humans—especially in the case of infertile couples attempting to have children—and the many safety and ethical concerns attendant on such a proposition. U.S. president Bill Clinton ordered a ban on federal funding of attempts to clone humans using this technique. He also instructed the National Bioethics Advisory Commission (NBAC) to study the issue and make recommendations to him within ninety days. Clinton had created the NBAC by executive order in 1995 to study and make recommendations on ethical issues arising from research on human biology or behavior.

The following selection is the executive summary of the NBAC's report. The NBAC states that the use of the new cloning technique (which is technically referred to as "somatic cell nuclear transfer") to create a human child would be "morally un-

National Bioethics Advisory Commission, *Cloning Human Beings* (Rockville, MD: National Bioethics Advisory Commission, June 1997). Available at http://bioethics.gov/pubs/cloning1/executive.htm.

acceptable." It therefore recommends a three- to five-year moratorium on federal funding of attempts to use the procedure on humans and calls for legislation to prevent such research in the government or private sector.

The idea that humans might someday be cloned—created from a single somatic cell without sexual reproduction—moved further away from science fiction and closer to a genuine scientific possibility on February 23, 1997. On that date, *The Observer* broke the news that Ian Wilmut, a Scottish scientist, and his colleagues at the Roslin Institute were about to announce the successful cloning of a sheep by a new technique which had never before been fully successful in mammals. The technique involved transplanting the genetic material of an adult sheep, apparently obtained from a differentiated somatic cell, into an egg from which the nucleus had been removed. The resulting birth of the sheep, named Dolly, on July 5, 1996, was different from prior attempts to create identical offspring since Dolly contained the genetic material of only one parent, and was, therefore, a "delayed" genetic twin of a single adult sheep.

This cloning technique is an extension of research that had been ongoing for over 40 years using nuclei derived from non-human embryonic and fetal cells. The demonstration that nuclei from cells derived from an adult animal could be "reprogrammed," or that the full genetic complement of such a cell could be reactivated well into the chronological life of the cell, is what sets the results of this experiment apart from prior work. In this report the technique, first described by Wilmut, of nuclear transplantation using nuclei derived from somatic cells other than those of an embryo or fetus is referred to as "somatic cell nuclear transfer."

Within days of the published report of Dolly, President Clinton instituted a ban on federal funding related to attempts to clone human beings in this manner. In addition, the President asked the recently appointed National Bioethics Advisory Commission (NBAC) to address within ninety days the ethical and legal issues that surround the subject of cloning human beings. This provided a welcome opportunity for initiating a thoughtful analysis of the many dimensions of the issue, including a careful consideration of the potential risks and benefits. It also presented an occasion to review the current legal status of cloning and the potential constitutional challenges that might be raised if new legislation were enacted to restrict the creation of a child through somatic cell nuclear transfer cloning.

The Commission began its discussions fully recognizing that

any effort in humans to transfer a somatic cell nucleus into an enucleated egg involves the creation of an embryo, with the apparent potential to be implanted in utero and developed to term. Ethical concerns surrounding issues of embryo research have recently received extensive analysis and deliberation in the United States. Indeed, federal funding for human embryo research is severely restricted, although there are few restrictions on human embryo research carried out in the private sector. Thus, under current law, the use of somatic cell nuclear transfer to create an embryo solely for research purposes is already restricted in cases involving federal funds. There are, however, no current federal regulations on the use of private funds for this purpose.

UNIQUE AND DISTINCTIVE ISSUES

The unique prospect, vividly raised by Dolly, is the creation of a new individual genetically identical to an existing (or previously existing) person—a "delayed" genetic twin. This prospect has been the source of the overwhelming public concern about such cloning. While the creation of embryos for research purposes alone always raises serious ethical questions, the use of somatic cell nuclear transfer to create embryos raises no new issues in this respect. The unique and distinctive ethical issues raised by the use of somatic cell nuclear transfer to create children relate to, for example, serious safety concerns, individuality, family integrity, and treating children as objects. Consequently, the Commission focused its attention on the use of such techniques for the purpose of creating an embryo which would then be implanted in a woman's uterus and brought to term. It also expanded its analysis of this particular issue to encompass activities in both the public and private sector.

In its deliberations, NBAC reviewed the scientific developments which preceded the Roslin announcement, as well as those likely to follow in its path. It also considered the many moral concerns raised by the possibility that this technique could be used to clone human beings. Much of the initial reaction to this possibility was negative. Careful assessment of that response revealed fears about harms to the children who may be created in this manner, particularly psychological harms associated with a possibly diminished sense of individuality and personal autonomy. Others expressed concern about a degradation in the quality of parenting and family life.

SOCIAL AND RELIGIOUS VIEWS

In addition to concerns about specific harms to children, people have frequently expressed fears that the widespread practice of somatic cell nuclear transfer cloning would undermine important social values by opening the door to a form of eugenics or by tempting some to manipulate others as if they were objects instead of persons. Arrayed against these concerns are other important social values, such as protecting the widest possible sphere of personal choice, particularly in matters pertaining to procreation and child rearing, maintaining privacy and the freedom of scientific inquiry, and encouraging the possible development of new biomedical breakthroughs.

To arrive at its recommendations concerning the use of somatic cell nuclear transfer techniques to create children, NBAC also examined long-standing religious traditions that guide many citizens' responses to new technologies and found that religious positions on human cloning are pluralistic in their premises, modes of argument, and conclusions. Some religious thinkers argue that the use of somatic cell nuclear transfer cloning to create a child would be intrinsically immoral and thus could never be morally justified. Other religious thinkers contend that human cloning to create a child could be morally justified under some circumstances, but hold that it should be strictly regulated in order to prevent abuses.

The public policies recommended with respect to the creation of a child using somatic cell nuclear transfer reflect the Commission's best judgments about both the ethics of attempting such an experiment and its view of traditions regarding limitations on individual actions in the name of the common good. At present, the use of this technique to create a child would be a premature experiment that would expose the fetus and the developing child to unacceptable risks. This in itself might be sufficient to justify a prohibition on cloning human beings at this time, even if such efforts were to be characterized as the exercise of a fundamental right to attempt to procreate.

Beyond the issue of the safety of the procedure, however, NBAC found that concerns relating to the potential psychological harms to children and effects on the moral, religious, and cultural values of society merited further reflection and deliberation. Whether upon such further deliberation our nation will conclude that the use of cloning techniques to create children should be allowed or permanently banned is, for the moment, an open question. Time is an ally in this regard, allowing for the accrual of further data from animal experimentation, enabling an assessment of the prospective safety and efficacy of the procedure in humans, as well as granting a period of fuller national debate on ethical and social concerns. The Commission therefore concluded that there should be imposed a period of time in which no attempt is made to create a child using somatic cell nuclear transfer.

MORALLY UNACCEPTABLE

Within this overall framework the Commission came to the following conclusions and recommendations:

I.   The Commission concludes that at this time it is morally unacceptable for anyone in the public or private sector, whether in a research or clinical setting, to attempt to create a child using somatic cell nuclear transfer cloning. The Commission reached a consensus on this point because current scientific information indicates that this technique is not safe to use in humans at this point. Indeed, the Commission believes it would violate important ethical obligations were clinicians or researchers to attempt to create a child using these particular technologies, which are likely to involve unacceptable risks to the fetus and/or potential child. Moreover, in addition to safety concerns, many other serious ethical concerns have been identified, which require much more widespread and careful public deliberation before this technology may be used.

The Commission, therefore, recommends the following for immediate action:

- A continuation of the current moratorium on the use of federal funding in support of any attempt to create a child by somatic cell nuclear transfer.
- An immediate request to all firms, clinicians, investigators, and professional societies in the private and non-federally funded sectors to comply voluntarily with the intent of the federal moratorium. Professional and scientific societies should make clear that any attempt to create a child by somatic cell nuclear transfer and implantation into a woman's body would at this time be an irresponsible, unethical, and unprofessional act.

THE NEED FOR REGULATION

II.   The Commission further recommends that:

- Federal legislation should be enacted to prohibit anyone from attempting, whether in a research or clinical setting, to create a child through somatic cell nuclear transfer cloning. It is critical, however, that such legislation include a sunset clause to ensure that Congress will review the issue after a specified time period (three to five years) in order to decide whether the prohibition continues to be needed. If state legislation is enacted, it should also contain such a sunset provision. Any such legislation or associated regulation also ought to require that at some point prior to the expiration of the sunset period, an appropriate oversight body will evaluate and report on the current status of somatic cell nuclear transfer technology and on the ethical and social issues that its potential use to create human beings would raise in light of public understandings at that time.

III. The Commission also concludes that:

- Any regulatory or legislative actions undertaken to effect the foregoing prohibition on creating a child by somatic cell nuclear transfer should be carefully written so as not to interfere with other important areas of scientific research. In particular, no new regulations are required regarding the cloning of human DNA sequences and cell lines, since neither activity raises the scientific and ethical issues that arise from the attempt to create children through somatic cell nuclear transfer, and these fields of research have already provided important scientific and biomedical advances. Likewise, research on cloning animals by somatic cell nuclear transfer does not raise the issues implicated in attempting to use this technique for human cloning, and its continuation should only be subject to existing regulations regarding the humane use of animals and review by institution-based animal protection committees.

- If a legislative ban is not enacted, or if a legislative ban is ever lifted, clinical use of somatic cell nuclear transfer techniques to create a child should be preceded by research trials that are governed by the twin protections of independent review and informed consent, consistent with existing norms of human subjects protection.

- The United States Government should cooperate with other nations and international organizations to enforce any common aspects of their respective policies on the cloning of human beings.

DELIBERATION AND EDUCATION

IV. The Commission also concludes that different ethical and religious perspectives and traditions are divided on many of the important moral issues that surround any attempt to create a child using somatic cell nuclear transfer techniques. Therefore, the Commission recommends that:

- The federal government, and all interested and concerned parties, encourage widespread and continuing deliberation on these issues in order to further our understanding of the ethical and social implications of this technology and to enable society to produce appropriate long-term policies regarding this technology should the time come when present concerns about safety have been addressed.

V.   Finally, because scientific knowledge is essential for all citizens to participate in a full and informed fashion in the governance of our complex society, the Commission recommends that:

- Federal departments and agencies concerned with science should cooperate in seeking out and supporting opportunities to provide information and education to the public in the area of genetics, and on other developments in the biomedical sciences, especially where these affect important cultural practices, values, and beliefs.

THE PASSING OF A BEAT GENERATION ICON: ALLEN GINSBERG DIES

ROBERT SCHEER

The poet Allen Ginsberg, one of the central members of the Beat Generation of writers of the 1950s, died on April 5, 1997, at the age of seventy. The Beats—which included Ginsberg, Jack Kerouac, William Burroughs, and Lawrence Ferlinghetti—were known for challenging the conservative post–World War II American status quo with writing that was unconventional in both form and content. As one of the preeminent Beats, Ginsberg is said to have influenced artists as diverse as the singer/songwriter Bob Dylan and Czech playwright and politician Vaclav Havel. Aside from being a prolific poet, Ginsberg was also a radical political activist and pacifist who was involved in the protest movements of the 1960s. In the following essay, Robert Scheer, contributing editor to the *Los Angeles Times*, recalls Ginsberg's courage in standing up for his convictions even when confronted with violent opposition.

I sold Allen Ginsberg's poetry back in the early '60s, when San Francisco police would occasionally come through the door of City Lights Books looking to bust my boss, poet publisher Lawrence Ferlinghetti, because one of the authors he published had used the "f" word.

Reprinted from "Poet Is Priest in a Time of Truth and Change," by Robert Scheer, *Los Angeles Times*, April 6, 1994. Reprinted with permission.

The officers' literary standards were quite specific, and my protestation that Allen Ginsberg, often the target of their inquisition, was the most remarkable poet of his time—even celebrated by the likes of William Carlos Williams—was to no avail.

These days there are streets near City Lights named after Beat poets, and even the cops in that now sophisticated town would likely agree with Williams, who wrote in his introduction to Ginsberg's first collection that "poets are damned but they are not blind, they see with the eyes of the angels."

News of Ginsberg's death sends me down to the Midnight Special bookstore on the Promenade in Santa Monica, where "angelheaded hipsters"—franchised now like the espresso from San Francisco's 1950s North Beach—do congregate but don't read and are probably not the best minds of their generation. Although that's what stuffy established people said about Allen Ginsberg and the Beats, and were they ever so wrong.

With a fevered haste that would have caused Ginsberg to giggle, I grabbed the last copy of his extraordinary pamphlet poem "Howl," which was once again missing from my bookshelf. It was borrowed often, but rarely returned, by those old enough to savor it as the obituary of the oppressive '50s and as the first screaming rebirth pains of the maniacal love of freedom that this funky reincarnation of Tom Paine would push past the batons of cops and into the hands of the young who never know better than to think that life doesn't have to be as it is.

Naked Courage

Ginsberg's naked courage is not always evident to us today because of the many battles that he helped win. The love of a man for a man, what Williams referred to in his 1956 introduction to "Howl" as the "effrontery to love a fellow of his own choice and record that love in a well-made poem," is admitted if not accepted as a fact of life. In the days when Ginsberg dared to celebrate his same-sex loves, gay was "fag" and it was, as I recall even in San Francisco, almost always used pejoratively.

Ginsberg's love was universal, and at a time when America, even in the North, was rigidly segregated, Ginsberg was one of those whites who plunged into the most alienated strata of ghettoized America, "dragging themselves through the Negro streets at dawn," as he wrote in "Howl," "looking for an angry fix" and ending with a poetry that was wedded to the sounds of [American jazz musicians] John Coltrane and Thelonious Monk.

A lifelong pacifist who eschewed violence no matter the cause in which it was employed, Ginsberg was one of the first—at a time when kids were ducking under desks in A-bomb civil defense drills—to mention the unmentionable: there would be no survivors, let alone winners, in a nuclear war; there were no good warriors, not Americans or Russians or Vietnamese, only humans led astray to kill.

No one was his enemy, not the police or protesters. I once came upon Ginsberg, a bearded Buddha chanting his calming mantra in the midst of a tear gas rain forest in the Yale yard. We were caught in a mini-riot following Richard Nixon's bombing of Cambodia, and I tried to explain to Ginsberg that events were out of control and he'd better get out of there. He had the most benighted but quizzical response to my entreaty to leave, and asked me how his departure could possibly make things go better for those being clubbed. He was right then as he was throughout the protests of those years, never betraying his pacifist faith to rage, rhetoric or the expediency of cause.

Allen Ginsberg with authors Timothy Leary and Ralph Metzner

"Poet is priest," I wrote of him back in 1960 in a tiny, brown shingle shack in Berkeley where Allen Ginsberg had previously lived and where we collated copies of *Root and Branch*, the first New Left magazine. It was a warning to myself, as much as to the readers, to heed the message of Ginsberg that truth is inevitably chaotic, personal and never organized and official.

A BRAVE AND GENTLE PATRIOT

For more than 40 years, he has been a shadow on our conscience, reminding us of the potential for harm by even the best intentioned. His was the anarchist's independent spirit, but one obsessively nonviolent and always governed by the temperament of the lover.

"America I'm putting my queer shoulder to the wheel," he wrote in 1956 in his poem "America." What a brave and gentle patriot and, of course, poet Allen Ginsberg was.

His unfettered love could be summed up in a line from one of his earliest poems, "Sunflower Sutra": "We're not our skin of grime, we're not our dread bleak dusty imageless locomotive, we're all beautiful golden sunflowers inside."

THE DEATH OF
PRINCESS DIANA

CHARLES SPENCER

On the night of August 31, 1997, Princess Diana of Wales was killed in a car crash in Paris at the age of thirty-six. Her death provoked an enormous response from mourners around the world who praised her for her charity work and her attempts to give her sons a normal life despite their royal heritage. On September 6, an internationally televised funeral service was held at Westminster Abbey. The following selection is the text of a eulogy delivered at the funeral by Diana's brother Charles Spencer. Spencer recalls Diana's sensitivity toward society's outcasts, criticizes the media's treatment of the princess, and pledges to continue to raise her sons as she planned.

I stand before you today the representative of a family in grief, in a country in mourning, before a world in shock. We are all united not only in our desire to pay our respects to Diana but rather, in our need to do so.

For such was her extraordinary appeal that the tens of millions of people taking part in this service all over the world via television and radio who never actually met her feel that they, too, lost someone close to them in the early hours of Sunday morning. It is a more remarkable tribute to Diana than I can ever hope to offer her today.

Diana was the very essence of compassion, of duty, of style, of beauty. All over the world she was a symbol of selfless humanity, a standard-bearer for the rights of the truly downtrodden, a very British girl who transcended nationality, someone with a

Reprinted from Charles Spencer's eulogy for Princess Diana delivered at Westminster Abbey, September 15, 1997.

natural nobility who was classless, who proved in the last year that she needed no royal title to continue to generate her particular brand of magic. Today is our chance to say thank you for the way you brightened our lives, even though God granted you but half a life. We will all feel cheated always that you were taken from us so young, and yet we must learn to be grateful that you came along at all.

Only now you are gone do we truly appreciate what we are now without, and we want you to know that life without you is very, very difficult.

We have all despaired at our loss over the past week, and only the strength of the message you gave us through your years of giving has afforded us the strength to move forward.

There is a temptation to rush to canonize your memory. There is no need to do so. You stand tall enough as a human being of unique qualities not to need to be seen as a saint. Indeed, to sanctify your memory would be to miss out on the very core of your being, your wonderfully mischievous sense of humor with the laugh that bent you double, your joy for life transmitted wherever you took your smile and the sparkle in those unforgettable eyes, your boundless energy, which you could barely contain.

INTUITION AND VULNERABILITY

But your greatest gift was your intuition, and it was a gift you used wisely. This is what underpinned all your wonderful attributes. And if we look to analyze what it was about you that had such a wide appeal, we find it in your instinctive feel for what was really important in all our lives.

Without your God-given sensitivity we would be immersed in greater ignorance at the anguish of AIDS and HIV sufferers, the plight of the homeless, the isolation of lepers, the random destruction of land mines. Diana explained to me once that it was her innermost feelings of suffering that made it possible for her to connect with her constituency of the rejected.

And here we come to another truth about her. For all the status, the glamour, the applause, Diana remained throughout a very insecure person at heart, almost childlike in her desire to do good for others so she could release herself from deep feelings of unworthiness of which her eating disorders were merely a symptom.

The world sensed this part of her character and cherished her for her vulnerability, whilst admiring her for her honesty. The last time I saw Diana was on July the first, her birthday, in London, when typically she was not taking time to celebrate her special day with friends but was guest of honor at a fund-raising charity evening.

Cherished Memories

She sparkled, of course, but I would rather cherish the days I spent with her in March, when she came to visit me and my children in our home in South Africa. I am proud of the fact that, apart from when she was on public display, meeting President Mandela, we managed to contrive to stop the ever-present *paparazzi* from getting a single picture of her.

That meant a lot to her.

These are days I will always treasure. It was as if we'd been transported back to our childhood, when we spent such an enormous amount of time together, the two youngest in the family.

Fundamentally she hadn't changed at all from the big sister who mothered me as a baby, fought with me at school and endured those long train journeys between our parents' homes with me at weekends. It is a tribute to her levelheadedness and strength that despite the most bizarre life imaginable after her childhood, she remained intact, true to herself.

There is no doubt that she was looking for a new direction in her life at this time. She talked endlessly of getting away from England, mainly because of the treatment she received at the hands of the newspapers. I don't think she ever understood why her genuinely good intentions were sneered at by the media, why there appeared to be a permanent quest on their behalf to bring her down. It is baffling. My own, and only, explanation is that genuine goodness is threatening to those at the opposite end of the moral spectrum.

It is a point to remember that of all the ironies about Diana, perhaps the greatest is this: that a girl given the name of the ancient goddess of hunting was, in the end, the most hunted person of the modern age.

Protecting Her Boys

She would want us today to pledge ourselves to protecting her beloved boys, William and Harry, from a similar fate. And I do this here, Diana, on your behalf. We will not allow them to suffer the anguish that used regularly to drive you to tearful despair.

Beyond that, on behalf of your mother and sisters, I pledge that we, your blood family, will do all we can to continue the imaginative and loving way in which you were steering these two exceptional young men so that their souls are not simply immersed by duty and tradition but can sing openly, as you planned.

We fully respect the heritage into which they have both been born, and will always respect and encourage them in their royal role. But we, like you, recognize the need for them to experience as many different aspects of life as possible to arm them spiritually and emotionally for the years ahead. I know you would have expected nothing less from us.

William and Harry, we all care desperately for you today. We are all chewed up with sadness at the loss of a woman who wasn't even our mother. How great your suffering is we cannot even imagine.

I would like to end by thanking God for the small mercies he has shown us at this dreadful time: for taking Diana at her most beautiful and radiant and when she had joy in her private life.

Above all, we give thanks for the life of a woman I am so proud to be able to call my sister: the unique, the complex, the extraordinary and irreplaceable Diana, whose beauty, both internal and external, will never be extinguished from our minds.

THE POPE VISITS CUBA

ANNA HUSARSKA

In January 1998, Pope John Paul II made a five-day visit to the communist nation of Cuba, marking the first time a Catholic pope had journeyed to the island since the communist takeover in 1959 and the subsequent restrictions on religious activity. In the following essay, written in anticipation of the Pope's arrival in Havana, Anna Husarska explains the historical and cultural significance of the papal visit. She compares the Pope's visit to Cuba with his sojourn to communist Poland in 1979. The Pope's visit to Cuba is a less momentous event than his visit to Poland, Husarska concedes, but it may nonetheless inspire the formation of a stronger civil society in the communist island nation. Husarska is a journalist and contributor to the *New Republic* magazine.

"There are only two ways that Cuba's economy may be saved—one possible, the other unlikely," goes a popular joke here [in Havana]. "The Virgin of the Charity of el Cobre could come down from the heavens to intervene—that's the more realistic scenario—or Cuba's socialist experiment could end up succeeding—that would take a miracle."

Many a truth is told in jest, and a miracle or two would certainly come in handy on this island. Perhaps that's why the townspeople of Pinar del Reo went to such lengths to welcome Pope John Paul II. Although its famed tobacco plantations make a visit to this little town to the west of Havana a must for cigar connoisseurs, Pinar del Reo was not initially included on the Pope's itinerary. Undaunted, the local bishop, Jose Siro Gonzalez, proposed a novel way to get his flock in on the action: Why not have the Pope's plane enter Cuban airspace by flying above the town? That way, Pinar del Reo would be the first diocese to greet the Pope.

A daring but euphoric signature-gathering campaign ensued. Even the local Communist Party leaders got involved, and a thick book with thousands of requests was soon forwarded to Rome. The Vatican was happy to comply, and it instructed Alitalia to change the pontiff's flight path so he could approach Cuba from the right direction. Delighted, the residents of Pinar del Reo prepared huge hand-painted welcome banners and arranged to stand outdoors and use little mirrors to shine reflected sunbeams toward the plane carrying His Holiness.

The sunbeam committee was organized by Dagoberto Valdes, a lay Catholic activist. I met Dagoberto because he is the editor of *Vitral*, a bimonthly social and cultural magazine published by the local diocese, and I had come to Cuba in search of Cuban Catholic texts to translate for publication in Poland. Although I was not on a journalistic visit, my stay afforded me ample opportunity to observe the preparations that he and his fellow Catholics across Cuba were making in anticipation of the Pope's visit.

COMPARING CUBA, 1999, WITH POLAND, 1979

Their obvious enthusiasm inevitably called to mind the heady days of June 1979, when Karol Wojtyla, then only recently elected Pope John Paul II, returned to his (and my) homeland for the first papal pilgrimage to a Communist-ruled country. That visit changed Poland forever. The huge crowds that came to greet the Pope were the first spontaneous gatherings in Communist Poland. And their immense numbers gave those who had come together an unprecedented sense of self-confidence. The climate of fear that had gripped Poland for so long suddenly evaporated, creating an atmosphere that was more conducive to change. Within a year the "Solidarity" trade union was born. And ten years later the totalitarian regime was replaced with a democratic system.

There are of course many more differences than similarities between the 1979 papal visit to Poland and this year's visit to Cuba. The Pope is a lot older, and his energy level and degree of familiarity with the nation hosting him are much lower this time. And, in contrast to the Soviet-backed Communist apparatchiks who ruled Poland in 1979, the man who runs Cuba came to power in a revolution and has never faced an internal revolt strong enough to seriously threaten his rule. Whereas the Polish opposition of 1979 was an experienced, united group that reached out to workers and peasants, the dissident movement in Cuba is still politically divided and is limited to intellectual elites.

Most significantly, the Cuban church has never enjoyed the national stature of its Polish counterpart. True, roughly 40 percent of Cubans are baptized, and according to Vatican sources the number of Cuban children attending catechism classes has quintupled over the past few years. But the practice of religion is still very limited: churches fill up only on Sundays and major holidays. As a result, the Cuban clergy makes for a rather small group: there are only 240 Cuban priests on the island, and they tend to be wary of provoking the government's wrath, sticking to pastoral work instead.

AN ANTI-RELIGIOUS CAMPAIGN

Nonetheless, as with the Polish church of 1979, the Cuban church remains the only other structured, national institution aside from the Communist Party. Perhaps not surprisingly then, its relationship with the revolutionary government has been troubled. Things started out amicably enough in January 1959, when Cuban church leaders issued a pastoral letter saluting the "triumphal entry" into Havana of Fidel Castro and his companions. By May 1960, however, the tone had changed, and church leaders felt "obliged to recommend and indeed instruct diocesans (and, if necessary, all Cubans) to refuse to cooperate in any way with communism." Half a year later the bishops complained to Castro that there was "an anti-religious campaign of national dimension, growing more virulent by the day." Relations were not improved when a number of priests chose to participate in the failed April 1961 Bay of Pigs invasion. Castro retaliated by expelling 130 priests from Cuba; 400 more chose exile, as did 2,000 monks and nuns. The state security police also detained two bishops for several days, and four priests were jailed for two years for serving as "chaplains of the counterrevolutionaries." Repression of the church peaked during the mid-1960s when the current archbishop of Havana, Cardinal Jaime Ortega, and auxiliary Bishop Alfredo Petit were sent to forced labor in the "Military Units of Production Support"—Cuba's version of the Gulag.

The anti-religious campaign was to have long-lasting consequences. Anyone with any religious beliefs was barred from government employment, and young people from practicing Christian families were not admitted to the university. Although social studies, literature, journalism, and law were therefore offlimits to the practicing Catholics, some technical faculties were less restrictive—hence, the disproportionate number of Catholics among Cuban architects and engineers.

AN IMPROVED RELATIONSHIP

Relations between the church and the state began to improve by the mid-1970s. In 1975, the Cuban Communist Party declared that every citizen had the right to decide whether or not to be religious. Ten years later, perhaps inspired by the marriage of Nicaraguan Sandinistas and liberation theologians (or perhaps in a bout of nostalgia for his own education with the Jesuits), Castro discussed his relationship with religion in a series of interviews, which later became the book *Fidel and Religion.* "We never required that every man be an atheist," Fidel explained to Brazilian priest Frei Betto. "The revolution is not an anti-religious proposition."

A series of mutually conciliatory steps soon followed. In 1985, Castro met with Cuban bishops. A year later, the Cuban church held a national meeting to explore "what socialism can bring to religious faith." Finally, in 1991, the Communist Party allowed believers into its ranks, and, not long after—hallelujah!—the state was officially declared to be secular (instead of atheist). This had the immediate effect of increasing church attendance. Father Nelson of the Sagrada Corazon Church in Central Havana has observed a marked change: "In my parish there are now a few party members who would not have dared to come to mass before 1991."

The government's new tolerance is not the only reason for the surge in church attendance. Eighty-year-old Rafael Cepeda, dean of the Evangelical Institute of Biblical and Theological Studies (an unofficial yet tolerated study center), offers another explanation: "It all started with the fall of the Berlin Wall. The Cubans were stunned, they felt that the earth moved under their feet, and they experienced a disconcerting spiritual void. They felt like ideological orphans, so they flocked to the church, or rather to the churches, because in the evangelical church we also saw our congregation grow."

The Cuban government's rapprochement with the church was sealed in November 1996, when Castro traveled to Rome for his historic tete-a-tete with John Paul. The papal pilgrimage to Cuba was announced shortly afterward (although preparations for it had been going on much earlier). Castro would not have invited the Pope had he not believed it to be in his own best interest. But he also moved quickly to try to prevent the Pope's visit from turning into a replay of Poland in 1979. Calling on all Cubans to welcome the pontiff with open arms, Castro ensured that the impact of any mass outpouring of affection for—or curiosity about—the pontiff would be neutralized. Now, no one could be sure how many of those who gathered to greet the Pope had come spontaneously and how many were following orders.

Nonetheless, there can be little doubt that the Pope has aroused genuine sympathy. Outside private houses all over Havana, people put up posters welcoming "The Messenger of Truth and Hope." At first, these houses tended to come in clusters, as if each resident had infected his neighbor with the courage to display such a defiant credo. The church groups also distributed Pope buttons. I obtained one from the Cuban office of Caritas (a Catholic humanitarian society that is the only nongovernmental organization authorized to operate in Cuba) and pinned the button on my t-shirt. It brought me a lot of friendly smiles, a ten percent price reduction on a collection of 1950s American film posters from an antique shop, and many inquiries as to where one could find more buttons.

Another bit of Pope paraphernalia in high demand was, ironically, the Communist Party's newspaper *Granma*. Crammed with endless pages of official speeches, complete with mentions of "applause" and "laughter," the party organ is not usually a hot item. But the paper made its black-market debut when it featured an address from His Holiness to the Cuban people that took up two-thirds of the front page in its December 20, 1997, issue. Copies of the issue were said to have fetched up to $10—a hundred times its nominal price and the equivalent of an average monthly salary here.

INSPIRING COMMUNITY ACTIVITY

But ultimately it was not the outward manifestations of support for the Pope that make his visit significant. Rather, it was the way in which his presence spurred local communities to organize themselves independently of the government. A group of local Havana parishioners passing out informational leaflets listing, for example, the precise gathering points for groups wishing to welcome the Pope were engaging in what was probably their first spontaneous community activity since the revolution.

The importance of these activities lies not so much in their immediate impact as in the mood that they inspire. As Dagoberto said of his fellow mirror-carrying citizens in Pinar del Reo, "We need to do things, to do them together." Thus, in the long run, apart from its pastoral dimension, the Pope's visit may end up serving to mobilize people, to help them shake off their inertia, and act as an independent community, even if they are starting with only small things. The crucial question is whether the Pope will indeed manage to provoke such lasting changes in the hearts and minds of Cubans. How much courage, self-reliance, and solidarity will he inspire? How will he and his visit reinforce or rather reconstruct civil society on the island? It is in this sense that the miracle that happened with the Holy Father's 1979 visit to Poland may repeat itself in Cuba, although on a smaller scale: it may plant the seeds for an open-minded civil society. . . . A strong civil society is the sine qua non for a peaceful transition in Cuba. It is a transition that the 77-year-old Pope fears may come too late for him, and that the 71-year-old comandante fears may come too early for him. But they both know that it will come.

TOWARD PEACE IN NORTHERN IRELAND

TONY BLAIR

In April 1998, all parties in the decades-long conflict over the political control of Northern Ireland signed a landmark accord known as the Good Friday Agreement. This agreement ended the Republic of Ireland's territorial claim to the North, established new governing bodies, set a timeline for the decommissioning of combatants, and called for the release of political prisoners.

The Good Friday Agreement, which was approved by 71 percent of Northern Ireland voters, paved the way for improved relations with the governments of Britain and the Republic of Ireland. On November 26, 1998, Tony Blair became the first British prime minister to address the Irish Parliament. In his speech, excerpted below, he expressed his optimism for peace in Northern Ireland and increased cooperation between Britain and Ireland.

M embers of the Dail and Seanad [the two houses of the legislature], after all the long and torn history of our two peoples, standing here as the first British prime minister ever to address the joint Houses of the Oireachtas [legislature], I feel profoundly both the history in this event, and I feel profoundly the enormity of the honour that you are bestowing upon me. . . .

Ireland, as you may know, is in my blood. My mother was born in the flat above her grandmother's hardware shop on the main street of Ballyshannon in Donegal. She lived there as a child, started school there and only moved when her father died; her mother remarried and they crossed the water to Glasgow.

Reprinted from Tony Blair's address to the Irish Parliament, November 26, 1998.

We spent virtually every childhood summer holiday up to when the troubles [violent conflict over political control of Northern Ireland] really took hold in Ireland, usually at Rossnowlagh, the Sands House Hotel, I think it was. And we would travel in the beautiful countryside of Donegal. It was there in the seas off the Irish coast that I learned to swim, there that my father took me to my first pub, a remote little house in the country, for a Guinness, a taste I've never forgotten and which it is always a pleasure to repeat.

Even now, in my constituency of Sedgefield, which at one time had 30 pits or more, all now gone, virtually every community remembers that its roots lie in Irish migration to the mines of Britain.

So like it or not, we, the British and the Irish, are irredeemably linked.

SHARED HISTORY AND PAIN

We experienced and absorbed the same waves of invasions: Celts, Vikings, Normans—all left their distinctive mark on our countries. Over a thousand years ago, the monastic traditions formed the basis for both our cultures. Sadly, the power games of medieval monarchs and feudal chiefs sowed the seeds of later trouble.

Yet it has always been simplistic to portray our differences as simply Irish versus English—or British. There were, after all, many in Britain too who suffered greatly at the hands of powerful absentee landlords, who were persecuted for their religion, or who were for centuries disenfranchised. And each generation in Britain has benefited, as ours does, from the contribution of Irishmen and women.

Today the links between our parliaments are continued by the British-Irish Parliamentary Body, and last month 60 of our MPs [members of Parliament] set up a new all-party "Irish in Britain Parliamentary Group."

Irish parliamentarians have made a major contribution to our shared parliamentary history. Let me single out just two:
- Daniel O'Connell, who fought against injustice to extend a franchise restricted by religious prejudice;
- Charles Stewart Parnell, whose statue stands today in the House of Commons and whose political skills and commitment to social justice made such an impact in that House.

So much shared history, so much shared pain.

And now the shared hope of a new beginning.

PROGRESS MADE

The peace process is at a difficult juncture. Progress is being made, but slowly. There is an impasse over the establishment of

the executive; there is an impasse over decommissioning. But I have been optimistic the whole way through. And I am optimistic now. Let us not underestimate how far we have come; and let us agree that we have come too far to go back now.

Politics is replacing violence as the way people do business. The Good Friday Agreement, overwhelmingly endorsed by the people on both sides of the Border, holds out the prospect of a peaceful long-term future for Northern Ireland, and the whole island of Ireland.

The Northern Ireland Bill provides for the new Assembly and

Executive, the North-South Ministerial Council, and the British-Irish Council. It incorporates the principle of consent into British constitutional law and repeals the Government of Ireland Act of 1920 [which established British control over all of Ireland]. It establishes a Human Rights Commission with the power to support individual cases. We will have an Equality Commission to police a new duty on all public bodies in Northern Ireland to promote equality of opportunity. We have set up the Patten Commission to review policing. We are scaling down the military presence. Prisoners are being released.

None of this is easy. I get many letters from the victims of violence asking why we are freeing terrorist prisoners. It is a tough question but my answer is clear: the agreement would never have come about if we had not tackled the issue of prisoners. That agreement heralds the prospect of an end to violence and a peaceful future for Northern Ireland. Our duty is to carry it out. That is a duty I feel more strongly than ever, having seen for myself the horror of Omagh. [On August 15, 1998, a bomb set by a group called the "Real" IRA killed twenty-eight people at a market in Omagh.] This was not the first such atrocity. But with all of my being, I will it to be the last. I will never forget the meeting I had, with Bill Clinton, with survivors, and with relatives of those who died. Their suffering and their courage was an inspiration. They will never forget their loved ones. Nor must we. We owe it to them above all to build a lasting peace, when we have the best opportunity in a generation to do so.

The Taoiseach's [primer minister; Bertie Aheru] personal contribution has been immense. I pay tribute to his tireless dedication. I value his friendship. I also salute the courage of our predecessors, Deputy Albert Reynolds, Deputy John Bruton and John Major; and I also salute Deputy Dick Spring, whose role in this process goes back a long way.

Like us, you are living up to your side of the bargain too. You have voted to end the territorial claim over Northern Ireland, essential to the agreement.

THE VICTORY OF PEACE

It is time now for all the parties to live up to all their commitments. Time for North/South bodies to be established to start a new era of co-operation between you and Northern Ireland—I hope agreement on these is now close. Time to set up the institutions of the new government. Time for the gun and the threat of the gun to be taken out of politics once and for all; for decommissioning to start.

I am not asking anyone to surrender. I am asking everyone to declare the victory of peace.

In Belfast or Dublin, people say the same thing: make the agreement work.

It is never far from my mind. My sense of urgency and mission comes from the children in Northern Ireland. I reflect on those who have been victims of violence, whose lives are scarred and twisted through the random wickedness of a terrorist act, on those who grow up in fear, those whose parents and loved ones have died.

And I reflect on those, who though untouched directly by violence, are nonetheless victims—victims of mistrust and misunderstanding who through lack of a political settlement miss the chance of new friendships, new horizons, because of the isolation from others that the sectarian way of life brings.

I reflect on the sheer waste of children taught to hate when I believe passionately children should be taught to think.

Don't believe anyone who says the British people don't care about the peace process. People in my country care deeply about it, are willing it to work. And in our two countries, it is not just the politicians who have a role to play.

No one should ignore the injustices of the past, or the lessons of history. But too often between us, one person's history has been another person's myth.

We need not be prisoners of our history. My generation in Britain sees Ireland differently today and probably the same generation here feels differently about Britain.

A CHANGED IRELAND AND BRITAIN

We can understand the emotions generated by Northern Ireland's troubles, but we cannot really believe, as we approach the 21st century, there is not a better way forward to the future than murder, terrorism and sectarian hatred.

We see a changed Republic of Ireland today:
- a modern, open economy;
- after the long years of emigration, people beginning to come back for the quality of life you now offer;
- a country part of Europe's mainstream, having made the most of European structural funds but no longer reliant on them;
- some of the best business brains in the business world;
- leaders in popular culture, U2, the Corrs, Boyzone, B-Witched;
- a country that had the courage to elect its first woman president and liked it so much, you did it again; and the politics of Northern Ireland would be better for a few more women in prominent positions too.

And you see, I hope, a Britain emerging from its post-Empire malaise, modernizing, becoming as confident of its future as it once was of its past.

The programme of the new Labour government: driving up standards in education; welfare reform; monetary and fiscal stability as the foundation of a modern economy; massive investment in our public services tied to the challenge of modernization; a huge programme of constitutional change; a new positive attitude to Europe—it is a program of national renewal as ambitious as any undertaken in any western democracy in recent times.

It is precisely the dramatic changes in both countries that allow us to see the possibilities of change in our relationship with each other.

It will require vision, but no more than the vision that has transformed Ireland. It will require imagination, but no more than that shown by the British people in the last two years. The old ways are changing between London and Dublin. And this can spur the change and healing in Northern Ireland too. The old notions of unionist supremacy and of narrow nationalism are gradually having their fingers prised from their grip on the future.

THE WISH TO BELONG

Different traditions have to understand each other. Just as we must understand your yearning for a united Ireland, so too must you understand what the best of unionism is about. They are good and decent people, just like you. They want to remain part of the UK—and I have made it clear that I value that wish. They feel threatened. Threatened by the terrorism with which they have had to live for so long. Threatened, until the Good Friday Agreement, that they would be forced into a united Ireland against the will of the people of Northern Ireland.

Yet they realize now that a framework in which consent is guaranteed is also one in which basic rights of equality and justice are guaranteed, and that those who wish a united Ireland are free to make that claim, provided it is democratically expressed, just as those who believe in the Union can make their claim.

It is all about belonging. The wish of unionists to belong to the UK. The wish of nationalists to belong to Ireland. Both traditions are reasonable. There are no absolutes. The beginning of understanding is to realize that.

My point is very simple. Those urges to belong, divergent as they are, can live together more easily if we, Britain and the Irish Republic, can live closer together too.

OPPORTUNITY TO WORK TOGETHER

Down through the centuries, Ireland and Britain have inflicted too much pain, each on the other. But now, the UK and Ireland as two modern countries, we can try to put our histories behind us, try to forgive and forget those age-old enmities.

We have both grown up now. A new generation is in power in each country.

We now have a real opportunity to put our relations on a completely new footing, not least through working together in Europe. I know that is what our peoples want and I believe we can deliver it.

Our ties are already rich and diverse—the UK is the largest market for Irish goods. And you are our fifth most important market in the world;

- in trade unions, professional bodies and the voluntary sector, our people work together to help their communities; in culture, sport and academic life there is an enormous crossover. Our theatres are full of Irish plays. Our television is full of Irish actors and presenters. Your national football team has a few English accents too;

- above all, at the personal level, millions of Irish people live and work in Britain, and hundreds of thousands of us visit you every year.

As ties strengthen, so the past can be put behind us. Nowhere was this better illustrated than at the remarkable ceremony at Messines earlier this month. Representatives of nationalists and unionists travelled together to Flanders to remember shared suffering. Our army bands played together. Our heads of state stood together. With our other European neighbors, such a ceremony would be commonplace. For us it was a first. It shows how far we have come. But it also shows we still have far to go.

The relationships across these islands are also changing in a significant way. . . .

FORGING NEW BONDS

I want to forge new bonds with Dublin. Together we can have a stronger voice in Europe and work to shape its future in a way which suits all our people. It is said there was a time when Irish diplomats in Europe spoke French in meetings to ensure they were clearly distinguished from us. I hope those days are long behind us. We can accomplish much more when our voices speak in harmony.

Our ministers and officials are increasingly consulting and coordinating systematically. We can do more. I believe we can transform our links if both sides are indeed ready to make the effort. For our part, we are.

This must also involve a dramatic new effort in bilateral relations, above all to bring our young generations together. We need new youth and school exchanges, contact through the new University for Industry, better cultural programs in both directions. We need to work much more closely to fight organized crime and drugs. We can do much more to enrich each other's experience in areas like health care and welfare.

None of this threatens our separate identities. Co-operation does not mean losing distinctiveness.

What the Taoiseach and I seek is a new dimension to our relationships—a real partnership between governments and peoples, which will engage our societies at every level.

We have therefore agreed to launch a new intensive process. The Taoiseach and I will meet again next spring in London, with key ministerial colleagues, to give this the necessary impetus and agenda, and will thereafter meet at least once a year to review progress. This will be part of the work of the new Intergovernmental Conference. The objective is threefold:

- first, revitalized and modernized bilateral relations where we can finally put the burden of history behind us;
- second, a habit of close consultation on European issues, marked by a step-change in contacts at every level, particularly in key areas such as agriculture, justice and home affairs, employment and foreign and security policy;
- third, working together on international issues more widely, for example UN peacekeeping, to which both our countries have been important contributors, arms proliferation and the Middle East.

BEYOND NORTHERN IRELAND

What I welcome above all is that, after keeping us apart for so long, Northern Ireland is now helping to bring us closer together. But I do not believe Northern Ireland can or should any longer define the relationship between us. Our common interests, what we can achieve together, go much, much wider than that.

Our two countries can look to the future with confidence in our separate ways. But we will be stronger and more prosperous working together.

That is my ambition. I know it is shared by the Taoiseach. I believe it is an ambition shared by both our nations. The 21st century awaits us. Let us confront its challenge with confidence, and together give our children the future they deserve.

INDIA AND PAKISTAN DEVELOP NUCLEAR WEAPONS

JASWANT SINGH

In May 1998, India surprised the international community by an-
nouncing it had conducted five underground nuclear weapons
tests. Two weeks later, India's neighbor Pakistan conducted its
own tests. These events heralded the entry of two more nations
into the "nuclear club"—the group of countries that possess nuclear weapons capability—and raised renewed concerns about
nuclear proliferation.

In the following essay, Jaswant Singh, the external affairs minister for Indian prime minister Atal Bihai Vajpayee, defends his
country's decision to proceed with the development of nuclear
weapons. It is unfair to expect India to forgo nuclear weapons,
Singh argues, when other countries claim they need them to
guarantee their security. Singh insists that India will not use its
nuclear weapons offensively and that his nation is committed to
the goal of global disarmament.

W hile the end of the Cold War transformed the political
landscape of Europe, it did little to ameliorate India's
security concerns. The rise of China and continued
strains with Pakistan made the 1980s and 1990s a greatly troubling period for India. At the global level, the nuclear weapons
states showed no signs of moving decisively toward a world free
of atomic danger. Instead, the nuclear nonproliferation treaty
(NPT) was extended indefinitely and unconditionally in 1995,

Reprinted from "Against Nuclear Apartheid," by Jaswant Singh, *Foreign Affairs*,
September/October 1998. Reprinted by permission of *Foreign Affairs*. Copyright 1998 by
the Council on Foreign Relations.

perpetuating the existence of nuclear weapons in the hands of five countries busily modernizing their nuclear arsenals. In 1996, after they had conducted over 2,000 tests, a Comprehensive Test Ban Treaty (CTBT) was opened for signature, following two and a half years of negotiations in which India participated actively. This treaty, alas, was neither comprehensive nor related to disarmament but rather devoted to ratifying the nuclear status quo. India's options had narrowed critically.

India had to ensure that its nuclear option, developed and safe-guarded over decades, was not eroded by self-imposed restraint. Such a loss would place the country at risk. Faced with a difficult decision, New Delhi realized that its lone touchstone remained national security. The nuclear tests it conducted on May 11 and 13 were by then not only inevitable but a continuation of policies from almost the earliest years of independence. India's nuclear policy remains firmly committed to a basic tenet: that the country's national security in a world of nuclear proliferation lies either in global disarmament or in exercise of the principle of equal and legitimate security for all.

INDIAN FOREIGN POLICY POST WWII

In 1947, when a free India took its rightful place in the world, both the nuclear age and the Cold War had already dawned. Instead of aligning with either bloc, India rejected the Cold War paradigm and chose the more difficult path of nonalignment. From the very beginning, India's foreign policy was based on its desire to attain an alternative global balance of power that, crucially, was structured around universal, nondiscriminatory disarmament.

Nuclear technology had already transformed global security. Nuclear weapons, theorists reasoned, are not actually weapons of war but, in effect, military deterrents and tools of possible diplomatic coercion. The basis of Indian nuclear policy, therefore, remains that a world free of nuclear weapons would enhance not only India's security but the security of all nations. In the absence of universal disarmament, India could scarcely accept a regime that arbitrarily divided nuclear haves from have-nots. India has always insisted that all nations' security interests are equal and legitimate. From the start, therefore, its principles instilled a distaste for the self-identified and closed club of the five permanent members of the U.N. Security Council.

During the 1950s, nuclear weapons were routinely tested above ground, making the mushroom cloud the age's symbol. Even then, when the world had witnessed only a few dozen tests, India took the lead in calling for an end to all nuclear weapons testing, but the calls of India's first prime minister,

Jawaharlal Nehru, went unheeded.

In the 1960s, India's security concerns deepened. In 1962, China attacked India on its Himalayan border. The nuclear age entered India's neighborhood when China became a nuclear power in October 1964. From then on, no responsible Indian leader could rule out the option of following suit.

With no international guarantees of Indian security forthcoming, nuclear abstinence by India alone seemed increasingly worrisome. With the 1962 war with China very much on his mind, Indian Prime Minister Lal Bahadur Shastri began tentatively investigating a subterranean nuclear explosion project. A series of Indian nonproliferation initiatives had scant impact. In 1965, to make matters worse, the second war between India and Pakistan broke out. Shastri died in 1966 and was succeeded by Indira Gandhi, who continued the fruitless search for international guarantees. In 1968, India reaffirmed its commitment to disarmament but decided not to sign the NPT. In 1974, it conducted its first nuclear test, Pokharan I.

RESISTING DISCRIMINATORY NONPROLIFERATION

The first 50 years of Indian independence reveal that the country's moralistic nuclear policy and restraint paid no measurable dividends, except resentment that India was being discriminated against. Disarmament seemed increasingly unrealistic politics. If the permanent five's possession of nuclear weapons increases security, why would India's possession of nuclear weapons be dangerous? If the permanent five continue to employ nuclear weapons as an international currency of force and power, why should India voluntarily devalue its own state power and national security? Why admonish India after the fact for not falling in line behind a new international agenda of discriminatory nonproliferation pursued largely due to the internal agendas or political debates of the nuclear club? If deterrence works in the West—as it so obviously appears to, since Western nations insist on continuing to possess nuclear weapons—by what reasoning will it not work in India? Nuclear weapons powers continue to have, but preach to the have-nots to have even less. India counters by suggesting either universal, nondiscriminatory disarmament or equal security for the entire world.

India is alone in the world in having debated the available nuclear options for almost the last 35 years. No other country has deliberated so carefully and, at times, torturously over the dichotomy between its sovereign security needs and global disarmament instincts, between a moralistic approach and a realistic one, and between a covert nuclear policy and an overt one. May

11, 1998, changed all that. India successfully carried out three underground nuclear tests, followed on May 13 by two more underground, sub-kiloton tests. These five tests, ranging from the sub-kiloton and fission variety to a thermonuclear device, amply demonstrated India's scientific, technical, and organizational abilities, which until then had only been vaguely suspected. A fortnight later, on May 28 and 30, neighboring Pakistan predictably carried out its own tests in the bleak vastness of the Chagai Hills in Baluchistan, near the Afghan border. Suddenly the strategic equipoise of the post–Cold War world was rattled. The entire nonproliferation regime and the future of disarmament were at the forefront of international agendas. . . .

COMMITTED TO RESTRAINT

India is now a nuclear weapons state, as is Pakistan. That reality can neither be denied nor wished away. This category of "nuclear weapons state" is not, in actuality, a conferment. Nor is it a status for others to grant. It is, rather, an objective reality. India's strengthened nuclear capability adds to its sense of responsibility—the obligation of power. India, mindful of its international duties, is committed to not using these weapons to commit aggression or to mount threats against any country. These are weapons of self-defense, to ensure that India, too, is not subjected to nuclear coercion.

India has reiterated its desire to enter into a no-first-use agreement with any country, either negotiated bilaterally or in a collective forum. India shall not engage in an arms race, nor, of course, shall it subscribe to or reinvent the sterile doctrines of the Cold War. India remains committed to the basic tenet of its foreign policy—a conviction that global elimination of nuclear weapons will enhance its security as well as that of the rest of the world. It will continue to urge countries, particularly other nuclear weapons states, to adopt measures that would contribute meaningfully to such an objective. This is the defining difference. It is also the cornerstone of India's nuclear doctrine. . . .

India's nuclear policy has been marked by restraint and openness. It has not violated any international agreements, either in 1974 or 1998. This restraint is a unique example. Restraint, however, has to arise from strength. It cannot be based upon indecision or hesitancy. Restraint is valid only when it removes doubts, which is precisely what India's tests did. The action involved was balanced—the minimum necessary to maintain an irreducible component of the country's national security calculus.

Even before 1990, when Congress passed the Pressler amendment cutting off economic and military aid to Pakistan to protest its development of a nuclear program, the genie of nuclear proliferation on the Indian subcontinent was out of the bottle. The much-quoted 1987 interview in which Abdul Qadeer Khan, the chief Pakistani nuclear scientist, verified the existence of Islamabad's bomb simply confirmed what New Delhi had long suspected. The United States, then still engaged in Afghanistan, continued to deny that Pakistan had crossed the nuclear threshold. The explosions at the Chagai Hills on May 28 and 30 testify to the rightness of India's suspicions.

After the tests, India stated that it will henceforth observe a voluntary moratorium and refrain from conducting underground nuclear test explosions. It has also indicated a willingness to move toward a de jure formalization of this declaration. The basic obligation of the CTBT is thus met: to undertake no more nuclear tests. Since India already subscribes to the substance of the test ban treaty, all that remains is its actual signature.

TROUBLE IN THE WHITE HOUSE: THE IMPEACHMENT OF BILL CLINTON

HENRY HYDE

In 1998, Independent Counsel Kenneth Starr, who had been appointed to investigate President Bill Clinton's business dealings, discovered that the president had engaged in a sexual affair with a White House intern named Monica Lewinsky. Clinton denied under oath that such an affair had occurred. However, when confronted with mounting evidence, he finally admitted wrongdoing. In a 445-page report released in September 1998, Starr provided detailed descriptions of the president's affair with Lewinsky, presented evidence that Clinton lied under oath and attempted to obstruct justice to cover up the affair, and recommended that Clinton be impeached for his actions.

In December 1998, in response to the Starr report, the U.S. House of Representatives approved two articles of impeachment against the president for perjury and obstruction of justice. Clinton thus became the second U.S. president ever to be impeached (the first being Andrew Johnson in 1868). Under the U.S. Constitution, the removal of an impeached president from office requires a trial in the U.S. Senate in which the president must be voted guilty by a two-thirds vote. Clinton escaped this fate, receiving 45 guilty votes on the perjury charge and 50 guilty votes on the obstruction of justice charge.

Prior to voting to impeach the president, members of the House

Henry Hyde, statement to the U.S. Congress, December 18, 1998.

of Representatives engaged in a lively debate. The forces for impeachment were led by Henry Hyde, the Republican representative from Illinois. The following selection was excerpted from statements Hyde made in the House on December 18, 1998, the day the articles of impeachment were introduced. Hyde insists that Clinton's guilt is beyond question and that to fail to remove him from office would undermine the rule of law in the United States.

M r. Speaker, my colleagues of the People's House, I wish to talk about the rule of law. After months of argument, hours of debate, there is no need for further complexity. The question before this House is rather simple. It is not a question of sex. Sexual misconduct and adultery are private acts and are none of Congress' business. It is not even a question of lying about sex. The matter before the House is a question of lying under oath. This is a public act, not a private act. This is called perjury. The matter before the House is a question of the willful, premeditated, deliberate corruption of the Nation's system of justice. Perjury and obstruction of justice cannot be reconciled with the Office of the President of the United States.

The personal fate of the President is not the issue. The political fate of his party is not the issue. The Dow Jones Industrial Average is not the issue. The issue is perjury, lying under oath. The issue is obstruction of justice, which the President has sworn the most solemn oath to uphold. That oath constituted a compact between the President and the American people. That compact has been broken. The people's trust has been betrayed. The Nation's chief executive has shown himself unwilling or incapable of enforcing its laws, for he has corrupted the rule of law by his perjury and his obstruction of justice.

AN IMPEACHABLE OFFENSE

Mr. Speaker, that and nothing other than that is the issue before this House.

We have heard ceaselessly that even if the President is guilty of the charges in the Starr referral [report of the independent counsel, Kenneth Starr], they do not rise to the level of an impeachable offense. Well, just what is an impeachable offense? One authority, Professor Stephen Presser of Northwestern University School of Law, said, and I quote:

'Impeachable offenses are those which demonstrate a fundamental betrayal of public trust; they suggest the federal official has deliberately failed in his duty to uphold the Constitution and laws he was sworn to enforce.'

So, Mr. Speaker, we must decide if a President, the chief law enforcement officer of the land, the person who appoints the Attorney General, the person who nominates every Federal judge, the person who nominates to the Supreme Court and the only person with a constitutional obligation to take care that the laws be faithfully executed, can lie under oath repeatedly and maintain it is not a breach of trust sufficient for impeachment.

The President is the trustee of the Nation's conscience, and so are we here today.

There have been many explosions in our committee hearings on the respective role of the House and the Senate. Under the Constitution, the House accuses and the Senate adjudicates. True, the formula language of our articles recites the ultimate goal of removal from office, but this language does not trump the Constitution, which defines the separate functions, the different functions of the House and the Senate. Our Founding Fathers did not want the body that accuses to be the same one that renders final judgment, and they set up an additional safeguard of a two-thirds vote for removal.

So, despite protests, our job is to decide if there is enough evidence to submit to the Senate for a trial. That is what the Constitution says no matter what the President's defenders say.

When Ben Franklin, on September 18, 1787 told Mrs. Powel that the Founders and Framers had given us a Republic 'if you can keep it,' perhaps he anticipated a future time when bedrock principles of our democracy would be mortally threatened as the Rule of Law stands in the line of fire today. Nothing I can think of more clearly illustrates that America is a continuing experiment, never finished, that our democracy is always a work in progress than this debate today, for we sit here with the power to shape and reconfigure the charter of our freedom just as the Founders and Framers did. We can strengthen our Constitution by giving it content and meaning, or we can weaken and wound it by tolerating and thus encouraging lies under oath and evasion and breaches of trust on the part of our chief executive.

THE 'SO WHAT' DEFENSE

The President's defenders in this House have rarely denied the facts of this matter. They have not seriously challenged the contention of the independent counsel that the President did not tell the truth in two sworn testimonies. They have not seriously attempted to discredit the facts brought before the committee by the independent counsel. They have admitted, in effect, he did it.

But then they have argued that this does not rise to the level of an impeachable offense. This is the 'so what' defense whereby

In 1998 Bill Clinton became the second U.S. president to be impeached.
He was charged with perjury and obstruction of justice for lying
about his affair with White House intern Monica Lewinsky.

the Chief Executive, the successor to George Washington, can cheapen the oath, and it really does not matter. They suggest that to impeach the President is to reverse the result of a national election as though Senator Bob Dole would become President. They propose novel remedies, like a Congressional censure that may appease some constituents and certainly mollify the press, but in my judgment betray lack of seriousness about the Constitution, the separation of powers and the carefully balanced relationship of checks and balances between Congress and the President that was wisely crafted by the framers. A resolution of censure, to mean anything, must punish, if only to tarnish his reputation, but we have no authority under the Constitution to punish the President. It is called separation of powers.

As my colleagues know, we have been attacked for not producing fact witnesses, but this is the first impeachment inquiry in history with the Office of Independent Counsel in place, and their referral to us consisted of 60,000 pages of sworn testimony grand jury transcripts, depositions, statements, affidavits, video and audio tapes. We had the facts, and we had them under oath. We had Ms. Monica Lewinsky's heavily corroborated testimony under a grant of immunity that would be revoked if she lied; we accepted that and so did they, else why did they not call any others whose credibility they questioned as their own witnesses? Now there was so little dispute on the facts they called no fact witnesses and have even based a resolution of censure on the same facts.

A Vote on the Rule of Law

Let us be clear. The vote that all of us are asked to cast is in the final analysis a vote on the rule of law.

Now the rule of law is one of the great achievements of our civilization, for the alternative is the rule of raw power. We here today are the heirs of 3,000 years of history in which humanity slowly, painfully, and at great cost evolved a form of politics in which law, not brute force, is the arbiter of our public destinies.

We are the heirs of the Ten Commandments and the Mosaic law, a moral code for a free people, who, having been liberated from bondage, saw in law a means to avoid falling back into the habits of slaves.

We are the heirs of Roman law, the first legal system by which peoples of different cultures, languages, races and religions came to live together in a form of political community.

We are the heirs of the Magna Carta, by which the free men of England began to break the arbitrary and unchecked power of royal absolutism.

We are the heirs of a long tradition of parliamentary development, in which the rule of law gradually came to replace royal prerogative as the means for governing a society of free men and women.

We are the heirs of 1776, and of an epic moment in human affairs when the Founders of this Republic pledged their lives, their fortunes and their sacred honors, think of that, sacred honor, to the defense of the rule of law.

We are the heirs of a hard-fought war between the states, which vindicated the rule of law over the appetites of some for owning others.

We are the heirs of the 20th Century's great struggles against totalitarianism, in which the rule of law was defended at immense costs against the worst tyrannies in human history.

The phrase 'rule of law' is no pious aspiration from a civics textbook. The rule of law is what stands between all of us and the arbitrary exercise of power by the state. The rule of law is the safeguard of our liberties. The rule of law is what allows us to live our freedom in ways that honor the freedom of others while strengthening the common good.

Securing the Structure of Freedom

The rule of law is like a three-legged stool. One leg is an honest judge, the second leg is an ethical bar, and the third is an enforceable oath. All three are indispensable to avoid political collapse.

In 1838, Abraham Lincoln celebrated the rule of law before the Young Men's Lyceum in Springfield, Illinois, and linked it to the perpetuation of American liberties and American political institutions. Listen to Lincoln, from 1838:

> Let every American, every lover of liberty, every well wisher to his posterity, swear by the blood of the Revolution never to violate in the least particular the laws of the country; and never to tolerate their violation by others. As the patriots of seventy-six did to support the Declaration of Independence, so to the support of the Constitution and laws, let every American pledge his life, his property and his sacred honor; let every man remember that to violate the law is to trample on the blood of his father, and to tear the character of his own and his children's liberty. Let reverence for the laws be breathed by every American mother to the lisping babe that prattles on her lap, let it be taught in the schools, in seminaries, and in colleges. Let it be written in primers, spelling books and almanacs. Let it be preached from the pulpit, proclaimed in legislative halls, and enforced in the courts of justice.

So said Lincoln.

My colleagues, we have been sent here to strengthen and defend the rule of law; not to weaken it, not to attenuate it, not to disfigure it. This is not a question of perfection; it is a question of foundations. This is not a matter of setting the bar too high; it is a matter of securing the basic structure of our freedom, which is the rule of law.

No man or woman, no matter how highly placed, no matter how effective a communicator, no matter how gifted a manipulator of opinion or winner of votes, can be above the law in a democracy. That is not a counsel of perfection; that is a rock bottom, irreducible principle of our public life.

THE PRESIDENT MUST BE REMOVED

There is no avoiding the issue before us, much as I wish we could. We are, in one way or another, establishing the parameters of permissible presidential conduct. In creating a presidential system, the framers invested that office with extraordinary powers. If those powers are not exercised within the boundaries of the rule of law, if the President breaks the law by perjury and obstructs justice by willfully corrupting the legal system, that president must be removed from office. We cannot have one law for the ruler and another law for the ruled.

This was, once, broadly understood in our land. If that understanding is lost or if it becomes seriously eroded, the American democratic experiment and the freedom it guarantees is in jeopardy. That, and not the fate of one man, or one political party or one electoral cycle, is what we are being asked to vote on today.

In casting our votes, we should look not simply to ourselves, but to the past and to the future. Let us look back to Bunker Hill, to Concord and Lexington. Let us look across the river to Arlington Cemetery, where American heroes who gave their lives for the sake of the rule of law lie buried, and let us not betray their memory. Let us look to the future, to the children of today who are the presidents and members of Congress of the next century, and let us not crush their hope that they too will inherit a law-governed society.

Let us declare, unmistakably, that perjury and obstruction of justice disqualify a man from retaining the presidency of the United States.

There is a mountain of details which are assembled in a coherent mosaic in the committee report. It reads like a novel, only it is nonfiction, it really happened, and the corruption is compelling. Read the report and be convinced.

What we are telling you today are not the ravings of some vindictive political crusade, but a reaffirmation of a set of values that are tarnished and dim these days, but it is given to us to restore them so our Founding Fathers would be proud.

Listen, it is your country. The President is our flag-bearer. He stands out in front of our people, and the flag is falling. Catch the falling flag as we keep our appointment with history.

NATO BOMBS SERBIA

IVO H. DAALDER AND MICHAEL E. O'HANLON

In the late 1990s, ethnic Albanians in Kosovo, a republic of Serbia, made increasingly strident demands for independence. The Kosovo Liberation Army (KLA) attacked Serbian troops and police, who in turn responded by driving ethnic Albanians from their homes. Attempts by the international community to orchestrate a peaceful settlement failed due to Serbian leader Slobodan Milosevic's unwillingness to sign. In March 1999, as the Serbian army prepared for a large-scale attack on the KLA, NATO began a bombing campaign designed to force Milosevic back into negotiations.

In the following essay, Ivo H. Daalder and Michael E. O'Hanlon chronicle the NATO effort, known as Operation Allied Force. Initially intended as a short bombing campaign, the authors write, the operation lasted for seventy-eight days, eventually forcing Milosevic to withdraw his forces from Kosovo and agree to a peace settlement. Daalder and O'Hanlon contend that the NATO campaign, while imperfectly executed, was ultimately successful. Other commentators have been more critical of the NATO campaign. Some point out, for example, that soon after the bombing commenced, the Serbs stepped up their violence toward Kosovar civilians, driving over 800,000 out of the country and killing 10,000.

Daalder and O'Hanlon are senior fellows in foreign policy studies at the Brookings Institution, a policy research organization. They are the co-authors of *Winning Ugly: NATO's War to Save Kosovo*, from which this selection was excerpted.

O n March 24, 1999, NATO went to war for the first time in its fifty-year history. Its target was not a country, but a man. As the Serb leader of Yugoslavia, Slobodan Milosevic had been most responsible for a decade of violence that accompanied the breakup of Yugoslavia. Well over a hundred thousand people had been killed and millions displaced in Croatian and Bosnian wars during the first part of the 1990s. Now a similar humanitarian catastrophe threatened in Kosovo, part of Serbia, the heart of the former Yugoslavia. Milosevic's security forces were arrayed against the Kosovo Liberation Army (KLA), a small insurgent force, and the ethnic Albanians who dominated the area's population. In the previous year of fighting, nearly two thousand people had been killed and many hundreds of thousands were driven from their homes. A full-scale war in Kosovo between Serbs and Albanians would likely have been particularly brutal, leaving untold death and destruction in its wake. Compounding the likely humanitarian disaster was the potential for large numbers of refugees engulfing the fragile border countries of Macedonia and Albania, with consequences for stability and security across the entire region.

So NATO went to war. For a decade, the alliance had wavered in its resolve to confront Milosevic. At times, the Serb leader had proven a willing partner in negotiating a halt to the region's violence. More often, he had been the source of that violence. For more than a year, the United States and its principal European allies had tried to head off a military confrontation by seeking to engage the man most responsible for the carnage that had befallen Kosovo, an approach similar to that followed in Croatia and Bosnia earlier in the decade. The Kosovo effort failed, not least because Milosevic displayed little interest in defusing a confrontation with a NATO alliance he assumed would soon founder in disagreement over how and to what extent to prosecute a war.

THE START OF A "BRIEF" CAMPAIGN

Late on the night of March 24, NATO warplanes began what was expected to be a brief bombing campaign. The purpose of the campaign was to force Milosevic back to the negotiating table so that NATO could find a way short of independence to protect Kosovo's ethnic Albanian population from Serb violence and political domination. This bombing campaign, it was emphatically stated, was not a war, and none of the NATO leaders had any intention of waging one.

Politics at home and abroad were believed to constrain the United States and its partners in the use of force. When hostilities began, President Bill Clinton had just survived his impeachment ordeal. He faced a Congress that was not just politically hostile but also increasingly wary of U.S. military action designed to serve humanitarian goals, including in the Balkans. Although Clinton had authorized the use of military force several times in his presidency, he had not ordered American soldiers into situations in which some were likely to be killed since the Somalia operation had gone tragically wrong in late 1993. Against this backdrop, the president failed to prepare the country for the possibility that NATO's initial bombing raids might be the opening salvo of a drawn-out war. Nor were he and his top advisers really prepared for this possibility themselves.

As alliance aircraft revved up their engines to start a short air campaign focused primarily on Serb antiaircraft defenses, the expected operation had the flavor of a number of other recent, short, and antiseptic uses of Western airpower. Three months earlier the United States and Great Britain had conducted a four-day bombing campaign against Iraq, and in August 1998 the Clinton administration had launched cruise missile strikes against suspected terrorist facilities in Afghanistan and Sudan in retaliation for the bombings of two U.S. embassies in Africa by the Osama bin Laden network. Neither of those recent military operations had achieved core U.S. strategic objectives. Saddam Hussein had not allowed weapons inspections to resume in Iraq, and the bin Laden network remained intact and, by all accounts, poised to strike again. These generally unsuccessful attacks did little to enhance the credibility of the United States. They were designed more to punish, and to "send a message," than to compel an adversary to change his behavior or directly achieve concrete strategic objectives.

NATO's security interests seemed even less engaged in the Balkans than they had been with Saddam Hussein or bin Laden. This was apparent in the alliance's goals for Kosovo, which were quite nuanced. NATO did not seek to defeat the Serb-dominated Yugoslav armed forces, cause a regime change in Belgrade, or gain Kosovo its independence. Rather it sought to convince Milosevic to resume negotiations that would allow an armed international force into Kosovo to quell the violence that had erupted there in March 1998. Beyond that the alliance objective was nothing more than autonomy for the ethnic Albanian majority in Kosovo. As a major inducement to Milosevic, it even promised to disarm the KLA. Under such circumstances, a protracted NATO bombing campaign seemed disproportionate—and thus unlikely—to most onlookers, be they in Belgrade, Brussels, Washington, or elsewhere.

WREAKING DESTRUCTION

However, what had started very much as a foreign ministers' battle soon became NATO's first real war. Seventy-eight days later, it finally ended as Serb forces left Kosovo and a NATO-led international force of 50,000 began to move in. But over the intervening weeks a great deal of destruction was wrought, by Serbs against ethnic Albanians and by NATO against Serbia.

Despite the fact that most of the world's best air forces were conducting combat missions over Yugoslavia from March 24 onward, the early phases of the conflict were dominated militarily by Serb units in Kosovo. NATO lost the war in the initial going, and the Kosovar Albanian people paid the price. Up to 10,000 or so died at Serb hands, mostly innocent civilians; thousands more were raped or otherwise brutalized. Some 800,000 people were forcefully expelled from Kosovo, and hundreds of thousand more were displaced within the territory. Ultimately perhaps 1,000 to 2,000 Serbs perished as well, both civilians killed inadvertently and regular and irregular Serb forces killed on the battlefield.

THE MOMENTUM SHIFTS

In the end, NATO prevailed. Although there was no clear turning point, the NATO summit in Washington on April 23–25, 1999—organized originally to celebrate the alliance's fiftieth anniversary—may represent the best dividing line between losing and winning the war. Before that time, the vast majority of Kosovar Albanians were forced from their homes. Despite an intensification of its air campaign, NATO remained powerless to prevent atrocities on the ground or to establish a public perception that it was truly committed to winning the war.

But the summit revealed an alliance unified in its conviction that the war against Serbia must be won. War planning became more systematic, and further increases in NATO's air armada were authorized. The alliance steeled itself sufficiently that even the accidental bombing of the Chinese embassy on May 7 by a U.S. B-2 bomber did not seriously threaten continuation of the war effort. Perhaps most significantly, on April 25 Russian President Boris Yeltsin called Bill Clinton, resuming U.S.-Russian ties that had been effectively frozen when the war began. Yeltsin, though still upset, committed to do what he could to end the war, setting in motion a negotiating process that would ultimately put a 360-degree diplomatic squeeze on Milosevic.

When it was all over, the alliance was able to reverse most of the damage Serbia had caused in the early period of the war. Notably, of the nearly 1.3 million ethnic Albanians driven from their homes, virtually all were able to return within a few short weeks of the end of the war. Serb forces left Kosovo, with NATO-led units assuming physical control of the territory. An international administration was set up to run Kosovo, effectively wresting political control over the area from Belgrade.

MILITARY SUCCESSES

Although overall political momentum began to shift in NATO's favor around the time of the Washington summit, the military tide of battle turned most dramatically in late May. By then, NATO air assets had nearly tripled and the weather had improved, making precision bombs far more effective. In addition, the alliance's political leadership had authorized attacks against a much wider range of targets in Belgrade and elsewhere. The KLA, though still a modest militia force, had begun to conduct limited offensives against Serb positions within Kosovo, in some cases forcing Serb troops to expose themselves, at which point they became more vulnerable to NATO attack aircraft.

By early June Serbia was reeling. In Kosovo Serb forces had lost substantial amounts of the equipment with which they had begun, and Serb soldiers were finding themselves at considerable personal risk. In Serbia electricity grids were being severely damaged, water distribution was adversely affected in all major cities, and the businesses and other assets of Milosevic's cronies were being attacked with growing frequency.

During the eleven-week air campaign, NATO flew nearly 40,000 combat sorties, about one-third the number flown in six weeks during the 1991 Desert Storm campaign. Fourteen of the alliance's nineteen members participated in the attacks. The air campaign was conducted very professionally and precisely by the armed forces of the United States and other NATO member countries. Although some 500 Serb and ethnic Albanian civilians were killed accidentally by NATO bombs, that toll is modest by the standards of war. Moreover, only two alliance jets were shot down in combat, and only two NATO troops died—U.S. Army pilots who perished in an Apache helicopter training accident in neighboring Albania.

NATO's air war had two main thrusts: a strategic campaign against the Serb heartland and a tactical campaign against the Serb forces doing the killing and the forced expulsions in Kosovo. NATO supreme commander General Wesley Clark rightly argued that, for understanding how NATO won the war, "the indispensable condition for all the other factors was the success of the air campaign itself." The Pentagon's report on the war reached a similar conclusion. But neither ultimate victory nor historically low losses demonstrate that the air war was well designed or properly conceived by top decisionmakers in Washington and other NATO capitals.

BEYOND BOMBING

Final victory required more than bombing. Two critical factors occurred on the political front: NATO's demonstrated cohesion as an alliance and Russia's growing willingness to cooperate in the pursuit of a diplomatic solution. On the military front, NATO's talk of a possible ground war (which alliance leaders had unwisely ruled out when the bombing began) and the well-publicized decisions to augment allied troop strength in Macedonia and Albania proved to be crucial as well. Whereas the air war inflicted mounting damage, these other factors probably convinced Milosevic that no plausible escape remained. Once that became clear to him, capitulation became his best course, both to minimize further damage to Serbia and its military and to secure his position in power.

Although U.S. domestic politics complicated the conduct of the conflict at times, and did much to shape the limited way in which it was initially fought, they did not fundamentally threaten the operation once it was under way. Most polls showed clear, though hardly overwhelming or impassioned, majorities of the U.S. public supporting NATO's air campaign. Indeed, once the war started, the Clinton administration faced more criticism from those who felt its war plan to be excessively cautious than from those who believed the use of force to be wrongheaded in the first place. As columnist E.J. Dionne Jr. wrote, liberals in particular supported this war for its humanitarian dimensions, getting over their "Vietnam syndrome" in the process. And while some conservatives objected to the war as not serving U.S. interests, much of the Republican foreign policy elite felt strongly that the conflict had to end in a NATO victory. . . .

NATO did meet reasonable standards of success in its 1999 war against Serbia. The outcome achieved in Kosovo, while hardly without its problems, represented a major improvement over what had prevailed in the region up to that point and certainly over what would have happened had NATO chosen not to intervene. It is in that relative sense that the policy was successful, not because it was properly designed at most major stages and not because it achieved the best plausible outcome to which NATO might have aspired.

Operation Allied Force was far from a perfect diplomatic and military accomplishment. The United States and its allies succeeded only after much suffering by the ethnic Albanian people on the ground. They prevailed only after committing a number of major mistakes, which future interventions must seek to avoid. In fact, NATO's mistakes were so serious that its victory was anything but preordained. Had Milosevic not escalated the conflict dramatically by creating the largest forced exodus on the European continent since World War II, and had alliance leaders not then realized they had to radically overhaul their military strategy, NATO could have lost the war. That would have held very serious implications for the future of the alliance and even worse implications for the peoples of the region.

THE WORLD'S POPULATION REACHES SIX BILLION

LINDA FELDMANN, HOWARD LAFRANCHI, LARA SANTORO, AND
ALEXANDER MACLEOD

October 12, 1999, was declared "Day of 6 Billion" by the United
Nations because that was forecasters' best estimate of when the
world's population would reach the 6 billion mark. In the following selection, Linda Feldmann and her colleagues report that
although reaching 6 billion is a landmark, the threat of overpopulation is not the cause for concern that it was in decades past.
Due to declining birth rates in many parts of the world, global
population growth has slowed significantly. Feldmann and
LaFranchi are staff writers for the *Christian Science Monitor*. Santoro and MacLeod are contributors to the *Monitor*.

T oday, the 6 billionth baby will be born, a milestone of multiple dimensions. In a way that child—probably born
somewhere in Asia or Africa—represents a triumph of human ingenuity in the face of dire predictions. No longer, by and
large, are demographers issuing Malthusian forecasts of global
destruction from overpopulation. Revolutions in food production have kept pace with population growth.

But child No. 6 billion also comes laden with concerns for the
future. In just 12 years, the planet is expected to add another billion people. And by 2050, according to the UN's projections,
global population will approach 9 billion.

"The question is, can we absorb another 3 billion over the next 50 years?" asks John Bongaarts, director of policy research for the Population Council in New York. "The answer is yes. But we would be better off if we had a magic wand and could make this population go away. Societies would be better off without this additional population growth."

The developed, industrial world has, on average, stopped growing. The United States' population is still rising, but only because of immigration. Japan's population is holding steady, and Europe is declining a bit. So the globe's next few billion people will be added to the poor countries of Asia, Africa, and Latin America. And within those countries, the growth will be focused on cities, and particularly the slums.

Most of the world's nations now understand the need to provide reproductive health services to couples, and in particular to offer choices, not mandates. By just filling unmet demand for birth control, advocates say, the global birthrate would drop by 20 percent.

Each corner of the world has its own challenges, and successes, in dealing with population growth. Following are reports from three continents, chronicling the efforts of each to anticipate population needs in the next millennium.

MIXED RESULTS FROM MEXICO'S EFFORTS

Mexico is an example of a country where the population "glass" is half full—and half empty.

One of the world's most successful fertility reduction programs has significantly reduced the average number of children born per woman over the past 25 years. Mexico's total of 100 million people is about 50 million less than what demographers projected in 1970 for 2000.

The smaller number of dependents per family presents an opportunity for increased family economic well-being that should allow Mexico to reduce its high poverty rates. Yet for too long, Mexico's policymakers placed too much stock in contraception and too little in accompanying human development programs.

The result is that while the average Mexican woman who had seven children in 1965 has what averages to 2.5 today, poverty rates have not declined accordingly—and in fact in recent years have increased.

"The mistake made was the supposition that with a substantial fall in the population growth rate alone, development levels would increase and average living conditions would improve," says Carlos Welti Chanes, a demographer at Mexico City's National Autonomous University. Mexico has learned that a population policy "is much more than just anticonception," he says.

Dr. Welti, coordinator of the regionwide Latin American Program for Population Activities, says the picture across most of Central and South America is similar to Mexico's. While most countries have done well in reducing fertility, insufficient attention and resources have been placed in such areas as education, women's development, rural development (to counter migration), and children's health.

The irony for Mexico is that a country long considered "young" is beginning to age rapidly. By 2010 a quarter of the population will be 65 or older. And smaller families will mean that the elderly will have fewer dependents to count on for their financial well-being. "The thinking was always that lower fertility rates would free up savings to spend on other population segments, but the problem is that the elderly are costlier than children," Welti says. And with more than 80 percent of the aging population outside Mexico's social-security system, the scenario is set for a major crisis among Mexico's elderly.

In Latin America, "the focus on a young population has made the problem of street children universally known, but in the future we're going to be increasingly confronted with street elderly," Welti says.

"In the past in demographic surveys, you'd find a lot of women saying they wanted many children because they felt assured that at least one would do well and take care of her in her old age," says Welti. "But with just two children to count on, the possibilities are considerably reduced."

CHALLENGES IN AFRICA

With 622 million people, sub-Saharan Africa has one of the highest populations in the world. And the average fertility rate is 6.1 percent, which causes the population to double every 25 years.

On average, only 18 percent of adults of reproductive age use contraception—and this in a continent where people are 22 percent poorer than they were in 1975. But largely because of the AIDS pandemic, African governments have taken increasingly aggressive steps to address the issues of reproductive health and population control.

Kenya, with a population of nearly 29 million, was the first country in black Africa to view unchecked population growth as a serious impediment to growth and economic prosperity. It was the first country to develop a population policy in 1967; Ghana followed in 1969. Today, 25 African countries have such policies, which include sex education, AIDS awareness programs, and promotion and distribution of contraception. Urbanization, ris-

ing costs, higher literacy rates, and better infant survival rates
have also restrained population growth.

In Kenya, where the fertility rate averages 5.1 percent, couples
now say they want an average of four children, down from seven
in the 1980s. Between 1982 and 1994, the availability of contraception grew at a faster pace in sub-Saharan Africa than in any
other developing region. Still, 13 percent of Kenya's population
has AIDS, according to the National AIDS and Sexually Transmitted Diseases Control Program. In many pockets, infection
rates far exceed the national average, soaring as high as 50 and
60 percent. There are 350,000 AIDS orphans and 66,000 children
with HIV.

According to Lewis Odhiambo of the University of Nairobi,
the mortality rate among Kenyans has increased from 9 per 1,000
population in the late 80s to 13 per 1,000 population. The rise,
says Dr. Odhiambo, is almost entirely due to AIDS.

The deaths of more than 4 million Africans are attributed to
AIDS, and more than 21 million people are currently living with
the disease. AIDS has also led to a sharp decline in life expectancy. Odhiambo estimates that Kenyans' life expectancy has
been cut by 10 years, from an average of 64.5 during 1995–2000
to 54.7 years.

AN AGING POPULATION IN EUROPE

Europe will soon be a "gray continent."

According to Eurostat, the European Union's statistical
agency, the trend across Europe will be for birthrates to be in
sustained decline.

The result, it says, will be a steadily declining and aging population, with increasing pressure on a contracting tax base to provide economic and social support for older people.

In 1997, Italy became the first nation in world history to have
more people age 60 and older than those age 20 and younger.
Last year Greece, Spain, and Germany edged closer to the same
situation.

Population numbers in the EU's 15 states, according to Eurostat, will grow slightly in the next 25 years. But by 2050 they will
have fallen back to the current 368 million, then keep on falling.

David Coleman, lecturer in demography at Oxford University,
says European women are choosing to have their first baby later
in life. In 1970, the average age for a European woman to have
her firstborn was 23½. "Now it is 27," Dr. Coleman says.

He says that the collapse of communism in Eastern Europe,
which caused a reduction or end to state-paid child-support policies, produced a sharp fall in birthrates in those countries. "In the

communist era people tended to vote against their regimes with low birthrates," Coleman says.

In Scandinavian countries, attempts to boost birthrates through tax incentives and cash support for larger families were launched two decades ago, and the trend was temporarily slowed. But between 1990 and 1998 it picked up again. In that period Sweden's birthrate fell from 2.12 per woman to 1.42 today.

In southern Europe the trend is much more pronounced. Even Roman Catholic countries, known traditionally to favor large families, are registering low birthrates.

In Italy and Spain, Eurostat reports, women nowadays bear what averages out to be only 1.17 and 1.18 babies respectively. By 2050, if current trends hold, Italy's population will have shrunk by about 20 million.

By the year 2050, Germany (current pop. 82 million) expects to have 5 million citizens over age 80. The effect of this will be felt most in the sphere of government pension obligations to citizens. According to government figures, state-funded pension liabilities amount to 127 percent of the gross domestic product. In tiny Luxembourg, the liability is 230 percent of the GDP.

How We Rang In 2000

Sharon Begley

As the end of the 1990s approached, technology experts and cultural commentators began to caution that New Year's Eve 1999 could bring calamity. Computer programmers warned that computers might read the new year as 1900 rather than 2000, causing systems to crash. Since many of society's infrastructure and transportation systems were run by computers, it was feared that the "Y2K computer bug" could result in widespread disruption of key services. Some predicted that power would go out, water would shut off, airplanes would fall from the sky, ATMs would cease to function, and nuclear weapons would launch automatically. These disruptions could lead to civil disturbances, it was argued, and terrorists might take advantage of the chaos to strike at a vulnerable government and public.

As *Newsweek* senior editor Sharon Begley notes in the following essay, none of these doomsday scenarios came to pass. Instead, people around the world celebrated the arrival of 2000 without any major computer failures or incidents of violence, marking a peaceful end to a turbulent century.

T hey sat side by side, these men who had spent their professional lives pointing nuclear missiles at each other, inside the windowless room at Peterson Air Force Base in Colorado. Officers of the U.S. Space Command and their Russian counterparts had gathered, the day before New Year's Eve, to keep the world from ending: together they would monitor the early-warning system so that no Y2K-befuddled computer would mistakenly signal an ICBM launch, precipitate an all-too-real response and make this a really short millennium. Russian Lt. Col. Viktor Grigorenko kept glancing nervously from his desktop computer to the wall clock showing the time in Moscow. Three minutes to midnight, someone called out. Two minutes . . . And then, as the room fell silent, the officers stared at the TV screen showing the first fireworks arcing over Red Square in the final seconds of the old millennium. Three Russians in the room grabbed their hot lines to Moscow. One minute . . . And then it came: rollover to 2000. After listening to the report from home, the senior Russian broke into a grin: midnight had marched from Petropavlovsk to Moscow without a single major Y2K disaster. As the officers shook hands, fireworks turned the gables and onion domes of St. Basil's Cathedral into a resplendent phantasm.

It was that kind of night. In counterpoint to the 10, 9, 8 . . . prefacing the pop of champagne corks and the rainbow bursts of fireworks, there was a parallel countdown: three, two, one . . . exhale.

Every New Year's Eve inspires a jumble of contradictory feelings—a yearning for an ever-receding past, apprehension about an unknown future, nostalgia, hope, memories and dreams. But the eve of this millennium outdid all other new year eves in uneasy contrasts. Even as pumped-up crowds gathered in Times Square, Coast Guard helicopters hovered over Manhattan. Even as celebrants stocked up on party hats, they laid in a supply of batteries. Even as the first seconds of 2000 fell upon Kiritimati and Tonga, it was impossible to hear a radio or television broadcast, read a newspaper or even have a casual conversation without being bombarded with warnings about New Year's Eve mayhem. On this calendar turn as on no other, a specter haunted the celebrants. New Year's Eve, it seemed, could be hijacked either by terrorists or by the Y2K computer bug.

But as 11:59 flipped into 12:00 across the 24 time zones of the world, you could almost hear the soft pffft of air going out of the alarmists' balloon. The lights stayed on in Sydney. The phones rang in Vladivostok. The traffic lights worked in Cairo. The crowd of 2 million at the luminous Brandenburg Gate partied joyously, safely. And as countries that seemed least prepared to weather Y2K did so without so much as a need to reboot, it became clear that the United States, too, would evade the new year demons. The worst of the glitches were on the order of key cards' not working at a few nuclear power plants (the problem was fixed immediately), and Amtrak train signals' not showing up properly on controllers' screens (they entered the data manually). Oh, and wind-shear detectors went out at six U.S. airports (there was no wind shear anyway).

It was not only the cyberthreat that was missing in action. In time zone after time zone, terrorists held their fire (though thieves stole a Cezanne landscape from a museum in Oxford, England, as the streets outside throbbed with celebrating crowds). Doomsday cultists refrained from mass suicide. Presented with such slim pickings, the press struggled to find signs of disaster—and came up only with a drunk who electrocuted himself on a light pole in Las Vegas, an 11-year-old wounded by a bullet fired into the sky in Los Angeles, a bomb threat in Anchorage, Alaska, and a handful of fireworks deaths in Italy, the Netherlands and elsewhere. And so, mercifully spared anything more global, the world partied on.

Hong Kong staged an $8 million blowout for which high-tech tycoon Richard Li flew in Whitney Houston, Sister Sledge and others to entertain 1,000 celebrants. Five mock UFOs landed on a rooftop in downtown Seoul and deposited several friendly aliens as light beams blazed from the ships. Havana's Tropicana hotel was hopping like at no time since Batista.

Not every celebration was an over-the-top extravaganza, however. Yes, with 11 glittering Ferris wheels along the Champs-Elysees and a diademed Eiffel Tower, Paris surpassed its appellation as the City of Light and became a city of enchantment. But South Africa held its official celebration, with dancers of every race, on Robben Island, where Nelson Mandela was imprisoned for 19 years, as if to underline that we forget the past at our peril. And yes, Cairo did greet its seventh millennium with a rollicking concert and light show at the Pyramids. But in Bethlehem 2,000 white doves of peace flew into the night sky to the strains of Ode to Joy and the theme from 2001, and in Derry, Northern Ireland, the voices of 2,000 Protestants and Roman Catholics filled the air with the melancholy strains of Danny Boy.

Still, for all the revelry, in cities where a public bash had come to seem a matter of civic duty, fear or prudence cast a pall over the party. Radio hosts in Portland, Ore., joked about stealing the Space Needle from Seattle, which had canceled its celebration in the face of terrorism fears, but the 15,000 Portlanders who filled the colonnaded square were surrounded by cops with billy clubs and guns. Metal detectors, from Barbra Streisand's Vegas concert to a Detroit Red Wings game, were as de rigueur as noisemakers. Most people—more than anyone predicted when entrepreneurs laid plans for concerts and parties earlier this year—avoided large public gatherings. Doomsday predictions kept the crowd on the Las Vegas Strip below last year's 410,000. Thousands decided not to travel (airlines canceled scores of flights). And those who did venture out had continuous reminders that the night was far from carefree: sharpshooters on rooftops kept a wary eye on the 2 million people who jammed Times Square and environs. Other New York police carried anthrax-antidote kits in case of a bioweapons attack. At the Pyramids, security came in the form of antiaircraft guns as well as cops on camels.

The mark of status was not an invitation to the most exclusive party, anyway, but being needed at the office. Joining the usual crew of cops and ER doctors working or on call New Year's Eve were hospital administrators, bankers and emergency teams from virtually every American city. Microsoft president Steve Ballmer and 6,000 other 'softies were at work or on call; so were CEO Louis Gerstner and tens of thousands of other IBMers. Every single one of Israel's 25,000 police officers was on duty Friday night. To show her faith that planes would not fall from the sky when the system with which global aviation keeps time (Greenwich Mean Time, or Zulu time in the vernacular) rolled over to midnight, Federal Aviation Administrator Jane Garvey was about 30,000 feet over the Mississippi River en route from Dallas to San Francisco.

As each time zone crossed into 2000, it seemed to be waving back to those bringing up the rear in 1999: come on, the future isn't as scary as you were led to believe. For one night, at least, the world was on its best behavior. The confetti is now litter, the champagne is flat and the lasers are off. The sun has risen on a new century, but the midnight celebrations will go on as long as there are memories, symbols of the hope we can once again try to find in tomorrow.

CHRONOLOGY

1980

April 24—Eight American servicemen die in a failed attempt to rescue hostages held in Tehran, Iran.

August—Sixty-two nations—including the United States, West Germany, and Japan—protest the Soviet invasion of Afghanistan by boycotting the Summer Olympics in Moscow.

August—Workers at the Gdansk Shipyard in Poland go on strike, led by Lech Walesa; the trade union Solidarity is formed; the strike ends with the signing of the Gdansk Agreement on August 31.

November 4—Ronald Reagan is elected president of the United States.

December 8—Former Beatle John Lennon is shot and killed by mentally deranged fan Mark David Chapman.

1981

January 20—American hostages in Iran are released minutes after Ronald Reagan is sworn in as president.

March 30—John W. Hinckley Jr. attempts to assassinate U.S. President Reagan; the president is shot but quickly recovers.

April 12—The first space shuttle, *Columbia*, takes off for the first time.

May 13—Pope John Paul II is shot and seriously wounded in St. Peter's Square, Rome.

August—IBM launches the IBM Personal Computer (IBM PC).

December 12—Martial law is imposed in Poland.

1982

April–May—In a brief, undeclared war, Britain regains control of the Falkland Islands from Argentina.

July—AIDS is identified, but its cause remains a mystery.

October—Colombian author Gabriel Garcia Marquez wins the Nobel Prize for literature.

1983

March 23—Reagan announces his Strategic Defense Initiative (SDI).

April 18—The U.S. embassy in Beirut, Lebanon, is hit with a car bomb, killing dozens and injuring hundreds.

July—Martial law is lifted in Poland.

October 23—A truck bomb explodes at the Marine headquarters in Beirut, killing 240 marines and sailors. U.S. forces invade the Caribbean nation of Grenada to impose order and protect U.S. citizens there.

November—Over 100 million people watch the television show *The Day After*, a movie depicting the aftermath of nuclear war.

1984

January—Apple launches its Macintosh personal computer.

May—The Soviet Union announces it will not take part in the 1984 Summer Olympic Games in Los Angeles.

April—Researchers in France and the United States independently announce they have discovered the virus that causes AIDS.

November 6—Reagan is reelected.

December 2–3—A chemical leak at a Union Carbide chemical plant in Bhopal, India, kills 2,500 people and injures over 50,000.

1985

March 11—Mikhail Gorbachev becomes leader of the Soviet Union.

July 13—The Live Aid concert, held simultaneously in London and Philadelphia, raises nearly $70 million for African famine relief.

1986

January—Gorbachev calls for a total ban on nuclear weapons by the year 2000.

January 28—The space shuttle *Challenger* explodes during takeoff, killing all seven crew members on board.

April 14—U.S. launches air attacks on targets in Libya in an attempt to force Colonel Muammer el-Qaddafi to cease his support of anti-American terrorists.

April 26—A reactor at the Chernobyl nuclear power plant in Ukraine explodes, killing thirty-one and forcing the evacuation of over 100,000.

October 11–12—Reagan and Gorbachev meet at a summit in Reykjavik, Iceland, but reach no agreements.

November—The first reports of the Iran/Contra affair begin to surface; the Tower Commission is appointed to investigate the issue on November 26.

1987

January—Gorbachev launches liberal social and economic reforms in the Soviet Union.

May 5—Iran/Contra hearings begin.

October—World stock markets make a strong turn downward.

December 8—At a Summit in Washington, D.C., Reagan and Gorbachev sign a treaty banning intermediate-range nuclear forces (INF).

December 8—A Palestinian uprising (*Intifada*) erupts in the West Bank and Gaza Strip.

1988

November—Nationalist and ethnic ferment increases in the Baltic States of the Soviet Union.

November 8—George Bush is elected president of the United States.

December 22—Pan Am Flight 103 explodes over Lockerbie, Scotland, killing all 259 on board and eleven on the ground.

1989

February—The Soviet Union withdraws its troops from Afghanistan. Iran's Ayatollah Khomeini pronounces a death sentence on Salman Rushdie, British author of *The Satanic Verses*.

March—The U.S. Senate ratifies the Montreal Protocol, an international agreement calling for major reductions in the production of chlorofluorocarbons (CFCs), a main cause of ozone layer depletion.

April—Students begin a peaceful pro-democracy demonstration at Tiananmen Square in Beijing, China.

May 4—Colonel Oliver North is convicted on charges stemming from the Iran/Contra affair.

May 20—Martial law is declared in Beijing.

June—The Corcoran Gallery in Washington cancels a show of Robert Mapplethorpe's photographs, sparking the debate over government funding of the arts in America.

June 3–4—Hundreds of citizens are killed when Chinese forces move into Tiananmen Square and clear it of protesters.

June 5—The first democratic elections in forty years bring an end to communist rule in Poland.

July—Gorbachev announces that Eastern European countries are free to decide their own political futures.

November 9—East Germany opens its borders with West Germany, and celebrators begin tearing down the Berlin Wall.

November 17—Czechoslovakia's "velvet revolution" begins; by the end of the year the communists have lost power; Vaclav Havel is appointed president on December 27.

December 22—The dictator Nicolae Ceausescu and his wife Elena are overthrown as the leaders of Romania; they are executed on December 25.

1990

February 11—Nelson Mandela, anti-apartheid activist and leader of the African National Congress, is released from prison in South Africa.

April 8—Hungary votes the Socialist Party out of power and replaces it with a center-right coalition.

August 2—Iraq invades Kuwait, and on August 6–7 U.S. President Bush sends troops to Saudi Arabia.

October 3—East and West Germany unite.

December 9—Lech Walesa is elected president of Poland.

1991

January 16—An international coalition of forces led by the United States begins Operation Desert Storm, a bombing campaign against Iraq aimed at forcing Iraq to withdraw from Kuwait.

February 27—The Gulf War ends; Kuwait's independence is restored.

June—The republics of Croatia and Slovenia declare their independence from Yugoslavia; civil war ensues as the federal government attempts to prevent their succession.

June 17—The legal foundation of apartheid is repealed by the South African Parliament.

August 19–21—A group of hard-line communists attempt to overthrow Gorbachev and reestablish a strong communist control of the county. The Communist Party, discredited by the failed coup, is disbanded on August 29.

September—The republic of Macedonia declares its autonomy from Yugoslavia and makes a peaceful transition to independence.

October 13—Bulgaria's ruling Socialist Party is voted out of office.

December 25—Gorbachev resigns as president of the Soviet Union; the Union is officially disbanded.

1992

January—Slovenia and Croatia are recognized as independent nations.

March—Bosnia and Herzegovenia (Bosnia) declares its independence from Yugoslavia. Bosnian Serbs object and go to war with the government.

April 29—The verdict in the Rodney King case ignites riots in Los Angeles.

June 3–14—An "Earth Summit" on economic development and the environment convenes in Rio de Janeiro, Brazil, attracting leaders from around the world.

November 2—Bill Clinton is elected president of the United States.

December 9—U.S. troops land in Somalia to deliver humanitarian aid.

December 17—The presidents of the United States, Canada, and Mexico sign the North American Free Trade Agreement (NAFTA).

1993

January—The two republics of Czechoslovakia (Czech and Slovak) become two separate countries: the Czech Republic and Slovakia.

February 26—The World Trade Center in New York City is bombed by four men associated with radical Middle Eastern terrorist groups.

April 19—The compound of the Branch Davidian religious group in Waco, Texas, burns down during a raid by U.S. agents, killing seventy-five.

September—Israeli and Palestinian leaders sign an agreement setting a timetable for a peace agreement within five years.

October—The fist graphics-based browser software is introduced to commercial markets, initiating exponential growth of the World Wide Web.

October 7—African-American author Toni Morrison is awarded the Nobel Prize for literature.

November 18—South Africa adopts a multiracial constitution.

1994

January—The Justice Department begins investigations into Clinton's business dealings.

April 6—Rwandan President Juvénal Habyarimana is assassinated when his plane is shot down; Hutu militias in Rwanda begin to kill Tutsis and their Hutu sympathizers, eventually killing more than 500,000.

April 12—Kurt Cobain, lead singer and songwriter of the alternative rock band Nirvana, commits suicide with a shotgun.

May 9—Nelson Mandela is elected president of South Africa in that nation's first multiracial election.

June 17—Former football star O.J. Simpson is arrested and charged in the murder of his former wife and her friend. He is subsequently acquitted on October 3, 1995.

December 11—Russian forces invade the republic of Chechnya in an attempt to prevent its secession.

1995

April 19—Timothy McVeigh ignites a truck bomb in front of the federal building in Oklahoma City, killing 168.

June—The Bulgarian artist Christo wraps the German Parliament building (the Reichstag) in brightly colored nylon fabric.

September—Israeli and Palestinian leaders sign an agreement on expanded Palestinian self-rule.

October 16—Nation of Islam leader Louis Farrakhan leads the "Million Man March" in Washington, D.C.

November 4—Israeli President Yizhak Rabin is assassinated by a Jewish religious extremist.

December 14—All parties in the war in Bosnia sign the Dayton Agreement.

1996

July 27—A pipe bomb explodes at a park during Olympic celebrations in Atlanta, Georgia, killing one person.

November—Clinton is reelected.

September 13—Gangsta rapper Tupac Shakur is killed in a drive-by shooting.

September 26—The Taliban take Kabul, the capital of Afghanistan, killing the former president and imposing strict rules on dress, work, and religious practices in an attempt to establish a fundamentalist Islamic society.

1997

February—Researchers in Scotland announce they have successfully produced the first-ever clone of an adult mammal.

April 5, 1997—Beat Generation poet Allen Ginsberg dies of liver cancer.

May 1—Tony Blair of the Labour Party is elected prime minister of Britain, ending eighteen years of conservative control.

August 31—Diana, princess of Wales, dies in a car accident in Paris.

1998

January—Pope John Paul II visits Cuba—the fist papal visit to the island nation since the communist takeover of 1959.

April—All sides in the conflict over the political control of Northern Ireland sign the Good Friday Agreement.

May—Both India and Pakistan announce they have successfully tested nuclear weapons, thus joining the "club" of nuclear states.

August 7—U.S. embassies in Tanzania and Kenya are bombed simultaneously, killing hundreds. Blaming Muslim fundamentalist Osama bin Laden for the attacks, the United States retaliates by bombing targets in Afghanistan and Sudan.

September—Independent Council Kenneth Starr releases a 445-page report detailing Clinton's affair with White House intern Monica Lewinsky and providing evidence that the president lied under oath and obstructed justice to cover up the affair.

November 26—Tony Blair becomes the first British prime minister ever to speak to the Irish Parliament.

December 19—The U.S. Congress approves two articles of impeachment against Clinton for lying under oath and obstruction of justice.

1999

February 12—The U.S. Senate votes Clinton not guilty of perjury and obstruction of justice, allowing him to remain in office.

March 24—NATO initiates a bombing campaign designed to force Serbian President Slobodan Milosovic into negotiations over the political fate of Kosovo. The Serbs respond by forcing Kosovars from their homes, killing thousands and forcing over 800,000 from the country.

October 12—The world population reaches six billion.

2000

January 1—The Y2K computer bug fails to materialize.

June 26—American scientists announce the completion of the Human Genome Project to map the human genome.

October 12—Suicide bombers attack the American destroyer U.S.S. *Cole* in Aden, Yemen, killing seventeen sailors.

November 7—The U.S. presidential race between Al Gore and George W. Bush is left unresolved when Bush's lead in Florida is declared too narrow to call. A legal battle ensues over whether hand recounts should be allowed in several counties. On December 12, the U.S. Supreme Court declares the ballot recount unconstitutional, leaving Bush the winner.

FOR FURTHER RESEARCH

Afghanistan

Mark Galeotti, *Afghanistan: The Soviet Union's Last War*. London: Frank Cass, 1995.

Milan Hauner, *The Soviet War in Afghanistan: Patterns of Russian Imperialism*. Philadelphia: University Press of America, 1991.

M. Hassan Kakar, *Afghanistan: The Soviet Invasion and the Afghan Response, 1979–1982*. Berkeley: University of California Press, 1995.

William Maley, ed., *Fundamentalism Reborn? Afghanistan and the Taliban*. New York: New York University Press, 1998.

Peter Marsden, *The Taliban: War, Religion and the New World Order in Afghanistan*. London: Zed Books Ltd., 1998.

Ahmed Rashid, *Taliban: Militant Islam, Oil, and Fundamentalism in Central Asia*. New Haven: Yale University Press, 2000.

Africa

Alain Destexhe, *Rwanda and Genocide in the Twentieth Century*. Trans. Alison Marschner. New York: New York University Press, 1995.

Lindsay Michie Eades, *The End of Apartheid in South Africa*. Westport, CT: Greenwood Press, 1999.

Philip Gourevitch, *We Wish to Inform You That Tomorrow We Will Be Killed with Our Families: Stories from Rwanda*. New York: Farrar, Straus and Giroux, 1998.

John L. Hirsch and Robert B. Oakley, *Somalia and Operation Restore Hope: Reflections on Peacemaking and Peacekeeping*. Washington, DC: United States Institute of Peace Press, 1995.

Fergal Keane, *Season of Blood: A Rwandan Journey*. London: Viking, 1995.

Sebastian Mallaby, *After Apartheid*. Boston: Faber and Faber, 1992.

Nelson Mandela, *Intensify the Struggle to Abolish Apartheid: Speeches, 1990*. New York: Pathfinder, 1990.

Nelson Mandela, *Nelson Mandela Speaks: Forging a Democratic Nonracial South Africa*. New York: Pathfinder, 1993.

Marina Ottaway, *South Africa: The Struggle for a New Order*. Washington, DC: Brookings Institution, 1993.

Gérard Punier, *The Rwanda Crisis: History of a Genocide*. New York: Columbia University Press, 1995.

Jonathan Stevenson, *Losing Mogadishu: Testing U.S. Policy in Somalia*. Annapolis, MD: Naval Institute Press, 1995.

The Balkans

Thomas Cushman and Stjepan G. Mestrovic, *This Time We Knew: Western Responses to Genocide in Bosnia*. New York: New York University Press, 1996.

Ivo H. Daalder and Michael E. O'Hanlon, *Winning Ugly: NATO's War to Save Kosovo*. Washington, DC: Brookings Institution, 2000.

David A. Dyker and Ivan Vejvoda, *Yugoslavia and After: A Study in Fragmentation, Despair and Rebirth*. New York: Longman, 1996.

Aleksander Pavkovic, *The Fragmentation of Yugoslavia: Nationalism in a Multinational State*. New York: St. Martin's Press, 1997.

Sabrina Petra Ramet, *Balkan Babel: The Disintegration of Yugoslavia from the Death of Tito to Ethnic War*. Boulder, CO: Westview Press, 1996.

Carole Rogel, *The Breakup of Yugoslavia and the War in Bosnia*. Westport, CT: Greenwood Press, 1998.

The Challenger Explosion

Claus Jensen, *No Downlink: A Dramatic Narrative About the Challenger Accident and Our Time*. Trans. Barbara Haveland. New York: Farrar, Straus and Giroux, 1996.

Malcolm McConnell, *Challenger: A Major Malfunction*. Garden City, NY: Doubleday, 1987.

Diane Vaughan, *The Challenger Launch Decision: Risky Technology, Culture, and Deviance at NASA*. Chicago: University of Chicago Press, 1996.

The Chernobyl Disaster

Nigel Hawkes et al., *Chernobyl: The End of the Nuclear Dream*. New York: Vintage, 1987.

Viktor Haynes and Marko Bojcun, *The Chernobyl Disaster*. London: Hogarth Press, 1988.

Gigori Medvedev, *The Truth About Chernobyl*. Trans. Evelyn Rossiter. New York: BasicBooks, 1991.

Cultural and Social Developments

Jacob Baal-Teshuva, ed., *Christo: Reichstag and Urban Projects*. Munich: Prestel-Verlag, 1993.

Allan Bloom, *The Closing of the American Mind: How Higher Education Has Failed Democracy and Impoverished the Souls of Today's Students*. New York: Simon & Schuster, 1987.

Elinor Burkett, *The Gravest Show on Earth: America in the Age of AIDS*. New York: Houghton Mifflin, 1995.

Douglas A. Feldman and Julia Wang Miller, eds., *The AIDS Crisis: A Documentary History*. Westport, CT: Greenwood Press, 1998.

S.H. Fernando Jr., *The New Beats: Exploring the Music, Culture, and Attitude of Hip-Hop*. New York: Anchor Books, 1994.

Nelson George, *Hip Hop America*. New York: Viking, 1998.

Todd Gitlin, *The Twilight of Common Dreams: Why America Is Wracked with Culture Wars*. New York: Metropolitan Books, 1995.

Mark S. Hamm, *Apocalypse in Oklahoma: Waco and Ruby Ridge Revenged*. Boston: Northeastern University Press, 1997.

Neil Howe and Bill Strauss, *13th Gen: Abort, Retry, Fail?* New York: Vintage, 1993.

Institute for Alternative Journalism, *Inside the L.A. Riots: What Really Happened and Why It Will Happen Again*. New York: Institute for Alternative Journalism, 1992.

Haki R. Madhubuti, ed., *Why L.A. Happened: Implications of the '92 Los Angeles Rebellion*. Chicago: Third World Press, 1993.

Tom McGrath, *MTV: The Making of a Revolution*. Philadelphia: Running Press, 1996.

Scott Nance, *Music You Can See: The MTV Story*. Las Vegas: Pioneer Books, 1993.

Neil Postman, *Amusing Ourselves to Death: Public Discourse in the Age of Show Business*. New York: Viking, 1985.

George Ritzer, *The McDonaldization of Society: An Investigation into the Changing Character of Contemporary Social Life*. Rev. ed. Thousand Oaks, CA: Pine Forge Press, 1996.

Ronin Ro, *Gangsta: Merchandizing the Rhymes of Violence*. New York: St. Martin's Press, 1996.

Tricia Rose, *Black Noise: Rap Music and Black Culture in Contemporary America*. Hanover, NH: Wesleyan University Press, 1994.

Jim Ross and Paul Myers, *We Will Never Forget: Eyewitness Accounts of the Bombing of the Oklahoma City Federal Building*. Austin, TX: Eakin Press, 1996.

Gilbert T. Sewall, ed., *The Eighties: A Reader*. Reading, MA: Addison-Wesley, 1997.

Andy Shilts, *And the Band Played On: Politics, People, and the AIDS Epidemic*. New York: St. Martin's Press, 1987.

Eastern Europe and the Soviet Union

Deborah Adelman, *The "Children of Perestroika": Moscow Teenagers Talk About Their Lives and the Future*. Armonk, NY: M.E. Sharpe, 1992.

John Borneman, *After the Wall: East Meets West in the New Berlin*. New York: BasicBooks, 1991.

John F. N. Bradley, *Czechoslovakia's Velvet Revolution: A Political Analysis*. New York: Columbia University Press, 1992.

Helene Carrere d'Encausse, *The End of the Soviet Empire: The Triumph of Nations*. Trans. Franklin Philip. New York: BasicBooks, 1993.

Robert Darnton, *Berlin Journal, 1989–1990*. New York: W.W. Norton, 1991.

Michael Dobbs, *Down with Big Brother: The Fall of the Soviet Empire*. New York: Alfred A. Knopf, 1997.

Carlotta Gall and Thomas de Waal, *Chechnya: Calamity in the Causasus*. New York: New York University Press, 1998.

Mikhail Gorbachev, *At the Summit: Speeches and Interviews, February 1987–July 1988*. New York: Richardson, Steirman & Black, 1988.

Mikhail Gorbachev, *The August Coup: The Truth and the Lessons*. New York: HarperCollins, 1991.

Bernard Gwertzman and Michael T. Kaufman, eds., *The Decline and Fall of the Soviet Empire*. New York: Times Books, 1992.

Andrei Melville and Gail W. Lapidus, eds., *The Glasnost Papers: Voices on Reform from Moscow*. Boulder, CO: Westview Press, 1990.

Catherine Merridale, ed., *Perestroika: The Historical Perspective*. New York: Edward Arnold, 1991.

John Miller, *Mikhail Gorbachev and the End of Soviet Power*. New York: St. Martin's Press, 1993.

Martyn Rady, *Romania in Turmoil: A Contemporary History*. New York: I.B. Tauris, 1992.

Nestor Ratesh, *Romania: The Entangled Revolution*. Westport, CT: Praeger, 1991.

Gale Stokes, *The Walls Came Tumbling Down: The Collapse of Communism in Eastern Europe*. New York: Oxford University Press, 1993.

Wisla Suraska, *How the Soviet Union Disappeared: An Essay on the Causes of Dissolution*. Durham, NC: Duke University Press, 1998.

Ann Tusa, *The Last Division: A History of Berlin, 1945–1989*. New York: Addison-Wesley, 1997.

Bernard Wheaton and Zdenek Kavan, *The Velvet Revolution: Czechoslovakia, 1988–1991*. Boulder, CO: Westview, 1992.

Environmental Issues

Seth Cagin and Philip Dray, *Between Earth and Sky: How CFCs Changed Our World and Endangered the Ozone Layer*. New York: Pantheon, 1993.

John Firor, *The Changing Atmosphere: A Global Challenge*. New Haven, CT: Yale University Press, 1990.

David E. Fisher, *Fire & Ice: The Greenhouse Effect, Ozone Depletion, and Nuclear Winter*. New York: Harper & Row, 1990.

Al Gore, *Earth in the Balance*. Boston: Houghton Mifflin, 1992.

Richard J. Somerville, *The Forgiving Air: Understanding Environmental Change*. Berkeley: University of California Press, 1996.

The Iran/Contra Affair

William S. Cohen and George J. Mitchell, *Men of Zeal: A Candid Inside Story of the Iran-Contra Hearings*. New York: Viking, 1988.

Theodore Draper, *A Very Thin Line: The Iran-Contra Affairs*. New York: Hill and Wang, 1991.

Jonathan Marshall, Peter Dale Scott, and Jane Hunter, *The Iran-Contra Connection: Secret Teams and Covert Operations in the Reagan Era*. Boston: South End Press, 1987.

Lawrence E. Walsh, *Final Report of the Independent Council for Iran/Contra Matters*. New York: Times Books, 1994.

Lawrence E. Walsh, *Firewall: The Iran-Contra Conspiracy and Cover-Up*. New York: W. W. Norton, 1997.

Ann Wroe, *Lives, Lies and the Iran-Contra Affair*. New York: St. Martin's Press, 1991.

The Iran Hostage Crisis

Warren Christopher et al., *American Hostages in Ian: The Conduct of a Crisis*. New Haven, CT: Yale University Press, 1985.

Russell Leigh Moses, *Freeing the Hostages: Reexamining U.S.–Iranian Negotiations and Soviet Policy, 1979–1981*. Pittsburgh: University of Pittsburgh Press, 1996.

Paul B. Ryan, *The Iranian Rescue Mission: Why It Failed*. Annapolis, MD: Naval Institute Press, 1985.

Gary Sick, *All Fall Down: America's Tragic Encounter with Iran*. New York: Penguin, 1986.

Gary Sick, *October Surprise: America's Hostages in Iran and the Election of Ronald Reagan*. New York: Times Books, 1991.

Ireland

Paul Bew, Henry Patterson, and Paul Teague, *Northern Ireland—Between War and Peace: The Political Future of Northern Ireland*. London: Lawrence & Wishart, 1997.

Neil Collins, *Political Issues in Ireland Today*. New York: Manchester University Press, 1999.

George Mitchell, *Making Peace*. New York: Alfred A. Knopf, 1999.

The Middle East

Lawrence Freedman and Efraim Karsh, *The Gulf Conflict, 1990–1991: Diplomacy and War in the New World Order*. Princeton, NJ: Princeton University Press, 1993.

F. Robert Hunter, *The Palestinian Uprising: A War by Other Means*. Berkeley: University of California Press, 1991.

Phil Marshall, *Intifada: Zionism, Imperialism and Palestinian Resistance*. Chicago: Bookmarks, 1989.

Michael J. Mazarr, Don M. Snider, and James A. Blackwell Jr., *Desert Storm: The Gulf War and What We Learned*. Boulder, CO: Westview Press, 1993.

Edgar O'Ballance, *The Palestinian Intifada*. New York: St. Martin's Press, 1998.

Don Peretz, *Intifada: The Palestinian Uprising*. Boulder, CO: Westview, 1990.

Itamar Rabinovich, *Waging Peace: Israel and the Arabs at the End of the Century*. New York: Farrar, Straus and Giroux, 1999.

Andrew Rigby, *Living the Intifada*. Atlantic Highlands, NJ: Zed Books, 1991.

Uri Savir, *The Process: 1,100 Days That Changed the Middle East*. New York: Random House, 1998.

Kirsten E. Schulze, *The Arab-Israeli Conflict*. New York: Longman, 1999.

Samuel Segev, *Crossing the Jordan: Israel's Hard Road to Peace*. New York: St. Martin's Press, 1998.

Micah L. Sifry and Chistopher Cerf, eds., *The Gulf War Reader: History, Documents, Opinions*. New York: Times Books, 1991.

Overviews

Richard W. Bulliet, ed., *The Columbia History of the Twentieth Century*. New York: Columbia University Press, 1998.

Martin Gilbert, *A History of the Twentieth Century, Volume Three: 1952–1999*, New York: HarperCollins, 1999.

J.A.S. Grenville, *A History of the World in the Twentieth Century, Volume II: Conflict and Liberation, 1945–1996*. Cambridge, MA: Belknap Press, 1997.

J.M. Roberts, *Twentieth Century: The History of the World, 1901–2000*. New York: Viking, 1999.

Poland and Solidarity

Neal Ascherson, *The Struggles for Poland*. London: Michael Joseph Ltd., 1987.

Timothy Garton Ash, *The Polish Revolution: Solidarity, 1980–82*. London: Jonathan Cape, 1983.

Colin Barker, *The Festival of the Oppressed: Solidarity, Reform and Revolution in Poland, 1980–81*. Chicago: Bookmarks, 1986.

A. Kemp-Welch, *The Birth of Solidarity*. 2nd ed. New York: St. Martin's Press, 1991.

Jadwiga Staniszkis, *Poland's Self-Limiting Revolution*. Princeton, NJ: Princeton University Press, 1984.

Alain Touraine et al., *Solidarity: The Analysis of a Social Movement: Poland 1980–1981*. Trans. David Denby. Cambridge, UK: Cambidge University Press, 1983.

Lech Walesa, *A Path of Hope*. London: Collins Harvill, 1987.

The Strategic Defense Initiative (SDI)

Donald Baucom, *The Origins of SDI, 1944–1983*. Lawrence: University of Kansas Press, 1992.

Philip M. Boffey et al., *The New York Times Complete Guide to the Star Wars Debate*. New York: Times Books, 1988.

Steven W. Guerrier and Wayne C. Thompson, eds., *Perspectives on Strategic Defense*. Boulder, CO: Westview Press, 1987.

Edward Reiss, *The Strategic Defense Initiative*. New York: Cambridge University Press, 1992.

Gerald M. Steinberg, ed., *Lost in Space: The Domestic Politics of the Strategic Defense Initiative*. Lexington, MA: Lexington Books, 1998.

Technology and Computers

Stan Augarten, *Bit by Bit: An Illustrated History of Computers*. New York: Ticnot and Fields, 1984.

Tim Berners-Lee with Mark Fishetti, *Weaving the Web: The Original Design and Ultimate Destiny of the World Wide Web by Its Inventor*. New York: HarperCollins, 1999.

Martin Campbell-Kelly and William Aspray, *Computer: A History of the Information Machine*. New York: BasicBooks, 1996.

Paul E. Ceruzzi, *A History of Modern Computing*. Cambridge, MA: MIT Press, 1999.

James Chposky and Ted Leonsis, *Blue Magic: The People, Power and Politics Behind the IBM Personal Computer*. New York: Facts on File Publications, 1988.

Jon Palfreman and Doron Swade, *The Dream Machine: Exploring the Computer Age*. London: BBC Books, 1991.

Robert H. Reid, *Architects of the Web: 1,000 Days That Built the Future of Business*. New York: John Wiley & Sons, 1997.

Jeffrey S. Young, *Steve Jobs: The Journey Is the Reward*. Glenview, IL: Scott, Foresman and Company, 1988.

The Tiananmen Square Protests

Liu Binyan, Ruan Ming, and Xu Gang, *"Tell the World": What Happened in China and Why*. Trans. Henry L. Epstein. New York: Pantheon, 1989.

Chu-yuan Cheng, *Behind the Tiananmen Massacre: Social, Political, and Economic Ferment in China*. Boulder, CO: Westview, 1990.

Lee Feigon, *China Rising: The Meaning of Tiananmen*. Chicago: Ivan R. Dee, 1990.

Han Minzhu and Hua Sheng, eds., *Cries for Democracy: Writings and Speeches from the 1989 Chinese Democracy Movement*. Princeton, NJ: Princeton University Press, 1990.

Yi Mu and Mark V. Thompson, *Crisis at Tiananmen: Reform and Reality in Modern China*. San Francisco: China Books and Periodicals, 1989.

U.S. Politics

Paul T. David and David H. Everson, eds., *The Presidential Election and Transition, 1980–1981*. Carbondale, IL: Southern Illinois University Press, 1983.

Rowland Evans and Robert Novak, *The Reagan Revolution*. New York: E.P. Dutton, 1981.

Richard A. Posner, *An Affair of State: The Investigation, Impeachment, and Trial of President Clinton*. Cambridge, MA: Harvard University Press, 1999.

Austin Ranney, ed., *The American Elections of 1980*. Washington, DC: American Enterprise Institute, 1981.

Susan Schmidt, *Truth at Any Cost: Ken Starr and the Unmasking of Bill Clinton*. New York: HarperCollins, 2000.

Jeffrey Toobin, *A Vast Conspiracy: The Real Story of the Sex Scandal That Nearly Brought Down a President*. New York: Random House, 1999.

F. Clifton White and William J. Gill, *Why Reagan Won: A Narrative History of the Conservative Movement, 1964–1981*. Chicago: Regnery Gateway, 1981.

INDEX